The Business of Greening

Industry cannot be separated from nature. Indeed, there is a growing sense that industrialisation has now caused damage to the environment that is difficult, if not impossible, to rectify. Environmental problems now feature in newspapers, party political speeches, academic journals, specialised conferences and educational courses at school and university.

The Business of Greening debates the relationship between business and greening, and where this relationship is heading. The book gives voice to industrial actors in context – employees, employers, managers, technical specialists, regulators – in their organisations, within industrial sectors or as part of wider institutional regimes. The business of greening is taken as socially constructed, shaped through tensions and competing interests. It produces outcomes that are sometimes unexpected, sometimes hopeful. These outcomes are explored by examining a range of workers, including estate agents, bankers, bakers, printers, regulators, in small and large corporations.

Contributors write from different social science perspectives – sociology, geography, organisational science, psychology. This is a unique collection of findings from field projects within the Global Environmental Change research programme of the UK Economic and Social Research Council, and will be of particular interest to students and researchers of environmental and business studies, and to those who shape environmental policy in government and industry.

Stephen Fineman is Professor of Organisational Behaviour, School of Management, University of Bath.

Routledge Research in Global Environmental Change Series

Already published in the Routledge Global Environmental Change Series:

The Business of Greening

Edited by
Stephen Fineman

London and New York

First published 2000
by Routledge
11 New Fetter Lane, London EC4P 4EE

Simultaneously published in the USA and Canada
by Routledge
29 West 35th Street, New York, NY 10001

Routledge is an imprint of the Taylor & Francis Group

© 2000 Stephen Fineman

Typeset in Garamond by
Exe Valley Dataset Ltd, Exeter
Printed and bound in Great Britain by
TJ International Ltd, Padstow, Cornwall

British Library Cataloguing in Publication Data
A catalogue record for this book is available
from the British Library

Library of Congress Cataloging in Publication Data
The business of greening/edited by Stephen Fineman.
    p.   cm. – (Global environmental change series)
  1. Industrial management–Environmental aspects.   2. Economic
development–Environmental aspects.   3. Sustainable development.
  4. Environmental law.   I. Fineman, Stephen.   II. Series.

HD30.255.B8784 2000
333.7'2–dc21   00–036630

ISBN 0–415–22433–0

Contents

Figures and tables

Figures

Tables

Contributors

Stephen Fineman, School of Management, University of Bath

Andrea Coulson, Department of Accounting and Finance, University of Strathclyde

Frances Drake, School of Geography, University of Leeds

Ken Green, CROMTEC, Manchester School of Management, UMIST

Simon Guy, Centre for Urban Technology, School of Architecture, Planning and Landscape, University of Newcastle

Brian Harvey, Manchester Business School, Manchester University

Jane Hunt, Centre for Study of Environmental Change, Lancaster University

Deborah Millard, Centre for the Study of European Law, University of Leeds

Barbara Morton, CROMTEC, Manchester School of Management, UMIST

Steve New, Hertford College and Said Business School, University of Oxford

Judith Petts, Centre for Environmental Research and Training, University of Birmingham

Martin Purvis, School of Geography, University of Leeds

Sujatha Raman, Centre for Science Studies and Science Policy, Lancaster University

Anja Schaefer, The Management Centre, King's College London

Elizabeth Shove, Centre for Science Studies and Science Policy, Lancaster University

1 The business of greening

An introduction

Stephen Fineman

The twentieth century was remarkable for the growth of industrial goods and services. Human ingenuity appears to be almost limitless in turning the natural substances of the planet into objects and processes that serve our needs, whims and fantasies. Upon such a platform we erect our economic order: producing, selling, buying, consuming. The computers, cars, televisions, aircraft, heating and cooling systems, plastics, fashion clothes, cosmetics, hamburgers, hi-fi players and building materials that define modern life are both coveted and accumulated.

But the shiny image of production and consumption has tarnished over recent decades. A trickle of indicators that all may not be well has now grown into a fast stream. Our economic system produces 'bads' along with its 'goods'. Scraping and digging the earth, harvesting the forests and seas, creating and discarding chemicals and gasses, burying our waste and, generally, feeding the insatiable industrial/economic machine, may be wrecking the very ecosystem on which our supposed good life depends.

For some, the evidence that something is amiss is plain to see: congested roads, polluted rivers, air that is difficult to breathe, shrinking green spaces and forests, barren farmlands, diminishing wildlife, and the detritus of consumption on our streets and country lanes. Less obvious signs are spoken of in metaphors such as 'ozone holes', 'melting ice caps' and 'Frankenstein foods'. But, in the apt jargon of sociology, we here enter contested terrain. Is it 'really' happening? How bad is it? What evidence do we believe? Which scientists can we trust? Whose responsibility is it to do something about it?

It is this last question that is the concern of this book, focusing specifically on the activities of business. The book takes for granted that, at the very least, some precautionary changes are required in the way industry is organised and controlled if we are going to alleviate concerns about the environment. Of course, industry cannot shoulder all the blame for environmental degradation. Industry is a product of many social forces and structures – governments, financial systems, the way capital flows internationally in market economies, legal systems, and consumer pressures and lifestyles. However, industries, often in a very powerful way, shape and influence these features. Indeed, it is now apparent that some corporations have more financial and political clout than do those of their host countries. Industry's perspectives and actions on environmental issues are, therefore, crucially important for us all.

This much has been realised by the academic community. Research programmes into various features of business and the environment have sprung up worldwide. Different social scientists have contributed to these endeavours, reflecting the complexity of the issues involved. Thus we see investigations from sociologists, anthropologists, psychologists, management researchers, political scientists, geographers, organisational scientists and economists. They have examined: the way organisations change, or fail to change, in the face of environmental pressures; case studies of exemplars in corporate greening; the reasons behind industrial environmental disasters; how managers think about and see environmentalism; the selling and marketing of 'green' goods and services; the institutional pressures that facilitate or block green change; the workings of mandatory and voluntary environmental regulation; international influences on environmental strategies; the social and organisational features of waste management and recycling; environmental auditing; the influence of lobbying groups on industry. Apart from the practical significance of such investigations, they have opened key debates – such whether the much-canvassed 'sustainable development' is meaningful and attainable by industry.

This book adds its own voice to these issues. Its genesis lies in a research programme of the UK's Economic and Social Research Council (ESRC). In 1995 the ESRC funded a major research initiative on Global Environmental Change. The programme, which ran until 2000, included a stream of field research projects on business and the environment. The researchers, from various UK universities, developed their own network of meetings to share their findings and dilemmas. Out of these, the present volume was created.

Taken as a whole, the book does not preach greening, nor does it offer tidy managerial prescriptions. But it engages with debates about where business is and where it might go. The book gives voice to industrial actors in context – employees, employers, managers, technical specialists, regulators – in their organisations, within industrial sectors or part of wider institutional regimes. There is a wide representation of businesses – public and private, small and large: estate agents, banks, bakers, printers, regulators. While the authors present their subject matter through their own conceptual lenses, there is much convergence in the way the political and negotiative context of greening is viewed. Greening, its means and ends, is explored as socially constructed, shaped through tensions, passions and competing interests. The book's revelations are sometimes surprising, sometimes hopeful. They should be of particular interest to advanced students and researchers of environmental and business studies, and those trying to shape our social policies.

This chapter will preview in more detail the different contributions to the book. But first, what issues underlie them; broad motifs to bear in mind when considering the 'business of greening'? Two will be considered here.

Is business 'there' to look after the environment?

The dominant view of neo-classical economists is that commerce, from the sole trader to the transnational corporation, survives by securing profit – financial surplus over and above the costs of production. There are variations on this theme suggesting that profit-maximisation is important, but not everything. There is the drive towards market share, the creation of customers, capturing resources, innovation, appeasing shareholders. These, in turn, can reflect the aspirations, machinations and interpretations of key business actors – to acquire power and prestige, create and protect careers, accumulate personal wealth, pursue personal ambitions.

Doubtless, businesses – private and public – are complexly 'bounded' in their rationalities, such that their fortunes will follow more than one plan. Yet it is hard to escape the logic of industrial leaders, and the institutions that serve them, that profit and growth is key to survival in a competitive market economy. This is more than apparent when we see the giants, as well as the minnows, of the business world flounder or fail.

But where does the environment fit into this? One answer is 'everywhere and nowhere'. In other words, the natural environment is treated as an externality, some 'thing' to be used to serve and service corporate ends. In Ernst Schumacher's economic language, the environment is treated as income to spend, not capital to conserve (Schumacher, 1973). In the interests of short-term goals, increasing sales, more profit, stimulating ever more 'wants' and consumption, the planet's use is taken for granted. After all, the air, land and seas have always been there, free for us all. This thinking applies as much to what is put into the creation of goods and services as to where they happen to end up. Most modern businesses have been built upon such premises, not in the belief that the earth has finite capacity. Claims about environmental damage, therefore, are ideologically disturbing for business and ripe for denial or avoidance.

In these terms, businesses are singularly ill suited to take on board the social changes advocated by some environmentalists: towards low growth, eco-sensitivity in business strategy and processes, small-scale enterprise and reduced consumption. Environmentalists' assertions that we are witnessing a global tragedy of the commons – irrecoverably plundering and polluting our public spaces – are met with unease or incredulity by industry. It is easier to bury one's corporate head in monthly profit and loss accounts – and continue business as usual.

But as green pressures mount, such a response becomes harder to maintain. 'Dirty' firms get noticed, pointed out, embarrassed, by green observers and the world's media. Citizens, seeing the obvious effects of pollution in their communities, urge their local and national politicians to take some action. Governments begin to campaign for a new social responsibility within industry, exhorting business towards greener practices. As social concern increases, fiscal measures and mandatory regulation attempt to spur industry along a greener path. Some investors, including banks, add their voice, favouring corporations that have demonstrated at least some measure of green responsibility. All these moves amount to a huge project – which has been called eco-modernism. It is an attempt to have our economic cake and eat it, but a cake now leavened with greener yeast.

Towards sustainable capitalism?

It is a coarse, but sobering, observation that a quarter of the world's people enjoy three-quarters of the world's resources. It is not without irony that many countries that have enjoyed most wealth from exploiting their own, and others', natural environments are now at the vanguard of greener technologies (and the new markets that they bring). Indeed, the irony is compounded when so called third world and developing countries have been urged to care for their environments in their economic expansion by those who plainly have not. The arguments rage about whether we are now slamming the stable door after the horse has bolted or whether a combination of technical adjustments to the way we run our economy can fix matters. Certainly, as I write, the latter view prevails in most Western industrial economies. It is expressed in terms of *sustainable development*.

Sustainable development has a reassuring aura: '. . . an economic state where the demands placed upon the environment by people and commerce can be met without reducing the capacity of the environment to provide for future generations' (Hawken, 1995: 139). Yet the seduction of sustainability is problematic, if not downright misleading. In Tim O'Riordan's words:

> 'The refuge of the environmentally perplexed is sustainable development, namely wealth creation based on renewability and replenishment rather than exploitation. The trouble is that this is essentially a contradiction in terms for modernist capitalist culture' (1989: 93).

Sustainable development may well be an oxymoron, but it is one that can just about survive the test of political acceptability. For governments unwilling to threaten lifestyles and vested interests built upon industrial growth, sustainable development seems a way out. So in its name we see a range of measures intended to shape industry towards greener ways. They include international treaties on atmospherically-damaging emissions, fishing quotas, forestry protection, waste minimisation and recycling programmes, standards on packaging, eco-labelling, environmental auditing and reporting, greener goods, green self-regulatory schemes, the creation of green corporate cultures, 'brown' site development for new industry, and a new breed of environmental experts – consultants, managers, government bureaucrats. Additionally, we see fiscal devices intended to foster less-damaging environmental practice – such as tax penalties on polluting fuels and tradable pollution-credit systems.

The authors of this book get inside such 'sustainable' business practices. Eco-modernism is observed through empirical study of actors – managers, professionals, officials – who shape the project on the ground, so to speak. How well does it operate? What lesson can we draw?

The chapters to come

The book is divided into four parts: *Constructing the environment, Regulating, Learning and change,* and *The green organisation?*

Part 1   Constructing the environment

In this part of the book the authors examine how central players in organisations construct and make meaningful, environmental issues and discourses. It examines the perceptual slants, social linkages and political networks that constitute the environment and responses to it.

In *The manager, the business and the big wide world* (Chapter 2), Purvis, Drake, Hunt and Millard examine the realities of the 'think global, act local' slogan that has been attached to sustainability. They studied small businesses (see also Chapter 9) whose refrigeration activities have been linked to ozone depletion and climate change. How do workers/managers in these enterprises link their own activities to these global concerns? What bridge is there between workaday issues and ones of planet Earth? The authors find that 'the local has, in effect, become the global'; where what cannot be seen or otherwise sensed is not counted – at least, not in the workplace. Such psychological or perceptual constriction tempers, if not disables, grander proclamations and international protocols on voluntary emission controls. It takes mandatory regulation to make a difference. The chapter suggests that, while there may be some deliberate evasion of environmental responsibility amongst organisational managers and owners, the core problem is elsewhere. There is often a genuine helplessness and disempowement in the face of remote environmental pronouncements – such as those of scientists and politicians. The authors speculate on ways of addressing such difficulties and whether it is possible to 'win' for both environment and business.

New, Green and Morton, in *Buying the environment: the multiple meanings of green supply* (Chapter 3), expose the pervasiveness and power of corporate purchasing: how, and from whom, companies buy things. Corporate procurement is itself a huge and financially risky activity which involves complex relations with suppliers – including how green they are. Indeed, the greenness of a company is inextricably tied to the greenness of those who supply it with goods and services, and to the greenness of the suppliers' suppliers, and so forth. Hence we can refer to the greening of the 'supply chain'. How some of the links of this chain are connected, and the meanings and social relations that constitute the connections, are examined. Despite professional literature advocating a bond between environment and supply, the authors observe very little in actual practice. Why this might be the case is explored through interviews with managers and purchasing staff active, or inactive, in green purchasing. They reveal how green purchasing decisions are politicised and bureaucratised within organisations; how suppliers can resist and be coerced; how compromises occur that may or may not benefit the environment; the place of the owner's or purchasing manager's ethical beliefs; the fending-off of criticism from consumers and activists. There is, conclude the authors, no single model of supply-chain greening.

Buildings are more than economic units; they constitute our 'man'-made environment and the way we use and abuse natural materials and site locations. So those who turn to environmentally-sensitive development practices ought to be of considerable interest to us. This is the staring point of Guy's *Framing environmental choices: mediating the environment in the property business* (Chapter 4). Guy identifies five key figures in the property business: architects, developers, occupiers, investors and agents. They interact in complex ways to influence the style and form of buildings and the meanings of their environmental impact. What do these actors want from buildings? Architects will seek tailored design solutions for their clients, which may include ecological considerations. For developers, in search of enhancing the economic value of the land they manage, environmental care counts only if it inflates the price of land or rental from buildings. Occupiers want space to fit their task and productivity needs, and/or to symbolise their corporate ethos. Environmental issues may be part of such considerations, especially if they affect the costs of running the building. For investors, like developers, buildings represent quantifiable assets; the environmental profile of the building is of little interest unless it contributes to market attractiveness. Finally, estate agents; they are central to how the market is constructed. Estate agents listen to other estate agents as well as to their clients. Environmental innovation may be presented as a handicap in the market or the opposite – a 'desirable'. Guy examines how these various discourses conflict and interact and the circumstances under which environmental innovation and greener buildings may prevail.

Coulson's chapter, *Banking on the environment: risk and rationality* (Chapter 5) takes us into the world of the banker. Banks are a key source of finance for industrial projects. Do the environmental implications of the projects matter to the bank? Coulson argues that they are beginning to, not for altruistic reasons, but because (a) the bank can now suffer reputational damage if associated with a polluter, (b) security, such as property, for a debt can be affected by its environmental condition or effects, and (c) the lender may be liable for the environmental risks of its borrower. How this operates in practice is the focus of the chapter. Coulson describes how bank lending officers make judgements about the environmental credentials of clients. She reveals the interplay and politics between the formal guidance rules on lending, the use of experts, and the lenders' 'mental models' and intuitions. While official bank policy states that it is not acting as an environmental expert, the bank is clearly able to shape the environmental profile of the industries it supports by how and when it grants loans.

Part 2   Regulating

In this part of the book we examine the nature and effects of environmental regulation – mandatory and voluntary – on what companies do, or fail to do. As national and international environmental regulations have grown, so has our need for targeted, in-depth studies on how they work. Regulation is examined as a culturally contextualised, live, negotiative phenomenon.

In Chapter 6 *Being a regulator*, I take mainly a regulator's-eye view of mandatory environmental control. Environmental law is only as good as the way it is applied. What precisely happens when the regulatory officer and the industrial operator meet? How is regulatory law made real and effective in the interactions between the two parties? What are the partialities, prejudices and politics of the encounter? The chapter draws upon a qualitative study of a UK mandatory environment agency, shadowing and interviewing its field inspectors. While environmental law loosely frames the regulatory encounter, much depends on the way *both* parties work to negotiate an agreement. Indeed, for the inspector, enforcement and prosecution is a mark of professional failure and an unwelcome complication for future regulatory visits. The inspector's moral order of offences and offenders, and his or her use of power, are key resources in the way regulation is worked. Fairness, for the inspector, is not treating everyone alike, because they are often not alike – it is not a level playing field. The chapter concludes by outlining the tensions and contradictions in the regulator's role, the place of external influences, such as green activists, and how some of the pressures can be resolved.

Regulation, be it mandatory or voluntary, does not exist in a cultural vacuum. Not only may one type of regulation facilitate another, the setting and context of the particular industry will moderate all regulatory effects. Hunt and Raman, in *Regulation matters: global environmental discourse and business response* (Chapter 7) develop this argument through their studies of four business sectors: baking, building construction, printing and refrigeration. These sectors contain different sizes of business, different types of products, technologies and market relationships (e.g. with suppliers, producers, distributors, customers). Formal and voluntary environmental regulation need to be seen within the cultural domains of these features. The authors examine how regulation has unfolded, with distinct degrees of potency, within each of the sectors. While mandatory regulation can act as a force to protect the environment, it can also create a social medium where other pro-environmental regimes can flourish.

Raman and Shove, in *The business of building regulation* (Chapter 8), further unroll the regulatory map to demonstrate the way an ostensibly simple shift in mandatory regulation can have extensive social/organisational ramifications.

Their case example is of an amendment to the energy-efficiency requirements of the UK's building regulations from prescriptive to performance criteria: environmental ends are more important than means. On the face of it, this seems a straightforward regulatory move for discussion between government and the building industry. However, Raman and Shove's research with key government actors and much secondary data, reveals a multifaceted picture of parties directly and indirectly involved in facilitating action, blocking, doing deals, and moulding the new regulation. We see actors politically manoeuvring to protect their interests – such as concrete producers, the air conditioning and refrigeration industry, different government departments, surveyors, property federations, house builders, boilermakers, architects and timber associations. The salient dimensions of these processes are outlined through different conceptual lenses on policy analysis, 'from institutions to interests, interests to networks, and networks to systems'. Through these, the line between regulation and business becomes progressively more blurred and the construction of environmental regulation more frail. The real business of regulation, argue the authors, is holding this structure together.

Part 3   Learning and change

The management literature on the greening of organisations has much to say on how to bring about green organisational cultures. It usually includes calls for top management support, new green structures and roles, mechanisms of green audit and control, and special training This part of the book casts a critical eye over this field, especially the recipes to 'go green'. What can we expect of change efforts that seek to bring about green cultural shifts or transformation at corporate level? Are there key psychological ingredients that enable organisations to 'learn to be green'?

Petts, in *Smaller enterprises and the environment: organisational learning potential?* (Chapter 9), argues that organisations that employ under 250 people have a key role to play, both economically and environmentally. The vast majority of businesses are of this sort – and they are relatively flat in structure. Typically, though, they have been overshadowed by attention to large corporations. Smaller enterprises may not have the economic resources or expertise of large companies, but they have potential flexibility in their size. But are they sufficiently psychologically predisposed to environmentalism? What do the existing realities of actors in smaller businesses tell us of their scope for green change? Petts explores such issues through interviews, questionnaires and focus groups with managers and non-managers in small and medium-sized organisations. She teases out the various facets of their personal and role-related beliefs about the environment. Noteworthy is the downbeat picture painted by her respondents, who found if hard to relate the wider rhetorics of environmental concern and sustainability to their own pragmatics of doing business. As one said: 'being environmentally friendly does not always get the work out the door'. Indeed, they felt little pressure from customers in the supply chain to change their old habits. So organisational learning remains largely latent. But there were some exceptions, firms that were clearly proactive environmentally. Petts analyses what makes them different, highlighting the role of the environmental champion, the business benefit of greener ventures and environmental training for employees.

The last chapter of this part is by Schaefer and Harvey – *Agents of change in corporate 'greening': case studies in water and electricity utilities* (Chapter 10). In their interviews with managers, Schaefer and Harvey probe the way water and power generation companies have turned towards, or stalled, greening. Where is the locus of change? Who are the key agents? What are the influences of internal factors compared with external social influences? The chapter exposes a spectrum of managerial players in environmental initiatives, as well as the different structures and techniques (e.g. policy statements, accreditation schemes, performance reports). The companies and their sectors are compared and contrasted, as are the effects of their social contexts. Concerning the latter, whatever initiatives occur 'in' the organisations cannot be separated from the influence of wider conditions, especially the law, public opinion and changes at the competitive and industry level. The chapter concludes that the commitment of an environmental champion is important for greening. Beyond this, an environmental manager's skills at persuasion are crucial – more so than his or her formal status. Environmental polices can be fairly hollow symbols of intent; better to have an environmental management system that speaks of deliverable targets in a language with which organisational members can meaningfully connect.

Part 4   The green organisation?

The closing part of the book looks more reflectively on the green organisation. In *Green myths, green realities* (Chapter 11) six of the authors each contribute a brief polemic on 'the green organisation', speculating on the foibles and fate of greening. Their provocative views deconstruct some of the assumptions about 'greening' and 'organisation' and offer paths through the analytic maze that has become the business of greening. The chapter concludes with my own thoughts on their thoughts: a vision of the precariousness of industrial greening in practice, but within a social milieu where environmental issues will not go away.

References

Hawken, P. (1995) *The Ecology of Commerce*. Guernsey: The Guernsey Press
O'Riordan, T. (1989) The challenge of environmentalism. In R. Peet and N. Thrift (eds) *New Models in Geography*. London: Unwin Hyman.
Schumacher, E. F. (1973) *Small is Beautiful*. London: Abacus.

10   *Stephen Fineman*

Further Reading

Bansal, P. and Howard, P. (1997) *Business and the Natural Environment*. Oxford: Butterworth-Heinemann.
Buchholz, R. A. (1993) *Principles of Environmental Management*. Englewood Cliffs, NJ: Prentice Hall.
Cairncross, F. (1991) *Costing the Earth*. London: Business Books.
De George, R. T. (1999) *Business Ethics*. Englewood Cliffs, NJ: Prentice Hall.
Eden, S (1996) *Environmental Issues and Business*. Chichester, Wiley.
Fineman, S. (1996) Emotional subtexts in corporate greening. *Organisation Studies*, 17 (3): 479–500.
—— (1997) Constructing the green manager. *British Journal of Management*, 8: 31–38.
Fineman, S. and Clarke, K. (1996) Green stakeholders: industry interpretations and response. *Journal of Management Studies*, 33 (6): 715–730.
Fischer, K. and J. Schot, J. (eds), (1991) *Environmental Strategies for Industry*. Washington, DC: Island Press.
Gore, A. (1992) *Earth in Balance*. London: Earthscan Publications.
Hannigan, J. A. (1995) *Environmental Sociology*. London: Routledge.
McDonagh, P. and Prothero, A. (eds) (1997) *Green Management: A Reader*. London: Dryden.
O'Riordan, T. (1998) *Transition to Sustainability*. London: Earthscan.
Smith, A. (1997) *Integrated Pollution Control*. Aldershot: Ashgate.
Smith, D. (1993) *Business and the Environment*. London: Paul Chapman.
Welford, R. (1995) *Environmental Strategy and Sustainable Development*. London: Routledge.
—— (1997) *Hijacking Environmentalism*. London: Earthscan.
Yearley, S. (1992) *The Green Case: A Sociology of Environmental Issues, Arguments and Politics*. London: Routledge.

Part 1

Constructing the environment

2 The manager, the business and the big wide world

Martin Purvis, Frances Drake, Jane Hunt and Deborah Millard

The 1990s saw both the emergence of a literature on business and the environment, and a growing scientific and political consciousness of the global scale of environmental change (Stern *et al.*, 1992; Welford, 1996; Yearley, 1996). Logically, the two areas of study are closely connected; processes of production and consumption orchestrated by business play an important role in shaping human impacts upon the global environment. Political diagnoses of actions to meet the global environmental challenge also place business centre-stage; not simply as a participant in wider behavioural changes, but leading the design and implementation of techno-logical and managerial innovations to counter environmental damage. The present chapter focuses on atmospheric change, where an international political process has defined targets and timetables for reduction in the production and emission of ozone-depleting and greenhouse gases (Haas *et al.*, 1993; O'Riordan *et al.*, 1998; Parry *et al.*, 1998; Rowlands, 1995; Tangen,1999; Victor *et al.*, 1998). Some larger businesses have participated directly in this diplomatic process, but many more are drawn into the attempt to meet the environmental targets. This begs a number of questions about the capacity of business to implement change, which have a wider resonance in academic attempts to understand relationships between business and environment.

Some of the literature which has emerged in the 1990s has been rather unquestioning in its approach to the two central terms of 'business' and 'environment'. The message is relatively simple: business (as an undiffer-entiated whole), has to display greater responsibility towards the environ-ment (as an undifferentiated whole). In so doing, it is argued, business will adopt a new leadership role, discovering efficiencies, technologies and market opportunities that will yield commercial as well as environmental rewards (e.g. Elkington, 1994; Enmarch-Williams, 1996). Such 'win–win' arguments are often supported by case studies of individual companies, disproportionately drawn from amongst the largest international businesses (Newton and Harte, 1997).

Normative models and selective case studies may be intended to have a powerful inspirational effect in promoting the greening of business, but they leave unanswered questions which are of real importance, given the political emphasis on companies as environmental problem-solvers. This is not just to argue for more detailed exploration of the technical ability of businesses to change their own operational practices and create environmentally-friendly products for consumers. We also need to know rather more about the ways in which business people frame the environment. Connections between business activity and the state of the global environment may seem clear and logical to academics and policy-makers. But do they have the same reality to company managers whose attitudes and understandings directly influence business practice? How do global concerns fare when set against other environmental or commercial priorities which may seem more immediate and important?

The chapter addresses these latter questions first, before turning to the commercial and environmental complexities of redesigning core products in the refrigeration industry. In so doing it explores issues raised by strato-spheric ozone depletion and climate change, as viewed from the perspective of business managers and owners drawn from companies rather smaller than the transnational corporations whose names recur in accounts of international attention to the global atmosphere. These smaller companies do not proclaim their global role and responsibilities in a way that is increasingly common amongst their larger counterparts (ICI, undated; ICL, 1992). They are not individually dominant players in terms of the scale of their activity or their apparent potential for environmental leadership through technical and managerial innovation (cf Fiksel, 1996; Florida, 1996; Schmidheiny, 1992). Nor have they been active participants in the international diplomatic process which shaped such environmental agreements as the Montreal Protocol on ozone depleting substances (cf Susskind, 1992). Hence, questions are asked relatively rarely about the global connections and consciousness of smaller businesses. Yet their collective importance should not be under-estimated.

In total, smaller businesses have a huge economic impact (cf DTI, 1995; DTI, 1997). Ranging from significant operations with several thousand workers, to the smallest micro-businesses, they form a considerable, if fragmented, reservoir of capital and employment. Many operate internation-ally and some are influential in shaping commercial and technological agendas for their own industries. All are ultimately embraced by global commercial systems and the economic and regulatory forces which now operate as much at this largest scale, as they do within individual national territories.

From an environmental perspective the mass of smaller businesses is also collectively significant, not least in the context of efforts to develop broad-based participatory responses to global atmospheric change. The drive to reduce emissions of ozone-depleting and greenhouse gases potentially embraces businesses of all types and scales, as well as consumer households (cf Hinchliffe, 1996; Uniclima, undated). This is explicit in attempts by

European governments to reduce greenhouse emissions from transport and energy use by establishing partnerships with business that include not only links with major corporations, but also initiatives targeted at smaller companies (Bundesumweltministerium, 1996; DoE, 1995a; DoE, 1995b; Energy Efficiency Office, 1993; Ministère de l'Environnement, 1995; O'Riordan and Jäger, 1996). Within the refrigeration industry, where concerns about ozone and climate come together with a particular potency, the potential players include not only the many users of refrigeration equipment, but also the small niche producers, maintenance and service contractors which exist alongside the major companies mass-producing white goods and the chemical giants supplying refrigerant gases.

It seems relevant, therefore, to consider the place of smaller businesses in any 'global' scheme. What understanding of global environmental issues do their owners and managers have? Do they acknowledge personal or professional responsibilities as part of economic systems which have caused global atmospheric change? Do they feel willing or able to contribute effectively to measures designed to combat global environmental change?

Business attitudes: a world apart?

There are claims, not least from the image-makers for the largest corporations, that business commands especial expertise in finding practical solutions to a multitude of environmental challenges. This is also the core of technocentric arguments about ecological modernisation (Hajer 1995; Hajer 1996; von Weizsäcker *et al.* 1997, pages 33–36 on refrigeration are especially relevant here). But do such arguments ring true? More particularly, how appropriate is this assertion of environmental competence and certainty when smaller companies are pitted against complex global problems? Responsibilities may be ascribed to business, both in causing and combating environmental change (cf HMSO, 1994). Yet there is no necessity that such responsibilities are accompanied by heightened understanding of environmental issues amongst business managers. Nor does it follow that understanding the nature of a problem leads logically to its solution. Problems, perhaps especially those cast at the global scale, may inspire bewilderment at their complexity and a sense of the insignificance of individual actions.

Despite the sloganeering and initiatives such as Local Agenda 21, many people seem to find it difficult to link the local and the global, seeing the latter as separate, both spatially and temporally, from the routine of daily life. Nor is there immediate sensory evidence of global change, making it difficult for lay people to judge the validity of the environmental rhetoric and expert claims relayed through the media. Even when individuals see benefits from action to defend global, as well as local, environments, they may not apply the logic of this recognition to change their daily lives. This is not necessarily a reflection of ignorance, or lack of concern, but may stem from a sense of disempowerment, and a lack of faith in participatory initiatives and the institutions that orchestrate them. These are amongst the conclusions of recent attempts to go beyond the rather superficial categorisation of public attitudes towards the environment based on surveys and opinion polls (e.g. Burgess *et al.*, 1998; Harrison *et al.*, 1996; Hinchliffe, 1996; Macnaghten and Jacobs, 1997; Macnaghten and Urry, 1998). Might these feelings find an echo in the personal and professional experience of business managers?

Talking to business about environmental change

The following material derives from interviews undertaken with 65 individuals associated with 52 companies and organisations in Britain, France and Germany, between May 1996 and June 1998. Three business sectors with contrasting environmental profiles were identified for study. Refrigeration was chosen as an industry whose commercial and technical practice has been directly affected by concerns about ozone depletion and climate change. Rather than concentrate exclusively on the larger producers (with over 500 employees), attention was paid to commercial refrigeration where small (under 50 employees) and medium-sized (under 500 employees) companies are active in production, installation and servicing. Baking and printing are both users of refrigeration equipment, and industries in which energy use is obvious in core production systems. The former, however, has a self-image as a 'clean' industry with little environmental impact, while the latter has received recent criticism for its poor environmental performance. In these sectors it was possible to include micro-businesses with fewer than 10 workers in the sample, as well as a balanced range of small, medium-sized and larger operations.

Companies participated in the study by invitation, themselves nominating a member (or members) of the management team with particular responsibility for the environment. Semi-structured interviews with these individuals addressed their personal and professional understanding of environmental issues, with particular reference to global atmospheric change. The interview method is particularly appropriate for exploring individual perceptions and attitudes (King 1994). It is important, however, also to acknowledge its limitations. Where a broader perspective on a business's operations is required, the accounts of individual interviewees need to be checked against company documentation and, where possible, the knowledge of other managers. Prioritising detail in individual interviews also imposes practical limits to the number of participants in the study.

Overall, our sample may have an over-representation of companies and individuals with well-developed environmental interests. In part, this reflects our inclusion of one or two companies from each sector which had received publicity for their environmental initiatives. Generally, those respondents with environmental interests are more likely to have responded positively to our approaches. However, the range of different views expressed and the apparent candour with which both 'pro' and 'anti' environmental attitudes were voiced – sometimes by a single individual – give us confidence in the value of our interviews. We cannot claim that the opinions and experiences analysed here form a representative or comprehensive cross-section. They are, however, interesting in their range and reveal some of the ideas and attitudes current within these business sectors.

Interviewees were, with only two exceptions, male and predominantly middle-aged. Most had operational responsibilities in technical, engineering and plant management, a bias which is indicative of the way the environment is framed by many businesses. For smaller businesses with simple managerial structures, it was common to speak to the owner or managing director. Differentiation within the sample could be attempted in various different ways; for the sake of clarity the present discussion will confine itself largely to comparisons between the three business sectors, complemented, where appropriate, with reference to the scale of a company's operations.

Speaking personally: defining the environment

Without exception, interviewees expressed personal environmental concerns and saw action against environmental damage as part of creating a better world. A minority, perhaps drawing on core religious values, voiced explicitly moral arguments about pollution and the wasteful consumption of resources (cf Kempton *et al.,* 1995). Issues highlighted most frequently had an immediate local impact and related to interviewees' own experience (cf Burningham and O'Brien, 1994; Macnaghten and Urry, 1998). Hence, urban litter, pollution and congestion were contrasted with enjoyment of the countryside through walking and fishing. Ambiguities in environmental attitudes noted by studies of public understanding were similarly displayed by our interviewees (Macnaghten and Urry, 1998). Cars, for example, were seen both as environmentally damaging and a socio-economic necessity. Clearly also, the environment was a flexible concept for interviewees. Although invited to reflect on the ecological environment, several acknowledged no boundary between this and a broad socio-economic realm. Discussions ranged over issues, such as drug dealing and the commercial power of supermarkets, bearing upon concerns about social change and loss of community.

Around half the interviewees displayed, unprompted, consciousness of larger or more distant environmental problems. One individual who had worked in Nigeria drew on personal experience in expressing concerns about Third World deforestation. Others were clear in framing problems, including those of atmospheric change, as global. Hence, as the general manager of a small refrigeration contractor observed, 'it's the world as a whole that has to unite' in the search for solutions. This was, however, accompanied by scepticism about the institutional pace of change. International political conferences might float 'great ideas and very good theories', but they did not necessarily trigger effective action: 'in another five years you have another big conference, and you're still talking about it. And . . . the [environmental] position is worse'.

Recognition of the scale of environmental problems also prompted reflections that impinged upon issues of global equity. Individual interviewees noted the potential impact of past and projected global development patterns. One identified both current high levels of energy consumption in Europe and the United States, and rapidly increasing demand from developing countries, as reasons to promote energy and resource efficiency. Another acknowledged arguments that responsibility for causation and solution of global environmental change rested more with industrialised states than currently developing countries, because of the former's substantial historical use of resources. More common, however, was a construction of differences between 'them' and 'us', which assumed that western countries and businesses were now acting responsibly, while environmental damage continued elsewhere. The record of past consumption was overlain by a view of the present in which others, typically developing countries or former Soviet-bloc states, needed to implement environmental reforms. As the managing director of a small refrigeration producer put it: 'in the UK we're doing our bit, but an awful lot of people aren't doing their bit. And no matter what we do, Russia will still chuck out . . . rubbish . . . which is going to cause global warming'.

Around one quarter of interviewees made sense of these larger challenges through overt expression of personal concerns about the world to be inherited by their children. But where global futures were seen to be endangered, interviewees more frequently rehearsed arguments akin to the 'limits to growth' thesis, than concerns about global environmental change. Several talked explicitly about rising levels of material consumption and population growth creating a drain on resources which 'can only go so far, because the well will dry out' (General manager, small refrigeration contractor).

Only a small minority expressed, unprompted, personal concerns about global atmospheric change, although interviewees from refrigeration were well aware of the significance of these issues in relation to innovations forced upon their industry. Climate change, in particular, seemed an abstract concept with little immediate relevance to daily life for most bakers and printers. Its causal mechanisms were sometimes poorly understood, with interviewees conflating climate change with urban pollution and ozone depletion (cf Kempton, 1991; Kempton, 1997; Rudig, 1995). This might reflect a popular understanding in which the specific causes of climate change and ozone depletion seem less relevant than their potency as symbols of the wider environmental damage inflicted by industrial society (Thompson and Rayner, 1998). Some interviewees, however, apparently found it difficult to relate climate change to a personal model which equated environmental damage with pollution by toxic emissions. As a naturally occurring and 'harmless' compound, carbon dioxide, the greenhouse gas most commonly cited, was hard to envisage as an environmental threat (cf Kempton *et al.*, 1995).

Some interviewees reflected an ambiguity about the consequences of climate change which they had detected in media and other discussion of the issue (cf Brown, 1996; Mortimer, 1996). Global warming, at least when viewed from a distinctly national perspective, was not necessarily a threatening prospect. The sales director of a medium-sized baking oven manufacturer noted potential dividends including improved fortunes for the English wine industry: 'Somebody said it's going to be two extremes, it's going to be very hot in the summer and very cold in the winter, and I can live with that'. Responding to this, a colleague, the company's technical director, developed a philosophical, almost Gaian, argument about the inevitability of environmental change:

> I think the majority of people think . . . the environment will look after itself, it has done for hundreds of year, so what's different? . . . [W]e understand what we are doing to this planet's environment. But why shouldn't environments change? Are we destroying the planet? Yes. We're destroying it as we know it, but this planet has evolved through many phases. And is this just a phase that has to happen?

Professional perspectives: business roles and responsibilities

The overwhelming majority of interviewees accepted that business has environmental responsibilities, typically expressed in terms of legislative compliance, but extending to technological innovation, waste minimisation and eco-efficiency. However, ambiguity towards the environment was as evident in the business attitudes of interviewees as it was in their more personal expressions of opinion. The principle of general business responsibility, for example, was sometimes accompanied by initial denials of the individual company's contribution to environmental problems. In identifying the environmental effects of their own business, interviewees often defined the question in terms of immediate pollution and the emission of toxic or controlled substances. For around half the bakers and a minority of printers, this was the basis for assertions of little or no environmental impact. Such arguments were often reinforced by comparison with the major environmental hazards associated with heavy industry. As the health and safety manager for a major bakery put it: 'in the food industry there is not this enormous potential for pollution as there is in heavy industry. . . . We haven't got a Bhopal here'. Small companies also cited the scale of their activities as further confirmation of their lack of serious environmental impact.

Acknowledgement of environmental responsibility was tempered by other considerations. Only a small minority of interviewees, from avowedly 'green' companies, explicitly endorsed 'win–win' arguments about the coincidence of commercial advantage and environmental good practice. Others, including the marketing manager for a domestic refrigeration producer, were clear that 'doing the right thing for the environment, . . . doesn't always fit with business and you don't always get advantage out of it' (cf Walley and Whitehead, 1994). Good will towards the environment has to be set in the context of other concerns, such as profitability and competitiveness, the inheritance of plant, machinery and infrastructure, funding investment and expansion, employment, and the marketability of goods. Information and environmental management systems are not the only missing variables standing in the way of the 'greening' of business. Moreover, as the general manager of a small refrigeration distributor acknowledged, information may not engender a positive reaction even though 'everybody knows what's at stake'. The global environment can become 'like all the rest of the atrocious things that scroll past on the television every evening when you go home, and they just become thoroughly banal and devoid of any interest whatsoever'. A sense of the environment as an unending series of intractable problems may only reinforce feelings of powerlessness and, hence, the irrelevance of environmental information (cf Macnaghten and Urry, 1998).

Some interviewees were ill-informed about the environment, but many more were not. However, even those with a personal sense of the global agenda found it difficult to relate the totality of the environmental challenge to their daily experiences, the pressures on them to attend to other economic and social priorities in both their domestic and professional life, and the limits of their individual capacities. It is unsurprising, therefore, that subsequent discussion focused on definitions of environmental impacts and concerns that derived from the company's own production processes and technologies. From this grounded perspective, even interviewees who had initially denied any environmental impact began to construct a rather different account. Printers noted issues associated with the recycling of paper and the disposal of inks, photographic chemicals and solvents. Bakers, too, were interested in waste minimisation, related to food waste and packaging; the latter being the subject of imminent regulation at the time of the interviews. They also tended to equate 'environment' with hygiene and hazard management in food production, although several drew additional links with chemical use in agriculture and 'healthy' food, free from additives and preservatives.

The dominant framing of the workplace thus obscured other ways of viewing many of the issues identified by interviewees, and their potential connections to wider environmental systems. The use and recycling of paper, for example, is not simply a matter of purchasing and waste disposal practices, it potentially relates to issues of land use and ultimately the role of trees in the carbon cycle. Yet there was no evident consciousness of the way that individual managers' decisions might relate to this larger picture, beyond the individual printer who bemoaned a false public perception that paper production contributed to the destruction of tropical rainforests.

Similar biases were evident in discussion of refrigeration, a topic perhaps more likely to lead, unprompted, to consideration of global atmospheric change. Bakers, as users of refrigeration, were generally aware of regulatory curbs on CFCs and the need to employ alternative refrigerants in new equipment. But often it was the banning of CFCs which was presented as 'the problem', rather than a more direct expression of concern about global atmospheric change. Even amongst managers in the refrigeration sector itself, it was common for ozone depletion and climate change to be discussed as 'the CFC issue', transforming the global problem of atmospheric change into a more immediate and technical challenge to find alternative ways of delivering refrigeration.

Generally relevant issues, including energy use and transport, which have a bearing on global atmospheric change, were raised without prompting only by a minority of interviewees. This perhaps reflected an initial perception that these were not primarily 'environmental' concerns. Several companies had, or were planning, measures to monitor and improve efficiency of resource use in energy and transport, but these were prompted chiefly by commercial considerations, particularly the opportunities for cost savings. Any environmental benefits were imprecisely framed and invariably seen as incidental.

Individuals made the connection between transport and the environmental effects of vehicle emissions, although these related to concerns about urban air quality, rather than climate change. Similarly, few drew attention to the link between energy efficiency and reduction of greenhouse gas emissions from power generation (cf Thompson and Rayner, 1998). Energy use was sometimes noted in tandem with monitoring of other inputs, particularly water consumption (cf a similar approach in some official documentation: Energy Efficiency Office, 1995). This created a context in which environmental arguments, if acknowledged at all, related to resource management, rather than environmental change. Although the connection was not made by interviewees themselves, this also seems consistent with wider concerns about the exhaustion of resources which some expressed. Only two companies outside the refrigeration sector – a small baker and a medium-sized printer – confounded the general reticence about engaging with global atmospheric change. Both had a self-proclaimed 'green' profile, reflecting the strong personal environmental stance of their owners. This was apparent not only in the interviews, but also in advertising material which related practices such as the baker's sourcing of fuel wood from coppiced trees to efforts to combat global warming.

All businesses which control their energy consumption may contribute, even if unconsciously, to efforts to reduce emissions of greenhouse gases. However, framing energy use as a local and commercial consideration for the individual business places particular limits on companies' interest in technical innovation or managerial change. Refrigeration producers noted that supermarket clients were paying increased attention to operational efficiency when commissioning new systems, in large part because of the scale of their energy costs. However, many other customers were unwilling to pay a small capital premium for more energy efficient equipment, even when it could be quickly recouped in lower running costs. Thus, argued the owner of a small refrigeration contractor, 'you can't do anything for environmental protection'. Similar points were made by oven manufacturers regarding the baking trade. Smaller businesses were seen to have little incentive to take energy efficiency initiatives, given the limited financial returns that were likely to accrue. Even in a medium-sized printer, the engineering manager noted that potential annual savings of a few hundred pounds on energy were 'not worth a lot of management effort. . . . [T]here are other lines in the accounts where we could lever and get a lot more response'. Where cost reductions rather than energy efficiency *per se* were prioritised, the renegotiation of energy tariffs was a more attractive option.

The local and the global: links and limitations

The construction of environmental change as a long-term, global challenge may seem logical to scientists and policy-makers (cf Taylor and Buttel, 1992), but it draws an ambiguous response from the wider public. When local–global links are drawn, the effect may be to subsume the totality of 'environment' to concern about specific local issues, rather than stimulate a popular consciousness of the cumulative impact of local actions (Burningham and O'Brien, 1994; Hinchliffe, 1996). This tendency for specific, and often geographically restricted, issues to dominate the total environmental agenda of particular individuals was found repeatedly amongst our interviewees. The 'local' has, in effect, become the 'global'.

A focus on the local can be valid, even praiseworthy. Nor need it necessarily be constructed as a 'zero-sum' form in which finite amounts of attention are applied to particular issues at the expense of other environmental matters. Individual larger companies studied used written environmental policies to claim a commitment to reduction of 'impact on the local, national and international environment'. Classic accounts of the emergence of environmental consciousness, including stage models of the 'greening' of business, propose that awareness and action spreads from specific concerns to inform a company's entire operations (Hass, 1996; Schaefer and Harvey, 1998). However, the optimism of such normative models may be tempered by engagement with the perspectives of business managers themselves. Our interviews suggest that managers have a clearer sense of constraining 'reality', than they do of the way forward to a 'total' environmental consciousness. Individuals, whatever their personal environmental convictions, defined their priorities within the workplace in quite specific ways, related to their job description and consequent responsibilities to negotiate relations between the company and external actors.

In the following discussion we concentrate on the ways in which structural influences shape the spatial scale of environmental definitions. However, it is important to acknowledge the significance of other scalar issues. Global atmospheric change is seen as distant in time as well as space, as the gravest consequences seem likely to be experienced beyond the lifespan of most people now living (Adam, 1994). Expressed concerns for interviewees' children or grandchildren made personal sense of attention to the long-term. Notions of generational survival were transferred to the business sphere by interviewees from family-owned businesses. However, most displayed a sense of time, in which immediate priorities crowded out attention to a future seen as unknowable. Indeed, the rapidity of recent change in an industry such as refrigeration only reinforced a sense of the unpredictability of the future. Inside 10 years, questioning the use of CFCs had gone from 'madness' to orthodoxy, while the safety and performance of replacement refrigerants remained, in some respects, unproven.

Interviewees noted the particular difficulties experienced by small businesses in allocating limited management resources to longer-term strategic planning. In larger companies, there were clearer divisions of responsibility between operational and strategic management. Yet environmental responsibilities were invariably allocated to the operational sphere. This framing of environment of itself encourages priorities that are more likely to be short-term rather than long-term and local rather than global. It perpetuates a perspective rooted in the specifics of business and regulation, rather than following principles of connectivity that echo those found in nature.

For many companies the greatest priority was given to the immediacies of their own factory, ensuring that it was a safe environment for workers, hygienic for food production and caused no obvious nuisance to neighbouring communities. Notions of environmental responsibility were seen as clearly defined 'because obviously there are regulations there [in the factory] we have to follow' (Technical director, medium-sized baking oven manufacturer). Equally 'we have to be neighbourly, . . . because . . . we've got a duty, if something's happening here and it's affecting them [the local community], there could be a court case' (Health and safety manager, medium-sized bakery). Regulations cited were often from the field of occupational health, including the Health and Safety at Work Act and procedures laid down by the Committee on Substances Hazardous to Health (COSHH). Similar priorities were embodied in site audits, which aimed to identify and eliminate environmental risks in the face of pressure from insurers or major commercial customers. Individual bakers felt that audits conducted by their supermarket clients, with an emphasis on hygiene and the safety of the finished product, ignored or even obstructed their efforts to promote other initiatives in energy efficiency, waste minimisation and recycling. However, for the most part, this was a framing of environment with which interviewees felt comfortable; problems were defined, targets set, and liabilities established. The necessity to defend, not the environment, but the company, against prosecution and loss of public and investor confidence, was clearly established.

Several interviewees argued that on-site health and safety management systems were a good indicator of a company's environmental credentials. These links, and the particular localised definition of environment which they encouraged, were often reinforced by the allocation of environmental and safety responsibilities to the same member of the management team. One such individual, employed by a large printer, graphically outlined the priorities that such a brief imposed on him. Immediate attention was given to changes necessary to avoid prosecution by the Health and Safety Executive or the Environment Agency, but

> what I'd be picking up on first would be the safety side of things, . . . the nature of people is, . . . and this is from the chief executive down to the bottom level of the shop floor, is you can't really notice global warming, but you can notice somebody getting their hand ripped off.

Comments elsewhere in the interview made it clear that this individual did not discount the importance of climate change as an environmental issue. However, the framing of his responsibilities in work made it difficult for him to accord it any priority.

A handful of interviewees identified climate change as a personal concern, but even where they were in a position to influence a company's policy, most saw little that an individual business could do to combat the problem effectively. Indeed, the smallest businesses drew parallels between their own energy use and that of private households, thus emphasising the gulf between individual actions and the global challenge (cf Hinchliffe, 1996). Smaller bakers and printers, in particular, were also locked in to the use of long-lasting machinery, including presses, ovens and refrigerators, thus slowing the introduction of the more energy efficient equipment now available. More generally, energy use was defended as essential, with limited perceptions of scope for savings. Some interviewees, such as the manager of a medium-sized bakery, reacted defensively by taking their argument to extremes. Presenting the choice as one between polar opposites of consumption and conservation obscured the potential for increased efficiency in resource use: 'We can't do without all plastics, we can't do without delivery transport, we can't not burn oil'.

The construction of global warming as something you 'can't really notice' is also revealing in relation to recent work on sensing the environment. As Macnaghten and Urry (1998) note, much of humanity's experience of the environment has been grounded in the visual, allied with other senses, especially smell. Atmospheric change cannot be understood in these sensory terms, with evidence of its reality coming not from direct experience, but from scientific and government 'experts' whose message is relayed through official channels and the wider media. The ambiguity of the media message and the public reading of it have been noted above. But there are perhaps also other more ubiquitous media constructions, which, through their familiarity, and perceived relevance, make global climate appear something of an alien concept. Weather, rather than climate, assaults our individual senses and its pattern of short-term variation is presented daily through the media. What may be significant, as Ross (1991) points out, is the dominant framing of weather in national or regional terms in bulletins and forecasts. This, rather than the global scale, is, for the most part, the way we think about atmospheric effects upon our lives.

Refrigeration and atmospheric change: earth-bound uncertainties

While the weather is a daily reality, global atmospheric change is not only the preserve of experts, but also the subject of continuing scientific debate. A threat that is uncertain as well as global might seem especially difficult for lay audiences, including business managers, to relate to their own experiences and responsibilities. In practice, the scientific uncertainty of atmospheric change was not widely acknowledged by interviewees, even in the refrigeration sector which has been most affected by concerns about CFCs and other chemicals.

The destructive impact of CFCs on the stratospheric ozone layer was widely regarded by interviewees as beyond dispute. Only the managing director of a company which had a particular interest in the continued promotion of HCFCs – an alternative refrigerant with a low rather than zero ozone depletion potential – struck a questioning note: 'My own view is that the hole's going to heal up and everybody's going to say . . . this is because . . . we banned CFCs. But I think it's actually a natural event. Nobody's ever proved it's not, have they?'. While commercial interests might dictate a particular stance for this one company, for most refrigeration producers there was no point in pursuing any regrets about the passing of CFCs and other ozone depleting chemicals, despite praise for them as efficient and effective refrigerants (Purvis *et al.*, forthcoming). Any environmental uncertainty was obscured by the reality of regulations proscribing CFC production and the commercial investment made in alternative technologies. As the service manager of a large refrigeration contractor put it, changing 'the refrigerant, it was just law, we had to do it, we didn't have an option'. From such a perspective engagement with the global or with the uncertainty of science seemed of little relevance.

If the 'banning' of CFCs and the increasing price of refrigerants helped to bring the challenge of ozone depletion down to earth, constructions were less clear cut in relation to climate change:

> As regards that [climate change], there are no laws as far as I know, and the bases, physical bases are on shaky ground, in my opinion. We know that scientists express very contradictory views on the greenhouse effect. However, it seems that . . . the dominant opinion is that greenhouse

gases are damaging. Although it has not been proven. Just last week I read an article where a highly regarded professor . . . said that all the calculations that have been made are all rubbish. The fact that the temperature on earth has risen in the last 50 years is for completely different reasons than greenhouse gases. So it doesn't have the same status [as ozone depletion] . . .' (Development manager, large refrigeration producer).

Significantly, while dwelling on the science, the interviewee began by noting the absence of regulation, the ultimate source of certainty in many other aspects of business's engagement with environment. The alternative of voluntary initiatives between business and government to establish a national commitment to reduce greenhouse gas emissions made no such impact and was mentioned only by the German interviewee quoted above (and by his equivalent in a major German bakery).

Climate change was a particular challenge for the refrigeration industry, faced with the task of minimising the total global warming impact of the equipment they produced. This involves attention to both the direct effects of refrigerants and foam blowing agents as greenhouse gases, and the indirect warming impact of the equipment in use related to its electricity consumption. The difficulties of this task were increased by the diversity of possible technical solutions. Suppliers of refrigerants and other key components created confusion, in the opinion of many interviewees, by actively championing their own products. Refrigeration producers faced disputed claims about the environmental and thermal properties of a range of different chemicals used as refrigerants and blowing agents, as well as wider debate about the safety and efficiency of alternative refrigeration technologies.

These disputes, and the implied priority of some environmental concerns over others, were impossible for interviewees, or their companies, to resolve individually. Some felt frustrated that their dependence on component suppliers was being abused. Rather than expressing confidence in the market to deliver the best technical solutions, interviewees – and not only those from the smallest companies – felt that uncertainties were being exploited for individual commercial gain. In particular, chemical companies and wholesalers supplying refrigerant gases were charged with defending their investments in existing productive capacity to the point of obstructing the adoption of environmentally and operationally superior alternatives. Moreover, a sense of the intractability of atmospheric change was reinforced by perceptions that 'solutions' often bred fresh problems. Hence, refrigerants with minimal direct impact on ozone depletion might be greenhouse gases; or were criticised for sacrificing energy efficiency and allegedly implicated in the production of carcinogens and acid rain (Purvis *et al.* forthcoming).

In practice, even regulation does not always create the certainty about the technical future of their industry, that many refrigeration producers would like to see. This is especially the case for companies that deal in several different national markets throughout Europe. The Montreal Protocol provides the ultimate international authority for the abandonment of the most potent ozone-depleting chemicals. However, political institutions much closer to home have enforced the move away from CFCs, creating a variety in responses to the need to adopt alternatives. In a context where the identification of technical solutions was of greater relevance to interviewees than the exploration of environmental change as a shared global experience, it is unsurprising that the specifics of particular national or sectoral circumstances were often stressed. Even within western Europe, differences in legislation, popular and political environmental consciousness, and commercial attitudes towards particular technologies gave specific alternatives to CFC-based refrigeration systems a much greater currency in some countries than in others.

Regulation affecting refrigeration is more stringent in Scandinavia, Germany, Holland and Luxembourg, than in Britain, France and, especially, southern and eastern Europe. Several of the first named countries have restricted the employment of direct expansion systems in larger, new commercial installations. This prohibits use of HCFCs, still widely used in France and eastern Europe, and HFCs, the mainstay of commercial refrigeration in Britain and many other countries despite growing attention to their global warming potential. In states where use of HFCs has been curbed, hydrocarbons and ammonia play an increasing role in commercial refrigeration (*RAC,* 1997; *RAC,* 1998). Many in the British refrigeration industry are aware of this, but remain sceptical about the safety and commercial acceptability of hydrocarbons, in particular (Purvis *et al.*, forthcoming).

Interviewees professed themselves frustrated by this technical and regulatory diversity. There was also a strong sense that they were reacting to developments, rather than themselves playing a significant part in shaping future agendas, either environmental or commercial. Few of the companies in our study could contemplate direct involvement in the national or international regulatory process in the way that major corporations claim environmental partnerships with governments. However, even suggestions of their collective representation through trade associations drew a mixed response. In the UK, the British Refrigeration Association (BRA) speaks for commercial refrigeration, in particular, but membership was far from universal amongst the companies studied. Small businesses, especially, felt that they had little to gain from involvement with the BRA and some seemed actively suspicious of what they saw as a closed-shop representing the vested interests of larger companies (similar attitudes were displayed to trade organisations in the printing and baking sectors). Even amongst interviewees who saw the BRA as effective in representing its members to government, there was still a sense that industry's role was reactive. In the division of labour between government and business, the latter's role was to comment on the technical feasibility of change. Responsibility for identifying environmental concerns remained with government as the sponsors of scientific research, for 'suggestions have still got to come from the scientists who actually study the environment' (Engineering manager, compressor manufacturer).

Conclusions and policy implications

Many of our interviewees were conscious of living in an increasingly inter-connected world in which decisions made by other people in distant places impacted on their personal and professional lives. In the refrigeration sector, where more companies were trading internationally, interviewees referred to economic globalisation, in the shape of competition with low-cost producers in Asia, north Africa and eastern Europe. To some extent also there were perceptions of common global environmental problems. Yet this contextual knowledge was often crowded out in managers' framing of their own environmental responsibilities. For bakers and printers, potentially important as energy users, concerns about global atmospheric change lacked the immediate reality which most interviewees saw in regulatory frameworks, the elimination of on-site hazards, the particularities of relationships with customers or local environmental health departments. For all the environmental rhetoric, the construction of mental links between the local and the global is not easy.

Does this marginalisation of the global matter? It does, in that the absence of an environmental logic sets limits to initiatives in energy efficiency. Interviewees saw the importance of avoiding waste in the use of energy and other resources. Yet efficiency was justified by the economies accruing to the company, and perhaps for some individuals, the status acquired through management of a successful project. The achievement that individuals feel in delivering these results for their companies is not easily transferred to a wider environmental agenda. Particularly in the case of climate change, even those who were most aware of the problem felt that there was little that they or their company could contribute to its solution. For some, a lack of a larger agency reflected the limitations of their own managerial responsibilities within the company. For others, especially those working in the smallest businesses, even the company as a unit seemed hardly more significant than did an individual private household, when set against the scale of global atmospheric change.

Some of the same pessimism about the impact of individual actions and the potential for collective environmental action was apparent in the reflective tone struck by the marketing manager for a large refrigeration producer:

> Just set another target for the EST [Energy Saving Trust], or something, it's not that fundamental, it's not going to make a difference. Until the rubbish is piling over the landfill sites and we can't see the sky any more because of pollution . . . people aren't really going to do anything. I think we are all playing around at the edges.

But atmospheric change was a more immediate reality in the refrigeration industry, as concerns about ozone-depleting and greenhouse gases had affected the technical specification of their core product. This highlights the role of business as 'problem-solver'; the repository of technical expertise to sustain existing technologies and living standards while protecting crucial environmental capital such as the ozone layer.

Win–win arguments proclaim the coincidence of economic and environmental priorities. The reality is more complicated, and it is often this, rather than a deficiency of information about the nature of the environmental challenge, which curbs managers' willingness and ability to create the perfect 'green' business. Szerszynski (1996) has written of the difficulty of 'knowing what to do' as an environmental dilemma characterising modernity. In a less philosophically elevated fashion, this is the dilemma that confronts many of our interviewees from refrigeration. No single technology is universally recognised as delivering the perfect environmental performance, which now includes attention not just to safety and ozone depletion, but also to global warming and energy efficiency. So how are decisions to be made about prioritising these criteria? Addressing such dilemmas takes us far beyond the apparent logic of ecological modernisation. The problems that the refrigeration industry faces may not be framed primarily in terms of the global environment. However, their complexity and resistance to straightforward scientific or technical reasoning is a warning of the limitations of business's capacity to deliver environmental solutions.

It is possible that in pleading a lack of agency, businesses may be attempting to evade environmental responsibilities. But some, at least, of the expressions of frustration and disempowerment appear genuine. Within the refrigeration sector companies clearly want to resolve uncertainties about the environmental impacts of different refrigerants and technologies. What is good for business in enabling longer-term planning and investment without fear of further regulation, is also good for the environment. That much of the win–win argument is true, but it does not make it any easier for managers to 'know what to do'.

While the total resolution of environmental and technical uncertainty remains elusive, more limited initiatives do offer a way forward. The attempt to construct a standard measure which assesses both the direct and indirect warming potential of refrigeration systems, the Total Equivalent Warming Index (TEWI), is welcome. But if it is to be effective as a means of testing the various claims made by manufacturers for the performance of their products, greater effort has to be applied to the regulation and, if possible, standardisation of operational conditions under which TEWI is measured. This is an area in which national and international trade associations could play a stronger role, perhaps as part of wider initiatives to review the quality of information provided to members from commercial sources such as refrigerant suppliers. Greater international co-ordination on the part of state regulatory authorities could also reduce some of the contradictions currently facing producers of commercial refrigeration by harmonising the technical specification of systems throughout European markets.

Realism about the potential of business to meet the largest, global environmental problems is important, for it refocuses attention upon the tools of information, regulation and fiscal reform available to political policy-makers. Environmental education might change cultural attitudes towards resource use and consumption in the longer-term. However, it is difficult to see how the general provision of information about atmospheric change and the role of individual companies and households in its causation and solution could lead to wholesale and immediate modification of the behaviour of producers and consumers. Even if the logic of the message were accepted by its intended audience, commitments to existing infrastructure, managerial routine and competitive behaviour exercise a powerful influence against change (cf Hinchliffe, 1996; Shove *et al.*, 1998).

Some of the same arguments apply to efforts to encourage energy efficiency through fiscal measures. But costs do matter to business, and interviewees were consistent in prioritising the financial advantages of initiatives in energy and waste management. Around a quarter of interviewees went further, acknowledging, albeit sometimes grudgingly, the potential of energy pricing and taxation to focus attention on energy efficiency. The priority that many companies were giving to waste management in the light of the introduction of taxation of landfill and new packaging regulations, also suggests that a greater political commitment to financial penalties for inefficient energy use would bear results. At the very least it seems illogical that so much attention is currently being paid to cutting energy prices. If energy markets have previously created excess profits then these are best returned to consumers indirectly, through subsidising energy efficiency initiatives.

Any change in pricing would, however, have to be Draconian to impact upon the behaviour of many of the businesses in the study where inter-viewees saw energy as a low priority because it contributed little to overall operating costs. Again this is an argument against any expectation of wholesale transformation. It is more practical to take a selective approach, focusing attention on individual companies at those points in their develop-ment when the potential for change is greatest. One such moment is when businesses are looking to expand or to replace existing plant and equipment. Interviewees in this position often recognised the potential for increased energy efficiency, and it was in this context also that one of our refrigeration companies had made the move to hydrocarbon-based systems. Where there are several practical options, business decision-making may not be driven by environmental considerations, but managers and owners are not averse to taking the 'greenest' route. The aim must be, therefore, that the potential for environmentally beneficial change in such circumstances is more fully exploited.

A more contingent approach requires greater attention to how and why businesses use energy and other resources, going beyond the mechanistic approach of existing audits. Again, insights may be derived from work reviewing household behaviour, here highlighting the impact of cultural as well as economic influences upon energy use (Shove *et al.*, 1998). Business use of energy is not simply determined by the maintenance of essential core productive activity, but also by a whole series of assumptions about the nature of the working environment, working practices, and the ways in which goods are distributed, promoted and marketed. Only through adopting this broader perspective upon business practice and culture can we begin to understand the range of different points of change and possible intervention to promote environmentally sound behaviour.

It is consistent with this focused approach that information for business is targeted more effectively. Rather than distributing environmental inform-ation indiscriminately, often creating new agencies in the process, greater effort must be made to harness those sources already used by business. Amongst our interviewees, few were familiar with national initiatives to promote, and even subsidise, energy efficiency. Smaller companies, in partic-ular, looked to various departments of local government for advice on a broad range of operational matters. These relationships, many of which seemed built on a degree of personal knowledge and mutual trust, should be exploited to convey a wider range of information on matters such as energy efficiency, ensuring that it is delivered at a time which is most appropriate to the individual company. Similarly, trade journals and industry associations could become a more effective conduit of information about commercial and environmental good practice. Information does matter, but it must be applied in the right place and at the right time if it is to be effective.

Acknowledgements

We would like to thank the interviewees for their time and trouble in participating in this study. The work was funded by the ESRC under award number L320253204.

References

Adam, B. (1994) Running out of time: global crisis and human engagement. In M. Redclift and T. Benton (eds) *Social Theory and the Global Environment*, pp. 92–112. London: Routledge.

Brown, P. (1996) Long range weather forecast: hot, dry and French. *Guardian*, 3 July.

Bundesumweltministerium (1996) *Updated and Extended Declaration by German Indus-try and Trade on Global Warming Prevention*. Bonn: Bundesumweltministerium.

Burgess, J., Harrison, C. M., and Filius, P. (1998) Environmental communication and the cultural politics of citizenship. *Environment and Planning A,* 30(8), 1445–1460.

Burningham, K. and O'Brien, M. (1994) Global environmental values and local contexts of action. *Sociology*, 28, 913–932.

Department of the Environment (DoE) (1995a) *SCEEMAS. The Small Company Environmental and Energy Management Assistance Scheme. User Guide*. London: Department of the Environment.

—— (1995b) *The Company, the Fleet and the Environment*. London: Department of the Environment.

Department of Trade and Industry (DTI) (1995) *Small Firms in Britain*. London: HMSO.

—— (1997) *Small and Medium Enterprise (SME) Statistics for the United Kingdom*. London: Department of Trade and Industry.

Elkington, J. (1994) Towards the sustainable corporation: win-win-win business strategies for sustainable development. *California Management Review*, 36(2), 90–100.

Energy Efficiency Office (1993) *Practical Energy Saving Guide for Smaller Businesses. Save Money and Help the Environment*. London: Department of the Environment.

—— (1995) *Energy, Water and Waste*. London: Department of the Environment.

Enmarch-Williams, H. (ed) (1996) *Environmental Risks and Rewards for Business*. Chichester: Wiley.

Fiksel, J. (1996) *Design for Environment. Creating Eco-Efficient Products and Processes*. New York: McGraw Hill.

Florida, R. (1996) Lean and green: the move to environmentally conscious manufacturing. *California Management Review*, 39(1), 80–105.

Haas, P. M., Keohane, R. O. and Levy, M. A. (eds) (1993) *Institutions for the Earth: Sources of Effective International Environmental Protection*. Cambridge MA: MIT Press.

Hajer, M. A. (1995) *The Politics of Environmental Discourse. Ecological Modernization and the Policy Process*. Oxford: Clarendon Press.

—— (1996) Ecological modernisation as cultural politics. In S. Lash, B. Szerszynski and B. Wynne (eds) *Risk, Environment and Modernity. Towards a New Ecology*, pp. 246–268. London: Sage.

Harrison, C. M., Burgess, J. and Filius, P. (1996) Rationalizing environmental responsibilities – a comparison of lay publics in the UK and the Netherlands. *Global Environmental Change – Human and Policy Dimensions*, 6(3), 215–234.

Hass, J. L. (1996) Environmental ('green') management typologies: an evaluation, operationalization and empirical development. *Business Strategy and the Environment*, 5(2), 59–68.

Hinchliffe, S. (1996) Helping the earth begins at home: The social construction of socioenvironmental responsibilities. *Global Environmental Change – Human and Policy Dimensions*, 6(1), 53–62.

HMSO (1994) *Sustainable Development. The UK Strategy*. London: HMSO.

ICI (undated) *ICI and the Environment*. London: ICI.

ICL (1992) *Built in from the Beginning. ICL and the Environment*. London: International Computers Limited.

Kempton, W. (1991) Lay perspectives on global climate change. *Global Environmental Change – Human and Policy Dimensions*, 1(3), 183–203.

—— (1997) How the public views climate change, *Environment* 39(9), 12–21.

Kempton, W., Boster, J. and Hartley, J. (1995) *Environmental Values in American Culture*. Cambridge, MA: MIT Press.

King, N. (1994) The qualitative research interview. In C. Cassell and G. Symon (eds) *Qualitative Methods in Organisational Research. A Practical Guide*. London: Sage.

Macnaghten, P. and Jacobs, M. (1997) Public identification with sustainable development: investigating cultural barriers to participation. *Global Environmental Change – Human and Policy Dimensions*, 7, 1–20.

Macnaghten, P. and Urry, J. (1998) *Contested Natures*. London: Sage.

Ministère de l'Environnement (1995) *France and the Greenhouse Effect*. Paris: Ministère de l'Environnement.

Mortimer, J. (1996) Sweaty socks in the sun-dried shires. *Guardian*, 7 July.

Newton, T. and Harte, G. (1997) Green business: technicist kitsch? *Journal of Management Studies*, 34(1), 75–98.

O'Riordan, T. and Jäger, J. (eds) (1996) *Politics of Climate Change. A European Perspective*. London: Routledge,.

O'Riordan, T., Cooper, C. L., Jordan, A., Rayner, S., Richards, K. R., Runci, P. and Yoffe, S. (1998) Institutional frameworks for political action. In S. Rayner and E. L. Malone (eds) *Human Choice and Climate Change. Volume One: The Societal Framework*, pp. 344–439. Columbus, OH: Battelle Press.

Parry, M., Arnell, N., Hulme, M., Nicholls, R. and Livermore, M. (1998) Buenos Aires and Kyoto targets do little to reduce climate change impacts. *Global Environmental Change – Human and Policy Dimensions*, 8, 285–289.

Purvis, M., Hunt, J. and Drake, F. (forthcoming) Global atmospheric change and the UK refrigeration industry: redefining problems and contesting solutions. *Geoforum*.

Refrigeration and Air Conditioning (RAC) (1997) Swedish store runs on HCs throughout. *Refrigeration and Air Conditioning*, 99 (1194), 34.

—— (1998) HCs – in from the cold. *Refrigeration and Air Conditioning*, 99 (1198), 32–33.

Ross, A. (1991) *Strange Weather. Culture, Science, and Technology in the Age of Limits*. London: Verso.

Rowlands, I. H. (1995) *The Politics of Global Atmospheric Change*. Manchester: Manchester University Press.

Rudig, W. (1995) Public opinion and global warming. *Strathclyde Papers on Government and Politics*, 101, 1–38.

Schaefer, A. and Harvey, B. (1998) Stage models of corporate 'greening': a critical evaluation. *Business Strategy and the Environment*, 7(3), 109–123.

Schmidheiny, S. (1992) *Changing Course. A Global Business Perspective on Development and the Environment*. Cambridge, MA: MIT Press.

Shove, E., Lutzenhiser, L., Guy, S., Hackett, B. and Wilhite, H. (1998) Energy and social systems. In S. Rayner and E. L. Malone (eds) *Human Choice and Climate Change. Volume Two: Resources and Technology*, pp. 291–325. Columbus, OH: Battelle Press.

Stern, P.C., Young, O. R. and Druckman, D. (eds) (1992) *Global Environmental Change. Understanding the Human Dimension*. Washington, DC: National Academy Press.

Susskind, L. E. (1992) New corporate roles in global environmental treaty-making. *Columbia Journal of World Business*, 27(3), 62–73.

Szerszynski, B. (1996) On knowing what to do: environmentalism and the modern problematic. In S. Lash, B. Szerszynski and B. Wynne (eds) *Risk, Environment and Modernity. Towards a New Ecology*, pp. 104–138. London: Sage.

Tangen, K. (1999) The climate change negotiations: Buenos Aires and beyond. *Global Environmental Change – Human and Policy Dimensions*, 9(3), 175–178.

Taylor, P. J. and Buttel, F. H. (1992) How do we know we have global environmental problems? Science and the globalization of environmental discourse. *Geoforum*, 23(3), 405–416.

Thompson, M. and Rayner, S. (1998) Cultural discourses. In S. Rayner and E. L. Malone (eds) *Human Choice and Climate Change. Volume One: The Societal Framework* pp. 265–343. Columbus, OH: Battelle Press.

Uniclima (undated) *L'Effet de Serre, C'est L'Affaire de Tous*. Paris: Uniclima.

Victor, D. G., Raustiala, K. and Skolnikoff, E. B. (eds) (1998) *The Implementation and Effectiveness of International Environmental Commitments. Theory and Practice*. Cambridge MA: MIT Press.

von Weizsäcker, E., Lovins, A. B. and Lovins, L. H. (1997) *Factor Four. Doubling Wealth – Halving Resource Use*. London: Earthscan.

Walley, N. and Whitehead, B. (1994) It's not easy being green. *Harvard Business Review*, 72(3), 46–52.

Welford, R (ed) (1996) *The Earthscan Reader in Business and the Environment*. London: Earthscan.

Yearley, S. (1996) *Sociology, Environmentalism, Globalization. Reinventing the Globe*. London: Sage.

3   Buying the environment

The multiple meanings of green supply

Steve New, Ken Green and Barbara Morton

It is unlikely that corporate purchasing policy has ever before been as much in the news as in the period 1998–1999. The extraordinary controversy over the use of genetically modified (GM) foods, crops and feedstocks has been a major focus of political debates and environmental and consumer activism. It has brought to the public's attention not just the activities of research scientists in remote laboratories supposedly 'playing God' with so-called 'Frankenstein foods', but also of the sourcing policies and marketing strategies of major retailers. Particularly in Europe, major corporations have had to be, depending on one's view, nimble and responsive to market pressures, or hypocritical and cynical in pandering to ill-informed Luddism. Suddenly, what firms buy and from whom they buy it, and how environmental issues are included in these considerations, has become the subject of media attention from tabloid headlines to leaders in, for example, the *Guardian* and the *Wall Street Journal*.[1]

This outbreak of interest is of course not unique: for many years, controversy has rumbled about the ethical issues associated with labour policies of suppliers, particularly in developing countries, and particularly in textiles, but also in the toys, sport products and electronics industries (for example, see Louie,1998). Activist groups such as the Ethical Consumer have long been active in guiding a small vanguard of shoppers in the avoidance of particular companies' output and particular products and ingredients.[2] What is different in the recent controversies is the scale of interest, and the level of response of major organisations. Previously, explaining the connection between corporate procurement and environmental issues often required some kind of argument from first principles. Now, the shape of the debate is laid out on the evening TV news.

What is perhaps a little hidden from the public debate, however, is the fact that environmental issues have the potential to affect nearly all organisations' purchasing activities; that is, not just retailers, and not just those associated with products or services with an intrinsically controversial element. The most mundane products and services still have associated environmental issues, so there could be extraordinary scope for corporate purchasing to affect the 'greening' of industrial and commercial systems.

Indeed, one has only to review a few facts to get the sense of the potential for change and the importance of the mechanisms. First, governments face daunting obstacles in attempts to regulate or legislate on environmental issues, not least in the case of massive global companies who wield power politically, financially and scientifically. Second, the one set of forces that are presumed to keep these companies in check is the operation of 'the market', the site of all buying and selling. Third, by a considerable margin, most buying and selling is that which goes on between organisations (with the public sector procurement playing a significant role). Fourth, there are already established patterns of corporate buying effecting change in the supply chain (consider, for example, the so-called 'Quality Revolution'). Fifth, the complexity of modern production systems and industrial structures is such that *any* significant corporate response to environmental issues is likely to entail some connection with procurement and supplier relations.

'Green supply' is the term we use to describe the web of actions that occur when firms put the environment on the agenda for procurement and the responses this stimulates from the supply chain. It is reasonable to surmise that green supply will be a vital element in progress towards a 'sustainable economy'. To explore this possibility, and to use the focus as a way of understanding broader issues about corporate environmental behaviour, we set out to examine the prospects for and realisation of green supply in a range of organisations. Using longitudinal case studies in the private and public sectors, and by working with members of a specially convened forum of practitioners, we tried to map out the major issues that arose.

This chapter reflects on our findings from that work, and sets out some pointers for ways in which regulation may effectively work in tandem with market-driven greening. The first step, however, is to outline some of the key features of corporate procurement.

Organisational buying

Organisations differ from consumers in the way they buy things. Examining the differences is instructive, as this highlights the wide scope for environmental issues to affect the process. We shall also point to some surprising similarities between end-consumer and corporate purchasing, and these will provide a further range of possibilities.

Scale

The first point to note is that corporate purchasing operates on a vastly different *scale* to the consumer purchasing familiar to us as citizens. The amounts of money involved are huge, and a single purchasing decision may involve the expenditure of millions of dollars. Contracts may last for many years. These facts justify a vastly higher level of thoroughness and analysis before a purchase commitment; the risks are higher, and there is a greater return on investment in systematic analysis. In many cases, the purchasing of goods and services is the major way in which money leaves an organisation. For manufacturing firms, the percentage of total revenue spent on purchasing things is often greater than 60%, and can be much higher (see Dobler and Burt, 1996). With the growth in the outsourcing of services, and the development of sophisticated systems of sub-contracting in many industries (for example, electronics), this figure has risen over recent years. Money saved on purchasing translates immediately to profit for organisations: sell an extra dollar's worth of product, and only the 'margin' in that dollar finds its way to the profitability of the firm; save a dollar on buying things, and profits increase by the whole dollar.

Complexity

The second issue is that the *complexity* of the procurement decision may be vastly greater than that for consumer purchasing. Contracts may be long and detailed and involve tortuous provisions for the monitoring of performance and service improvement. Consider the case of an automotive manufacturer contracting for the provision of a vital component. The procurement cycle will involve the specification of the requirement, possibly with the supplier playing a key role in terms of research and development. The design stage may involve joint collaboration, often entailing the exchange of electronically-manipulated drawings through interconnected or even integrated information systems. The component will go through structured processes of prototyping and testing. Coming to the finalised design may involve collaboration not just between the manufacturer and supplier but also the supplier's suppliers, and so on along the chain. The contract for supply will not only have to specify the product but also the quality, inventory and planning systems that the supplier uses in the manufacturing process. It will also have to cover precise details for delivery, which might – in the case of just-in-time systems – entail hourly delivery 24 hours every day.

What the purchaser buys here is not just a one-off box of stuff, but an intricate complex of services, each with carefully managed contractual issues about risk and liability. The customer may even own some of the equipment (for example, tooling for machine tools) used by the supplier. At any time, a considerable number of the supplier's staff may be working on-site at the customer's factory, and *vice versa*. All this has to be wrapped up into a commercial relationship and a price agreed. The pricing may have to incorporate factors which reflect the supplier's own exposure to exogenous risk, but also to reflect estimates of economies of scale and learning curve effects. Some contracts entail the supplier sharing the customer's fortunes in terms of the success of the final product. This type of complexity is vastly different from the relative simplicity of individual consumer purchasing, and is a long way from the atomistic, impersonal and discrete market exchanges imagined by some economists (see Green *et al.*,1999a).

Control

The third feature we should note here is that of *control*. In organisational purchasing the people who are doing the purchasing are spending other people's money; corporate buying always involves some form of the so-called 'principal-agent problem'. Corporations naturally are keen to ensure that money is spent wisely and honestly, and this means that organisations normally couch buying activity within a system of bureaucratic control. This usually means that for a firm to purchase anything, a process of form-filling and authorisation is required; to come to a purchasing decision you have to follow some standard procedure. For example, many organisations use the 'sealed bid' tender process: potential suppliers are provided with a detailed specification of the purchase requirement, and asked to submit a bid in a sealed envelope on a particular date. When the bids are opened, the work is awarded to the lowest quotation, as long as it conforms to the original specification. The idea behind the process is that it is supposed to guarantee that the purchasing process is fair and systematic. Sealed bid tendering is used extensively in the public sector, where concerns about financial probity are particularly acute, but it is also used in the private sector. Many organis- ations use less rigorous methods which have the same basic intent; for example, buyers may be required to obtain at least three quotations from suppliers, and make a formal case if they choose one that is not the cheapest. Often, suppliers may only be used who have won a place on an 'approved' list by fulfilling some objective criteria. All these approaches are based on the idea of making the buying process rational and transparent.

These procedural mechanisms are important because of the combined risks of corruption and incompetence. The potential for corruption in corporate procurement is a significant problem, and may extend from straightforward bribes to the favouring of friends or relatives or even the exercise of dis- crimination for or against suppliers from particular ethnic or religious groups. Moreover, purchasing that does not follow a structured system is vulnerable to criticism that it could have been done better, and – with huge sums of money at stake – purchasing managers need to defend their actions. As well as requiring strict procedures, this point also means that purchasing departments' activities may be strongly skewed by the need to demonstrate cost savings. While it is broadly agreed that the costs on which purchasing should focus are the total costs (the phrases 'total cost of ownership' or 'life cycle costs' are often used), it is clear that by far the easiest costs to monitor are the prices that are paid.

This raises the important question of potential dysfunction in procure- ment systems: if the total costs that an organisation incurs are tricky to evaluate, the need to measure the purchasing process may encourage the choice of the 'cheapest' rather than the best value. For example, a purchasing manager might be able to make herself look effective by driving down the initial price paid for some supplies, even if this results in poor quality and ultimately more expense in terms of scrap. This point is particularly salient to the costs associated with environmental issues, which are notoriously difficult to measure.

A dynamic environment

The fourth difference between corporate and personal purchasing concerns the dynamic nature of the activity. For much personal buying, the end consumer plays a relatively passive role. Advertisers inform of us of the astonishing match between the needs that they have determined for us and the products and services they have on offer. A vast system of marketing and distribution exists to ensure that goods are placed under our noses and that we are aware of the potential benefits. For corporate customers, the marketing systems in place are less sophisticated; purchasers may need actively to investigate possibilities of supply and the procurement process may require more effort on the buyer's side. This does not just stop at the task of finding potential suppliers – organisations may seek to intervene in the supply market to ensure that goods and services are available to be sourced. At the governmental level, this is seen most explicitly in the commonplace interference of states in the development and survival of defence equipment; in the private sector, a good example is the effort made by Japanese transplant automotive firms to develop effective supply bases in US and European industry (for example, see Carr and Truesdale, 1992). In both cases, the purchasing task involves much more than merely selecting from some pre-existing list of choices; the purchaser actively invests effort in building up the capabilities and performance of the suppliers.

Strategic importance

This more 'strategic' element of the procurement process leads neatly into the final difference to be discussed here, which is the strategic importance of supply. For organisations, there are many issues in which buying decisions are of great importance for long-run competitive success. One issue concerns the structure of the supply base: should the organisation deal with many suppliers, perhaps using short-term contracts and 'churning' between them, or focus on a 'tiered' arrangement in which a relatively small group of key suppliers are selected for longer-term relationships in which they play a role in the co-ordination and management of second- and third-tier suppliers? Another issue is the degree of overlap that is permissible between the supply base and that of competitors: does it matter if key suppliers (perhaps providers of key technologies or those privy to future marketing plans or sensitive cost information) are also suppliers to competing organisations? These strategic issues are representative of the fact that for many organisations purchase decisions have a major impact on the ability of the organisation to maintain competitive advantage, and so become much more than the routine drafting of contracts and the whittling down of prices through negotiation.

By comparing organisational and personal buying, then, it is possible to see how significant purchasing is to corporations. Given this, it is interesting to consider the scope of actions which connect environmental issues to purchasing, but before doing so it is worth making some further comments about the character of purchasing in organisations. These put the procurement activity in the context of organisational culture and construction of reality in social interaction.

Buying as behaviour

As with any functional area of business (for example, marketing or accounting), procurement regimes exist within organisations in the context of broader patterns of corporate behaviour, and so reflect lived experience of those who participate in them. Hence, even though there is greater scope for system, method and rationality than in personal purchasing, there is no guarantee that a given instance of corporate purchasing will in fact be rational or systematic. Purchasing is, like other aspects of organisational life, heavily influenced by the human factors; inter- and intradepartmental politics, risk aversion, game playing, together with more extreme features such as deceit and fraud, will be inevitable in complex corporations. These issues are exacerbated by the fact that purchasing as an activity spans organisational boundaries, amplifying the scope for human behaviour which departs from the rational norm of idealised machine bureaucracy. Purchasing is also about relationships and money – and so is a natural locus for emotions within organisations, and in particular for the notion of 'trust'. The nature of complex contracts is that they are always incomplete, and both within and between organisations, ideas of loyalty, honour and decency (and their opposites) play a large part in actors' understanding of procurement processes and supplier–buyer relationships.

This issue runs parallel to the associated point that procurement in organisations is always difficult to understand, perhaps more than any other functional area of a business. This is because of three facts which work against transparency. First, the complexity mentioned above means that purchasing arrangements are often oriented to multiple, potentially conflicting objectives. Second, the amount of data relevant to understanding even a small firm's purchasing is often huge, and is likely to buried in contractual provisions or held in documents on different sides of the commercial boundary. Finally, much of the most important information (for example, the exact prices paid) is commercially confidential, and is often not bandied around even within an organisation, lest it leak to a competitor. So, whereas a manufacturing production system might be complex, at least it is possible in many cases to go to the shop floor and look at the physical manifestation. An accounting system, although dealing with the intangible, has strict systems of codification in which some of the 'reality' is crystallised into standardised documents. A purchasing system, on the other hand, necessarily involves intangible data which are difficult to collate and codify, and problematic to interpret. Moreover, as procurement involves at least a dyadic relationship between buyer and supplier (more in the case of complex supply chains), there are at the very least two 'realities' that apply. A good example of this is the difficulty of making sense of claims of buyer–supplier cooperation or 'partnership', which some have argued is often public relations 'gloss' covering rather exploitative relationships between major purchasers and weaker suppliers.

To sum up so far, it is fair to say that the realm of organisational procurement is a more challenging area of investigation than might at first appear. The complexity is matched by the range of ways in which the environment may be brought to bear on the buying process.

Buying green

The concept of the incorporation of the environmental agenda into corporate procurement has now been promoted from a number of quarters for several years (see Lamming and Hampson, 1996; Russel, 1998). Two main lessons have become apparent: first, there exists a huge range of options and tactics for organisations; second, very few organisations have really begun to exploit all the avenues that are available.

The range of possibilities implied by green supply is difficult to enumerate due to the wide spread of different types of purchasing organisation and the wide range of products and services secured; much of what follows will not apply to every organisation. The classification below works by starting with the simplest potential model and working towards greater complexity. The first main category of actions is based on possibility of purchase decisions being made on environmental grounds.

The simplest situation is procurement based on the choice of a 'greener' product compared with a 'browner' alternative. This is a straightforward choice. As an example, one might consider the selection of an environmentally-friendly cleaning fluid over a conventional one (in our study, this particular example came up within a local authority). The selection may be made 'in the marketplace', as it were, with the analysis of technical information or manufacturers' claims that are freely available in the public domain. In this case, the relationship between the buyer and seller may be at some distance, and there may be no interaction other than the transaction itself – 'the market' in its supposedly purest form. The effects of this purchase decision can be considered as fourfold: first, there is the immediate environmental consequence that a greener fluid will be tipped into the drains; second, there is the financial encouragement of an extra sale to the provider of the green good; third, there is the tacit message of the lost sale to the suppliers of conventional cleaner, which may promote product innovation; finally, there is the internal message in the organisation to its employees and possibly customers that green issues are being taken seriously and that buying the greener cleaner is an acceptable and sensible thing to do.

There are, of course, a number of issues which arise in considering the efficacy of any or all of these potential greening effects – a complex question which arose in a number of our case studies. We next turn to the possibility of purchasing not on the basis of a green product, but on a green *process*. For example, an organisation may select a supplier on the basis of an environmental accreditation (such as ISO 14000), or on the basis of some differentiating factor such as an environmental policy or the fact that the supplier does not do something which breaches some other code. This purchase decision is thus not based on the product or service, or any consequence of its use. It is entirely about the operations of the supplying company. Nevertheless, there is an element of 'greening' here, as the supplying firm is encouraged by the increased business, and its competitors may imitate the greener process in order to strengthen their position at the next sales opportunity.

So far, both of the cases have been based around a discrete purchase; but environmental considerations may be brought to bear even if the use of green criteria stops short of actually buying anything. For example, environmental consideration may be used to 'pre-qualify' those from whom the purchaser will select; again, this can relate to product and process. Here, the actual purchase decision is not finally made on the basis of environmental considerations, but may be based on other criteria; however, some environmental hurdle has been set before the selection. Again, this may or may not result in a substantive environmental benefit – but the supply base receives a message that environmental issues are important, and this is communicated to both successful and unsuccessful suppliers. Even without formal processes of pre-qualification, this 'softer' approach to green supply allows the buyer to communicate some priorities to the vendor. *Some* kind of pressure is applied just by raising the issue that, for example, it is expected that potential suppliers will have an environmental policy or be pursuing the development of an environmental management system. Given possibly ambiguous signals, the supplier has to make a judgement about how serious the buyer is, and whether at some stage in the future a low-key enquiry may evolve into something stricter. Faced with this, it may be sensible for the supplier to evaluate the potential pressures which the client may face, thus weighing the relative costs of action against inaction.

This spectrum of possibilities illustrates some of the approaches in which – albeit weakly – environmental pressures may be spread along the supply chain. Obviously there are additional complexities, and other variations on the main themes. The point is that purchasing behaviour can influence the supply base even if environmental criteria do not become the pivotal issue in a purchasing decision. Furthermore, there is a parallel range of mechanisms which apply to existing suppliers – the possibility of new work is merely translated into the prospect of keeping current business, and so on.

The second main category concerns the opportunities that present themselves for buyer and supplier to collaborate jointly on environmental initiatives. The exemplar case of this is packaging – there are many examples in which waste has been removed by buyers and suppliers merely devising systems which save both sides money. This type of collaboration can also affect more fundamental issues of product design, and also apply to consideration of logistics and scrap reduction. Here the supply relationship may be a conduit for inter-organisational learning and technology transfer. This type of cooperation is important because many industrial systems span commercial boundaries, and no significant improvements are really viable without the application of multiple players in the supply chain. In some cases, the collaboration may be mediated by industry groups or agencies.

The scope for green issues to affect the purchasing relationship, then, is considerable. There are many ways in which an organisation's own environmental agenda can be exercised in procurement. In principle, one might expect to see purchasing as the key area of environmental activity in firms. Curiously, this is not quite the case. Although many organisations have made some effort, and the idea of environment and supply being linked is reflected in the official publications and training syllabuses of professional institutions (CIPS/BIE, 1993), it is not obvious that there is a great deal of 'green supply' around. Our research has sought to understand why that might be, and the rest of the paper will focus on this matter, drawing on the case studies developed in our research.

Investigating green supply

In our research, we have worked closely with a wide range of organisations within the UK and a handful from overseas. Our methodology was simply to trace the development of green supply ideas within the organisations, and attempt to understand the meanings attached to the initiative by the various organisations, and to develop an empathetic understanding of the problems that faced the firms with whom we dealt. We interviewed managers and purchasing staff, and worked as 'consultants' and as a sounding board for managers -sometimes environmental managers, sometimes purchasing managers – and we attended meetings and examined documents. We also organised meetings of an Environmental Supply Chain Forum, at which practitioners came along to report their aspirations, confusions and (occasionally) progress.

Our rather pragmatic and reactive approach was based on a series of initial case studies in which we learnt that a more conventional cross-sectional, survey-based approach would be hindered by serious methodological difficulties. The first of these was that the range of actions possible, and the complexity of many organisations, would render any simplistic questions about organisational practice incomprehensible. For example, questions like 'Do you base purchase decisions on environmental criteria?' would generate answers that were likely to be uninterpretable, given the lack of consensus on what can be included in the word 'environment'. Second, we were aware that, for many organisations, the 'PR' aspects of green supply were paramount: without careful deconstruction and triangulation it would easy to be mislead by organisations who, for honest or cunning reasons, might confuse aspiration with actuality. Third, we realised that understanding the impact of organisations' own specific cultures, and the roles of the specific people involved, would be crucial to tell a complete story: this was a texture of explanation that would be missed by ticks in boxes on a cross-sectional questionnaire survey.

Our approach was not without its problems. Obviously we were not unseen observers silently collecting data: as with all research that is closely involved with organisational members, we became participants in the dramas we were investigating, and this has required us to be cautious in our interpretations of events. Furthermore, we found the process of working so closely with the research partners extremely demanding – we had to clarify our roles on some occasions, when some of the organisations came to expect us to provide almost limitless free advice and support. With the Forum activity, we faced the curious problem that a great deal of energy was absorbed coping with various organisations (some from our case study, others sometimes official bodies and consulting operations) who wished to develop the Forum into a continuing entity, but according to their own preferred model. Nevertheless, our approach had the merit of allowing the organisation's own agenda of meanings and interpretations to emerge and be examined over time.

We now turn to examine some of the organisations with whom we dealt, and in doing so, we illustrate the range of approaches we discovered. We begin with two organisations in the public sector, and these provide an illuminating comparison.

Green supply as constraint and opportunity

One organisation in our case study sample was a large government agency, whom here we will label *GovCorp*, which fulfilled a major administrative part of government. It employed thousands of employees, mostly at one major UK location. During the two years of our study, we met regularly with a group of managers charged with the development and implementation of 'leading edge' environmental policy, and who were regular attendees and contributors to our Forum meetings. The motivation for this was the need for government agencies to live up to governmental rhetoric, and a strong sense that there was a civic obligation to work in the best way possible. The function of the agency was largely bureaucratic, and a great deal of effort had been expended on the management of the office facilities. However, the organisation had struggled to make much headway on the issue of the incorporation of environmental criteria in procurement, and the key reason for this was a concern about the potential for breaking public procurement rules.

The public sector is in a particular position in regard to the control of the procurement process. Sensitivities are high in regard to the potential for corruption, and so public procurement is often more highly constrained in regard to procedures and rules. One aspect of this is that public contracts have to be advertised and awarded with demonstrable fairness. This means that appending 'extra' criteria to purchasing can potentially fall foul of the law (and, because of its complexity, particularly European Union law), and this means that many public sector organisations are wary of anything that could smack of discrimination for or against any particular group. The effect of this concern for GovCorp was that whilst these obstacles were not deemed completely insurmountable, substantive progress over an extended period was not great. Nevertheless, the representatives of the organisation appeared to derive benefit from involvement in the Forum, and this seemed to be in some ways a proxy for immediate action; the political context in which this organisation worked required there to be demonstrable action, and participation in a network was at least some signal that the issue was under consideration.

CityCouncil, on the other hand, was a local authority who had, by the bold initiative of a particular purchasing manager, made the connection between the environment and procurement a central theme. The individual concerned had managed to galvanise the organisation into acting in a particular way which meant the profile of his department was significantly enhanced. This had been done by interweaving the environmental imperative with concerns about local economic development. The argument went that if CityCouncil was an environmentally demanding customer and gave assistance to local companies in, for example, developing environmental policies, then those same companies would be better placed to get business from other regions. In other words, environmental purchasing would help regional competitiveness. Whether this argument is true or not is debatable; the point here is that the council were persuaded of the logic, and – such was the enthusiasm and energy of the manager in question – the idea was put into practice. CityCouncil organised seminars for local companies and provided help, especially to smaller firms, many of whom responded to the initiative. The council at no stage made environmental criteria the principal decision criteria for supply – normal tendering processes were still used, although the purchasing manager used what he saw as the scope of the pre-qualification stage to include some environmental considerations, which were largely at the level of requiring information on policies. One internationally-renowned firm of consultants who had omitted to provide an environmental policy, and were reminded of this, rapidly complied; the purchasing manager later found out that the firm was shaken into action when word had got around that CityCouncil would refuse to use their services in the future. This was a stronger interpretation than the one intended or indeed than was realistic –

nevertheless, the council's actions had effectively communicated that environmental issues were serious. The manager's enthusiasm also extended to trying to open up suppliers to becoming more proactive; part of a contract for office stationery included a provision that the supplier would be measured in part by its success in shifting the council (whose employees could order directly from a catalogue of approved products) towards the greener products.

These cases contrast strongly in some ways, yet they share a common feature; in both, green purchasing (in the first case, even interest in green purchasing) has a 'symbolic' value which means the organisations' adoption of green supply policies cannot be seen as just the outworking of some straightforward ethical motivation: there is more going on than organisations simply translating an environmental 'concern' into 'action'. Here we see that behind the external actions (or lack of them) lie intricate organisational politics, in which the *meaning* of the activity is important.

Green supply as ethics in action

Two organisations in our study were retail organisations. One – *Jojoba Ltd* – was a well-known manufacturer and retailer of cosmetics. The other – *BuyGroup* – was a purchasing consortium which supplied student organisations' retail outlets. Both are untypical organisations. Jojoba maintains a very high public image of environmental and ethical probity, and has well-documented criteria for its highly monitored purchasing operations. BuyGroup, because of its connection with student politics, is overseen by an ethics and environment committee which seeks to apply the aspirations of the parent body to the procurement operations.

For both organisations, there is a relatively unproblematic notion of environmental values – unlike some organisations in which the existence of an articulated ethical regime might require some justification against a traditional capitalist notion of profit maximisation. Jojoba had been active in this way since its inception, although the rapid international growth of the organisation had stimulated a continuing re-evaluation of processes and procedures. BuyGroup, however, despite being a well-established organisation, was still developing its approach, and at the time of this research was making some initial progress in establishing environmental purchasing policies. Several features of this development are worthy of note, and it is interesting to reflect on the comparisons with the activities of Jojoba.

First, BuyGroup's ethical imperative struggled to find a way of overcoming the more traditional approaches to purchasing used by the professional buyers. This latter group were experienced purchasing professionals for whom the chief objectives had been the traditional ones of price and delivery – quality was less of an issue than for many purchasing organisations, as BuyGroup largely purchased branded consumer products. So it was not in the position of major retailers (for example, Marks and Spencer) who might, as a matter of course, discuss the detailed specification and manu-

facturing of products with vendors. Despite the scale of BuyGroup's operations, the organisation remained a relatively small player compared with
major retail purchasers, and this meant that hard negotiation was required to
get good prices, which meant exercising the threat of substitution to suppliers.
The new environmental imperative sat uneasily with this traditional
approach: how could BuyGroup enact its green agenda?

The first element of the work was to seek to collect information from
suppliers about the environmental aspects of the products being purchased.
One of the first product groups to be considered – beer – shows up some of
the key difficulties in implementing green ideas in purchasing. The brewers
with whom BuyGroup dealt were generally very large established organisations, used to conducting business based on prices and promotions.
Enquiries from a relatively small customer about environmental aspects of
both the product and production operations did not fit with normal patterns
of customer relations, and some suppliers – despite being sophisticated
organisations – struggled to generate coherent responses to BuyGroup's
requests for information. An important issues here is the multiple interpretations of 'environmental'. There are an enormous range of environmental
aspects to the brewing industry – including the use of chemicals and energy
in the production process, the sourcing of raw materials, the design and
recovery of packaging and the complexities of the logistics process. However,
several questionnaires returned to BuyGroup claimed that there were no
environmental issues that affected the supply of beer. A second issue is that
in this particular supply market there is an absence of any particular green
differential between the suppliers – none of the beer companies projected a
deliberate 'green' image, nor made any marketing capital out of their
environmental credentials. This meant that a supplier could make the
judgement that even if its own response to BuyGroup was rather weak, it
would be unlikely that any of its competitors would do much better.

These issues also affect the operations of Jojoba, but for this organisation
three things assisted in reinforcing the credibility and impact of the environmental message. First, Jojoba found it easier to exercise simple commercial
power: the high degree of competition in the supply markets, and Jojoba's
relative size, meant that it faced less of a challenge in eliciting appropriate
information from the supply base. Second, Jojoba's high profile and clear
organisational commitment meant that suppliers knew that the environmental criteria laid down had to be fulfilled or they would be unable to win
the business. Third, the organisation separated out the functions of supplier
assessment and qualification from the rest of the purchasing process. Different
groups within Jojoba discharged these responsibilities, and this enabled the
hard business of price negotiating to be carried out without contaminating
the environmental assessment. This is an important point because the
credibility of the 'green' message can be easily undermined by suppliers perceiving that they might trade environmental aspects against price. Jojoba's
market, despite the organisation's strong green brand identity, is highly

competitive and price sensitive. There is little 'green premium' available from the consumer, and the control of purchase costs is a major component of the business strategy. The separation of qualification from price negotiation avoids the complexity of a supplier responding to a demand for a lower price by trying to renegotiate the environmental requirements set by the purchaser. This reduces the complexity of the discussion, and helped Jojoba send a consistent message. For BuyGroup, it is understandable if the initial approaches are simply not taken seriously by the suppliers, as they must first be convinced that the BuyGroup will actually do something with the information gleaned.

This leads to the second issue that faces organisations such as Jojoba and BuyGroup in regard to the implementation of green supply. What to do with information that suppliers provide, and how to act in a way that achieves the effects desired? The first stage of the BuyGroup process – the collection and collation of information – resulted in a large amount of non-commensurate data being obtained. One organisation might claim to be good at green logistics, another at recycling packaging waste, another avoids a chemical in production processes that may or may not have some biological risk to the environment. How can these different merits be compared? Moreover, if the organisation sets out a checklist of particular 'sins' which suppliers must avoid, what happens if the checklist fails to capture an important extra component, which suggests that a 'failing' supplier might actually be the best choice. An even thornier issue is that of suppliers whose current performance might be sub-optimal, but who are making strenuous efforts at improvement. How much emphasis should be placed on *aspiration* – perhaps embodied in the form of policies or formal statements – relative to 'real' substantive greening?

There is, of course, no clear answer to these problems and all of the organisations in our study struggled with them. The issues reflect what we can label the 'Paradox of Green Supply Pragmatism'. This paradox starts with the need for an organisation's communication with suppliers and potential suppliers to be clear and unequivocal about environmental requirements and expectations. This is necessary for purchasers to be taken seriously by the supply base, and is something that Jojoba were more advanced in than BuyGroup. However, the complexity of environmental issues, the difficulty of objective measurement and assessment, the advance of scientific understanding about environmental impacts, and the simple fallibility of human organisations, all add up to the fact that suppliers will perpetually fall short of environmental aspirations. For example, a supplier to Jojoba might commit itself not to test products in a particular way, and then – as the supplier changes its own sourcing relationships – find that the assertion no longer holds; or, a commitment to remove a particular chemical from a production process might turn out to be technically impossible. In these events, the sourcing company has to face the issue of what can be done: should the supplier be 'de-listed'? In many cases the most sensible approach will be to stick with the failing supplier and work for (or hope for) improvement, or maybe even to relax a particular requirement if it turns out to be impractical. This means that the buyer must be pragmatic, and must be prepared for its own environmental aspirations to be limited by the performance of its suppliers.

This is the nub of the paradox – effective green supply requires both consistency and compromise at the same time. This paradox is not, though, just played out as a moral or strategic issue within the buying organisation; it affects the relationship with the suppliers, who now must work out the meaning of the communications and signals presented by the customer. This second-guessing of what an organisation 'means' by the inclusion of green criteria is important for the suppliers, who will need to interpret carefully the arrival of, for example, questionnaires. The cost of providing very detailed information may be high, and of course may allow a supplier's shortcomings to be identified. The response of some of BuyGroup's suppliers – to offer paltry responses, and even to ignore the requests altogether – makes some sense if the supplier takes the view that enough of its competitors will do the same, or if the buying organisation is not serious about acting coherently on the data to be provided.

For Jojoba, the potential for public embarrassment from failures in its sourcing policy acted as a signal to its supply base of its serious intent, and so gave its actions greater credibility. Nevertheless, periodically, activist groups have pilloried the organisation for not being 'really green', and this has been the result of pragmatic responses by the organisation to failures by its suppliers. For organisations such as Jojoba, the paradox means that there are significant risks in green supply. For less developed organisations such as BuyGroup, the paradox means that trying to build up coherent policies from an 'ethical' base is fraught with complexity. In the next section, we turn to another case in which the emergence of green supply is constrained by issues of communication and credibility in the supply chain, but where the issue is the scientific credibility of environmental claims and counter claims.

Green supply as science and judgement

A major part of our study concerned the green supply issues relating to one particular kind of product – medical equipment, especially relating to intravenous therapies (IV) – made from the plastic polyvinyl chloride (PVC). For a variety of reasons, PVC is considered by some to be an environmentally disastrous product. First, a series of noxious chemicals are used and released in its production, and these are also normally present when PVC is incinerated. There is no realistic way of recycling PVC in quantity, and so PVC goods are typically dumped in landfill, which means both damage to the environment in the dumping, and a waste of the resources used to make a one-off product. Furthermore, there is some debate about whether some particular chemicals used in PVC production to give it increased plasticity can leach out of the material and into biological systems (or, in an IV bag, into the drug or blood being delivered to the patient, or into the saliva of a child sucking a plastic toy), where they may simulate the effect of the hormone oestrogen, and so affect, amongst other things, male fertility rates (see Green *et al.,*1999b).

On the other hand, if these negative effects of PVC do exist, then the causal link would be very difficult indeed to trace. PVC is ubiquitous in the Western world, and it exists alongside a great many other modern products which, by the same principle, might be considered dangerous or damaging to the environment. Further, these worries have to be set against the fact that for many purposes, especially in medicine, PVC is almost the perfect material for many applications. It is light, flexible, transparent, unbreakable, easy to sterilise and cheap enough to dispose of after a single use. It is perfect as a replacement for fragile, heavy glass, and does not entail the complexity of re-using and sterilising and storing without breakage, all major problems for hospitals.

In our study we examined the environmental controversies surrounding PVC, and in particular explored the uptake in different countries of non-PVC alternatives in IV therapies. All the major manufacturers are actively seeking to develop replacement materials, as in some markets, notably Scandinavia and Germany, the use of PVC has been constrained by both legislation and procurement practice. We set out to understand the fine detail of the issue, in particular in regard to the purchasing of IV equipment by the UK National Health Service (NHS). The study illustrated several general principles which have wider applicability for the understanding of green supply, and also helped illustrate the idea of the multiple meanings in this context.

One of the first features that emerged was that, despite the controversy, the health services in both the UK and the US (the latter being by far the dominant market, due to the scale and cost of the health care system there) were still purchasing PVC equipment. In the US, though, this was in the context of a well-publicised debate on the environmental merits. In the UK, where health care products purchasing is dominated by the NHS, the controversy was less well understood and there existed negligible pressure from purchasers on the dominant suppliers. Both of these markets shared two key features. On the one hand, the health care industry is highly fragmented, with a vast array of users: in the US, a complex web of hospitals, groups of hospitals and insurance companies; in the UK, a complex hierarchy of quasi-independent 'trusts' and regional bureaucracy. On the other hand, both exhibited a high degree of use of consortia purchasing, in which the supply chain for goods between manufacturer and users was mediated by purchasing organisations which exist to achieve economies of scale in terms of both purchasing power and administration. In both countries, such purchasing consortia have always been surrounded by debate as to whether they really do reduce costs, and so are always striving to deliver bottom-line cost reductions.

This places a severe practical constraint on these purchasing organisations working on non-price areas, particularly in an exploratory way, on issues that do not feed back to the key criteria on which they are judged: the prices paid.

In these situations, we found that the complexity of the procurement process, and the introduction of an extra tier of authority, meant that it was difficult for some kinds of information to flow between users and manu-facturers. In some senses, this was an amplification of the agency problem discussed above, in which the mandating of a specialist unit to deal with the purchasing process limits the ability for non-price criteria to be considered in the process. In this context, the blockage worked in two ways: even though there exists considerable (if, we noted, sometimes rather vague) interest in environmental improvement within the NHS, users find it difficult to translate this into substantial changes to the specification of their requirements, specifications which are then passed to the consortia with the mandate to buy as cheaply as possible. This is particularly the case where the environmental issue in question would require significant extra spending, or where the benefits might not accrue to the budget-holding unit responsible for the purchase. The second type of block was that the existence of the consortia partially limited the ability of the major manufacturers to com-municate directly with the ultimate users. The selling organisations with whom we worked invested considerable effort in trying to read between the lines of official policy statements and environmental initiatives; nevertheless, the routine procurement and supply relationship was dominated by price negotiation.

This combination of fragmentation and consolidation in the purchasing organisations had the effect of recasting the notion of 'customer pressure' in this context. What the (final) customer – the user – wanted, or could be persuaded to buy, did not always translate into what the (immediate) customer – the consortium – was able to pay for. The dominant manufacturer of the products we studied was in the position of trying to gauge how to respond to the rather confused signals it received: should it maintain a firm line that its current products were completely safe, or begin to introduce premium-priced alternatives to allay potential fears? What emerged from our investigation very strongly was that in such complex situations, a simple description of green innovation being 'driven' by a straightforward mixture of customer pressure and 'technology push' was inadequate. The 'customer' in this case was ill-defined, and the 'demand' was not a simple outflow from some ethical agenda. The high degree of contingency, and the varied perception of the different players, mean that it will always be difficult to trace simplistic causal lines between the factors involved.

Conclusions

These examples from our research show that green supply is by no means a straightforward alternative or even adjunct to other advocated methods of achieving greater environmental performance (never mind 'sustainability') in firms and other organisations. The greening of the supply chains that we have discussed has been subject to a number of 'drivers'. Clearly expressed pressure by end-consumers (whether represented by activist organisations or opinion polls, as in the current story of GM foods in the UK) is very rare. Of course, current events show how powerful such action can be – forcing large retailing chains to execute a U-turn on ingredients they will accept in the foods they sell and making biotechnology companies radically review their business and technology-development strategies. But the other examples we have mentioned have either been much more protracted (as in the continuing campaign against PVC) or less dramatic in their outcome.

Other drivers that are much more common and more likely to succeed in delivering some environmental progress would seem to be: purchasing managers' pursuit of the environmental agenda as a means of improving their position in the managerial pecking order ('putting purchasing on the map');[3] the personal commitments of individuals (including owners and managers) to ethical and/or sustainable ends; managers' calculations of the need to reduce the risk of consumer criticism and/or activist campaigning, not to mention possible financial claims, by excluding the risks they buy in in the form of their suppliers' components and services.

Some firms, though not as many as the business literature on greening seems to recommend, do see selling green products as a competitive advantage, making proactive attempts to green their customers (one might call this 'demand chain greening'). But even this is fraught with difficulty, as we have shown with our example of PVC products in the NHS. Even in this supposed era of globalisation, the continued existence of 'regional' markets in health care products means that signals for alternative greener products induced by regulations and pressure group campaigns are still often 'national'. This prevents firms from acting 'globally', since those signals may be much weaker in another country. Proactive firms might feel they need to induce market change to even out these competing pressures but, as our example has shown, in the Byzantine world of health care provision this is fiendishly difficult. Pressure groups seeking to persuade firms to offer greener products need to understand these constraints on firm's strategic action if they want to have an influence globally. And so do regulators: green supply is not an 'alternative' to tighter environmental regulation, but it is the means whereby the full effectiveness of regulation can be realised.

Our simple conclusion is that there is not one model of how corporate buying can induce supply chain greening. Firms' ability to influence suppliers depends on, *inter alia*, the style of green discourse in the sector, as well as the diverse pressures from different geographical regions and other, adjacent, supply chain systems. Criteria that might usefully predict interfirm influence on other matters (e.g. relative size, commercial dependency) are a poor guide for assessing the impact of green purchasing. In some cases, there may be a temptation for firms to overestimate the degree of influence that their green purchasing might have. In others, however, the opportunities to harness suppliers' environmentally innovative capabilities have yet to be appreciated.

Notes

1 'Test fields of conflict', *Guardian*, August 5th, 1999; 'Greenwar', *Wall Street Journal* August 11th, 1999.
2 Examples of campaigning organisations are the *Ethical Consumer Research Association* (ECRA), Unit 21, 41 Old Birley Street, Manchester M15 5RF UK, and *Labour Behind the Label*, 38–40 Exchange Street, Norwich, NR2, UK.
3 The annual publication by the UK's Business in the Environment organisation of 'league tables' of the environmental performance of top UK companies, one table being devoted to firms' green purchasing policies, is awaited with some apprehension by senior managers keen to be seen as greener than their industrial sector competitors.

References

Carr, C. and Truesdale, T.A., (1992) Lessons from Nissan's British suppliers. *International Journal of Operations and Production Management*, 2, 49–57.
Chartered Institute of Purchasing and Supply/Business in the Environment (CIPS/BIE) (1993) *Buying into the Environment*. Stamford: CIPS.
Dobler, D.W. and Burt, D.N. (1996) *Purchasing and Supply Management: Texts and Cases*. New York: McGraw-Hill.
Green, K. Morton, B. and New, S.J. (1999a) *Greening Organisations: Purchasing, Consumption and Innovation*. Paper presented to British Academy of Management Conference, Manchester, September 1999.
—— (1999b) *Deconstructing Green Supply: PVC, Healthcare Products and the Environment*, Working Paper No: 9913, UMIST: Manchester School of Management.
Lamming, R. and Hampson, J. (1996) 'The environment as a supply chain issue', *British Journal of Management*, 7, S45–S62.
Louie, M.C. (1998) Life on the Line. *New Internationalist*, 302, 20–22.
Russel, T. (ed.) (1998) *Greener Purchasing*. Sheffield: Greenleaf Publishing.

4   Framing environmental choices

Mediating the environment in the property business

Simon Guy

> Look at our cities: 100 storey towers of steel and glass, dehumanising in
> scale, loom as clones of one another. Hubris characterises their demeanour.
> The glass on all four sides mockingly attests to the lack of concern for
> energy conservation. There is defiance, not deference, towards nature.
>
> (Woods, 1992: 2)

Property development is one of those businesses that receives a lot of bad
environmental press. In the absence of the word 'sustainable', the idea of
'development' appears synonymous with environmental degradation. As a
result, the greening of the property industry is a tense and uncertain process.
However, despite the scepticism of critics a lively environmental debate has
surfaced in the development industry. While many design and real-estate
actors remain cautious about environmental issues, others are starting to
translate ecological concerns into commercial practice. As Deyan Sudjic has
pointed out, 'for any architect not to profess passionate commitment to
green buildings is professional suicide' (1996: 7). This chapter explores the
contested nature of environmental innovation in the property business[1]. In
particular, it identifies the commercial framing of environmental choice in
design practice and the mediation of environmental issues in development
processes.

The potential for reducing the environmental impact of office development is well documented (Rydin, 1992). Energy-saving technologies,
materials have been successfully identified and manufactured, energy-efficient
building designs have been constructed, tested and widely promoted, and
extensive monitoring of local, national and international building stocks
means we know more than ever before about the precise potential for
improved energy performance. Based upon this knowledge the Energy
Efficiency Office (EEO) believes the potential exists for saving some 20 per
cent of the energy consumed in the United Kingdom, using proven technology and cost effective measures (Environment Committee, 1993: 2). Ever
more sophisticated, energy-conscious ventilation systems have been successfully developed. Dynamic insulation now allows buildings to 'breathe',

maintaining air-flow and reducing energy costs by around 30 per cent, and thereby minimising CO_2 emissions and the potential for building 'sickness' (Halliday, 1996: 176). At the same time, advances in solar architecture and power are pointing the way towards self-sustaining buildings which consume little or no external energy, thereby radically reducing their 'ecological footprint' (see Vale and Vale, 1991; Behling and Behling, 1996; Hawkes, 1996). However, the best efforts of building scientists and energy efficiency policy-makers to promote best environmental practice seems to be falling on deaf ears. As Sandy Halliday has pointed out, the 'last 23 years have seen concerted and substantial efforts at energy conservation within the UK which have failed to produce net savings. Energy use per square metre in buildings has increased alongside a net overall growth in consumption' (1996: 175).

The central question of this chapter relates to the adoption, or otherwise, of environmentally sensitive development practices. Hitherto, research has tended to ascribe the failure of the property business to adopt environmentally sustainable principles to either the ignorance or apathy of individual real-estate professionals, or the blindness of market processes to environment priorities (Weir, 1990). This analytical polarisation of individual decision-makers and market processes has been methodologically reinforced by an over-reliance on questionnaire surveys, which assume that changing individual attitudes is the key to environmental innovation, and/or econometric analysis which reduces market innovation to narrow economic categories of use and exchange value (Luithlen, 1994).

The perspectives of environmental advocates are similarly polarised. Here, a very loose community of environmental actors share in the pursuit of sustainability. Any precise definition of sustainability in relation to buildings is rarely forthcoming. Instead, differences in the concerns and aims of advocates are put aside in the call for increased environmental awareness and stricter building regulations. The result is that the debate over the greening of the property industry is reduced to arguments about the setting of tighter standards, while environmental innovation becomes defined in terms of narrow technical parameters which can be conveniently measured and monitored. As a consequence, green buildings have too often stressed 'function over form', earning environmental design a 'reputation for being less attractive and less appealing to the market' (Chaffin, 1998: viii). Not surprisingly, commercial property actors have often resisted efforts to legislate or morally cajole their business activities, again encouraging a view of real-estate actors as unconcerned, or even ignorant about environmental innovation.

The response of environmental researchers to this conceptual impasse has been to map the environmental attitudes of real-estate professionals and to devise information and marketing campaigns designed to persuade what are seen as the key property industry decision-makers to adopt environmental best practice techniques and technologies. How, environmentalists ask, do we 'persuade those who have a vested interest' in ignoring environmental issues to reconsider their development strategies (Lees, 1992: 7). For example, in response to the use of non-renewable materials such as mahogany, one of the 'Friends of the Earth's objectives is to turn front doors into the emotional equivalent of a plague sign' (Lee, 1992: 4). These campaigns appear to meet with little success. The main problem here is the narrow focus on individual attitudes. The analytical assumption is that there are 'structures residing inside the person which are part of that person's make-up and which determine or at least greatly influence what the person does, thinks and says' (Burr, 1995: 49). Thus, there is 'something enduring in people which the scale is measuring – the attitude' (Potter and Wetherell, 1987: 45). At once this vocabulary of attitudes isolates real-estate actors from the organisational settings in which they work, and the changing market contexts which frame their real-estate strategies.

Researching environmental issues

> Actors, agencies and their relationships are . . . the critical elements linking demand generated by production and consumption to finance, to building capacity and to landowners and property development and management companies.
>
> (Healey, 1991: 101)

This view of the design and development process has blinded analysis to potential connections between environmental concern and commercial real-estate practice. We will develop a more relational approach by first, developing an understanding of the differing perspectives of real-estate actors operating within the property business, and second, by identifying the changing inter-relationships between commercial processes and environmental innovation. The starting point is an assumption that the decisions of real-estate actors are guided, not simply by technical potential or environmental attitudes, but by a commercial logic conditioned by prevailing market conditions, that frames the possibility of environmentally sustainable development practices.

Here, the 'market' is interpreted not simply in economic terms, but rather as a cultural entity, shaped by dynamic organisational, social, legal, regulatory, ecological and economic factors. By examining the inter-linkages between these 'market' mechanisms and the re-fashioning of office design specifications, we should develop a greater understanding of the constraints and opportunities for environmental innovation in the property business. In this way the chapter takes a different view to attitudinal environmental research by illustrating:

(a) the need to understand the differing, and changing, development strategies of inter-linked real-estate actors

(b) how design specifications act as a crystallisation of these differing strategies
(c) how the changing context of development activity is enabling the production of design specifications that reflect particular aspects of the environmental agenda
(d) the need for a new relational policy framework to promote greener office buildings.

The research question has now switched from identifying key decision-makers to one of unpacking the changing logic of environmental innovation. Rather than merely examining the attitudes of individual actors we turn our attention to *the social organisation of the property business*. In order to develop a finer-grain understanding of the ways in which contrasting real-estate strategies frame environmental debates about building design, it was necessary to go beyond the analytical confines of attitudinal or econometric approaches. To enable this, in-depth qualitative interviews were complemented with observations of office practices, participating in site visits and sharing informal meetings. Analysis involved a number of stages.

First, the case-studies of each development actor were compared and contrasted in order to produce a typology of organisational cultures (see Table 4.1). The emphasis here was on differences between organisations and the particular forms of value they sought to extract from the development process. Organisational studies literature was utilised (see, for instance, Ahrne, 1994) to focus the comparison and the interview transcripts were analysed to uncover key organisational traits. In particular, analytical effort went into delineating the competing story-lines which characterised particular ways of seeing buildings, and how these translated into justification for particular configurations of design specification.

The second analytical task was to explore how these differing strategies translated into a final design specification, and eventually into a physical building. Here, science studies literature was found to be useful for its emphasis on how technical objects differ not by form alone, but most importantly by the wider social 'scripts' inscribed in them. That is, the design conventions or protocols, built up over time, that provide a set of default guidelines for the technical specification of buildings. In particular, studies of the social shaping of other 'technical systems' such as utility meters (for example, Akrich, 1992), and medical protocols (for example, Timmermans and Berg, 1997), provided new ways of thinking about the development process, shedding light on the ways in which design process is socially negotiated.

Finally, the growing literature on policy discourses helped illuminate how environmental concern is a locus of differing viewpoints (for example, Hajer, 1995), and how the direction of environmental innovation is contingent on the ways in which social actors define problems and solutions (for example, See Myerson and Rydin, 1996).

Understanding the business of property

> Surveying and related professions are about land and property manage-
> ment; they highlight the ways in which day-to-day decisions on the use,
> exchange and development of landed resources are taken. While the
> prevailing ethos may suggest an economic goal of maximising returns
> when taking decisions, this is not inevitable.
>
> (Rydin, 1997:6)

Commercial property development is a difficult industry to conceptualise. It
is made up of a set of contrasting commercial businesses that share a stake in
the property market but embody profoundly different interests. While
property development provides the bread and butter for developers and
agents, it is only one of many possible options for investors. Similarly,
architects will often work beyond the market for private commissions, while
for occupiers property is simply a necessary venue for whatever business they
pursue. These differing interests are powerfully reflected in the contrasting
organisational worlds that real-estate actors inhabit, and the different forms
of value that each real-estate actor seeks to extract from the development
process. Buildings look very different when viewed from within each of these
organisational settings, and these competing ways of seeing fashion the
design interests and strategies of each real-estate actor. Nevertheless each of
these parties (and many others such as engineers and facilities managers)
must of necessity gather around a table and come to a shared view about the
form and specification of buildings.

Table 4.1 summarises the organisational worlds inhabited by the five real-
estate actors studied in this research, and delineates their resulting ways of
seeing buildings. It is important to note that each category is not claimed to
be representative of the range of real-estate actors currently operating.
Organisations in each category can vary widely in size and culture, and may
be involved in a variety of development activities. For instance, developers
may also operate as investors, while occupiers and investors can also act as
developers. Nor is it designed to be exhaustive. Other actors – engineers,
planners and quantity surveyors – also inhabit and influence the property
business. Rather, these organisational snapshots are simply meant to illustrate
the wider institutional framing of design and development practices and show
how these relate to alternative development goals in a form of 'theoretical
collage'. As Goran Ahrne puts it, 'Organisations are the locus of connection
between individuals, and through them human actions are transformed into
social processes' (1994: 2). Actors working in particular organisational frameworks can be then be regarded as 'organisational centaurs: part human and
part organisation' (Ahrne, 1994: viii). Thus, working in a different 'organisational context implies a particular rhythm of doing things' (Ahrne, 1994:
35). There is an intimate connection between particular ways of seeing (buildings), and different ways of doing (design and development). Competing

Table 4.1 Real-estate actors and their development goals: an organisational snapshot

Logic / Actor	Way of seeing	Culture of practice	Source of knowledge	Units of assessment	Value extracted	Development goal
Architect	Image/ machine	Creative collaborators	Previous practice	Design solutions	Fees and reputation	Shape buildings/ cities
Developer	Multipliable asset	Team-based entrepreneurs	Local knowledge and gut instinct	Residual valuation	Enhance value of land	Renew urban environ ment
Occupier	Work space/ symbol	Team-based specialists	Business operation	% Space utilisation Max. efficiency	Min. overheads	Appro- priate space
Investor	Quantifiable asset	Hierarchical experts	Investment performance	Compar- able % returns	Income stream/ capital gain	Grow capital/ hedge risk
Agents	Market comparable	Individual entrepreneurs	Latest deals	Letting rates/ market demand	Fees and market control	Construct market

styles of working, alternative forms of knowledge and differing valuation methodologies, are all linked to the diverse development goals that shape the actions of each real-estate actor. Moreover, while the search for profit characterises all businesses, each real-estate actor takes a different route to financial reward. It is within these complex and dynamic organisational worlds that environmental choices are framed.

The contrasting ways of seeing of the real-estate actors studied in this research are briefly summarised below. The aim here is to explore how real-estate actors are caught within a 'never-ending paradox of moral complexity, balancing the competing imperatives of ecological sensitivity and economic sensibility' (Chaffin, 1998: viii). In this way we may begin to understand the particular rationality that underpins the perspective of each real-estate actor, and to link the resulting development strategies to the contrasting organis-ational settings in which they operate.

Shaping buildings: the role of the architect

Architects are in the business of providing tailored design solutions to specific development challenges, for different types of client. At the same time, to prosper, architectural practices must develop a recognisable 'style' that can be translated into reputational capital which may attract new and repeat business. The culture of practice is therefore geared to generate design packages that reflect a discernible architectural ethos, while simultaneously satisfying the diverse needs of clients. In this way, architects generate value by both collecting individual fees and by visibly reinforcing their reputation. Seen from here, buildings represent both 'machines for living' and symbols of contemporary culture. This cultural role extends the interest of architects from individual buildings to debates about the future of cities as a whole. The pursuit of the sustainable city has come to the forefront of architectural debate and ecological issues are rarely absent from architectural manifestos where architects often strive to position themselves as champions of urban environmental innovation.

For instance, Norman Foster and Partners have built a reputation for 'linking form and function', meshing the needs of the client with 'more efficient ways of dealing with social, ecological and cost concerns'. The 'Foster method' has been developed through 30 years of building design in which a style, reputation and set of architectural techniques has evolved. His architectural ethos operates through a collective decision-making process represented by the open-plan working space of their Riverside Three head office and by the Monday morning 'directors meeting' in which the five key principals meet with key personnel to discuss and co-ordinate the huge variety of international papers underway at any one time. Here, designs are developed in the context of previous practice, creating a link between pathways of architectural innovation and local contexts of development. Working from concept sketches, the design evolves with team members working collectively and in collaboration with the client's research team. Aesthetic concerns are blended with technical functionality as Foster strives to promote his vision of technologically smart, low-energy buildings with a minimal environmental impact. Foster and Partners have pursued this strategy through a number of landmark buildings including the Commerzbank in Frankfurt, the world's first naturally ventilated skyscraper. For Foster, environmental issues are central to the practice of architects. As a member of his practice puts it:

'The sorts of buildings that we have done in Germany, for example – which were self sufficient in terms of power through pumps and solar collection – have got to be the coming thing. In the long term it would be irresponsible to build a building which has a great environmental cost.'

However, the enthusiasm for environmental innovation is tempered by an awareness of the economic realities of the British real-estate market.

'In terms of this country it would be nice if the timber came from renewable sources, it's all sort of warm cuddly stuff, but if you want a seriously environmentally friendly building it's going to cost a lot of money. If you are doing it on a goodwill basis only the most unusual tenant is going to say well yes, I'm going to increase my rent by 50 percent. In the commercial market, people will just say "right well I'm going down the road then".'

Renewing the urban environment: the role of developers

This market realism starts to explain why it is very rare to find any environmental zeal amongst property developers. To understand further we must identify how developers extract value from the development process. Unlike architects, developers do not make money by the construction of buildings *per se*. Rather, developers extract value by enhancing the economic value of land they manage to purchase relatively cheaply. The value of land is increased by the development of buildings that will attract secure rental income and, therefore, investment capital. The culture of practice is dedicated to identifying and exploiting feasible development opportunities. Knowledge of local market conditions, meshed with an almost 'mystical' instinct, is mobilised in entrepreneurial initiatives which are checked and balanced by making 'residual' financial calculations (price of land minus development costs) of the economic return gained by the act of developing land. Buildings merely represent a multipliable asset and development is taken for granted, as value can only be extracted when and where cityscapes are renewed. From this perspective, environmental issues are only considered when and where they make a positive difference to the price of land or the rental and/or investment value of buildings. As a development director at MEPC put it;

> 'So it comes back to the market. The difficulty we have as developers is actually going it alone and saying, right we are going to do it, we are going to be the ones to provide this non-air-conditioned building and then finding that no one wants it. Clearly if it's our money, we spend millions of pounds on this building and if it remains empty we've made a pretty bad business decision. We clearly can't afford to make those sorts of decisions, so whilst we are in a risk game in development, the biggest risk is . . . the state of the market come the completion of the development. Having accepted that fairly major risk, you don't want to actually increase the level of risk by doing things which are actually going to limit that market come completion in two or three years time. You clearly want to provide a building which will be of maximum appeal to reduce your overall risk.'

MEPC is a good example: a large, mature development company which has steadily built its property portfolio through acquisitions, take-overs of other property companies and, until the 1990s, an aggressive development programme. MEPC has organised its entrepreneurial activity into teams managed by development and budget managers who constantly monitor the worth of buildings through 'development expenditure analyses' which monitor the changing value of land holdings. With a reputation for caution, particularly since the 1999 property crash, MEPC tend to resist design innovation and focus on providing what the 'market' has traditionally demanded. Development feasibility is judged in relation to the overall business strategy, administered by the director of development, which in turn structures the 'view' taken on design and specification issues by development personnel. Any development activity, from simple refurbishments to large scale development, must have a multiplier effect on economic value, with company growth linked to constant renewal of buildings and cities. Energy performance is taken seriously, with a specialised energy manager appointed in the early 1990s. However, this work, along with other 'fringe' activities, has now been outsourced, as MEPC focuses on core business concerns. Time and time again, efforts to introduce energy efficiency measures run counter to perceived market demand and/or development budgets. As the development director at MEPC suggests:

> 'We are conscious of the issues as a company and we have debates internally. I was asked by our group manager the other day why we are looking at providing air conditioning in this City building. My response was because the market demands it; and we as speculative developers and as a commercial organisation can't afford to buck the market, we can't tell it what it wants. If we were the sole developer in the UK, and provided all products, then we could say this is all you are getting and the tenant would have to accept it – because he would have no other choice. We are very small fish in a big pond.'

The search for appropriate space: the role of the occupier

It quickly becomes clear, when considering the commercial contexts of development activity, that environmental issues have to be considered alongside more mundane business priorities. Any view of green development as an 'altruistic pursuit carried out by developers willing to lose money in the name of the environment' is seriously misplaced. Rather, environmental innovation has to be considered as a 'way to achieve multiple benefits – for the developer, for the investors, for the occupants, and for the natural environment' (Wilson, 1998: xi). Turning, then, to the consumers of development activity, we need to understand what shapes their way of seeing and using buildings.

Occupiers view space either as simply a background to their core operation, or more significantly as a reflection of their business practices. Value is extracted from design and development practice by either minimising the cost of occupying buildings (rent and services), or by organising office space to maximise efficiency and encourage productivity. Occupiers vary hugely in where they sit on this scale. What is certain is that occupiers' requirements for space is subject to rapid change. A real-estate manager for IBM suggests that:

> 'We have senior managers who have been used to showing their prestige by having a bigger office, but a lot of these things are changing. The fact of the matter is that the need for space is dissipating. No doubt about it. We don't need space. We hang on to it for historical reasons.'

IBM's property strategy has evolved through three generations, from basic post-war buildings, to fully specified air-conditioned buildings, to their current focus on flexible space that promotes good working practices. As IBM have re-engineered their business in response to wider industry challenges, their need for space has also altered. Driven by the need to cut costs and promote more efficient working practices, IBM have assembled a team of space utilisation experts from a variety of disciplinary backgrounds – architecture, psychology, surveying – who are charged with translating their knowledge of the commercial practices of IBM's component businesses into appropriate units of space. Space utilisation or SMART (Space, Morale and Remote Technology) studies resulted in the reconfiguration of existing space and the procurement of new forms of office. In turn, new configurations of space have encouraged new patterns of working, and IBM are now committed to a form of perpetual revolution in their use of space. Thus, IBM's desire is not so much for 'buildings' as for appropriate space which represents a material embodiment of their organisational aims. Environmental issues are here translated into concern for human comfort and creativity as a route to greater commercial productivity.

> 'You can bring all this back to the environment if you want. The best way that environmental things work is that there is a cost attached. If we're looking at an office, here we have an asset under-utilised which is costing us a fortune. It costs us a fortune to buy it or to lease it and to run it, heat it, light it. Whether there are people here or not, you still have to do that. Yet we're not using it, so why have we got it? It's crazy.'

Growing capital, avoiding risk: the role of the investor

In the world of the occupier, the language of the environment has to be translated into a vocabulary of space utilisation and resource efficiency. Real-estate investment also has its own specialist language. For investors, buildings purely represent quantifiable assets. Their interest in buildings is as undervalued assets to purchase, or regular and reliable income streams to manage as part of their existing property portfolio. When expert investment valuers assess the current and future economic value of individual developments, they are rarely interested in the environmental profile or aesthetics of building design. Instead, a building's worth is judged, on one hand, against the past investment performance of similar stock, and on the other hand against the investment performance of other investment mediums such as gilts and equities. It is rarely 'sustainability, diversity or ecology' that interests investors, but 'return on investment, bottom line, and cash flow . . . What they want to know about are the projected cash flows, revenues, and expenses' (Wilson 1998: 244). Design issues are of critical importance, but only in terms of the contribution of specification features such as air-conditioning to market attractiveness or rental growth. Similarly, environmental issues are of interest, but only in so much as they are marketable, or on the other hand, serve to increase the risk of investment through, for instance, vulnerability to environmental regulation or liability to health or contamination claims. As a portfolio manager for the Prudential argues:

> 'I think you'll find we are very socially responsible. We have done things like working on environmental policies for the company. However, we are a financial institution and what we do is central to what Granny Perkins' bonus policy is going to be. In that sense we have to endeavour to try and treat property as an income stream.'

The Prudential is the largest institutional investor in property, although buildings only correspond to about 5 per cent of its overall investment portfolio. Even so, managing this portfolio requires around 300 staff involved in all aspects of property management. Expertise is grouped by task and by type of fund. Each 'expert' contributes to the assessment of the asset value of particular buildings in relation to the degree of risk represented by the form, design and location of the development. The Prudential is developing innovative new analytical techniques designed to divorce the material aspects of buildings from their investment value, which is extracted by securing guaranteed high level, long term rental income and maintaining the overall asset value of the portfolio. Responsibility for portfolio selection is graded by levels of value with decisions taken at weekly and, for larger investments, monthly investment meetings attended by senior staff. The rate of investment in property is by no means certain, with the final view related to the ability of property stocks to grow capital and/or hedge the risk of other investment media. Again, environmental issues may connect directly to traditional investment concerns. Greener office buildings, both more efficient and healthier than traditional property, may attract higher valuations than hitherto as long as utility and flexibility are maintained. Similarly, greener buildings may help to offset investment risk:

> 'Contaminated land is a good example. How do we price for that extra risk and how much do we knock off for contamination. I think one can bring these same parallels into the energy side in terms of where is the

legislation leading, and how should we try and price for it now. It's the investor dilemma, trying to price for things that are only just on the margins of perception.'

Constructing the market: the role of estate agents

When environmental concerns mesh with commercial concerns, opportunities for green design emerge. Many commentators seem to assume that the language of the environment and the market are mutually opposed. However, green buildings can offer many potential commercial benefits: 'reduced operating costs of buildings and landscapes, improved sales or leasing rates, higher property values, increased absorption or occupancy rates, reduced liability risk, better health and productivity of workers, avoidance of regulatory delays during permitting processes, and even reduced capital costs' (Wilson, 1998: 6). Much depends upon how the 'market' is constructed by the changing priorities of real-estate actors. Critically here, market assessment is often a retrospective affair. The shape of the market is gauged by yesterday's design, development and investment activity, rather than tomorrow's. Real-estate agents are central to this process of market reconstruction. Agents sell their services as arbiters of the 'market', comparing and contrasting letting rates and rental values in relation to newly available or recently let buildings. By their knowledge of the 'latest deal', they are able to make 'introductions' to potential occupiers or investors, so shaping market demand. Value is extracted through fees but also through their control of market processes through which they promote themselves as independent judges of market acceptability. As a London estate agent argues:

'Agents are salesmen, but when they do look after a client they will try and understand what a client is looking for, what their key criteria are, and then what building matches these key criteria. Does it get six out of ten or zero out of ten etc. There's no point in putting a building with X if it doesn't match what they need.'

The interest of agents in environmental innovation is therefore strongly shaped by the priorities of other real-estate actors. The environment may be viewed by agents as a potential hazard, driving down market value or, in another context, as providing a market edge.

'At the end of the day a developer wants to build a product that needs to satisfy the occupier and satisfy the investor so it's got to fulfil two criteria. He will take on board a number of advisors to help him get the ultimate price because he is in it for the profit. Some take care over the environment and design, others couldn't care less.'

BH2, an offshoot of a larger established practice, have established themselves as experts in the City of London marketplace, meshing expertise in the valuation of buildings with intimate knowledge of occupiers' needs. BH2 position themselves as cutting edge specialists in the most important UK, and arguably global, property market, and are often associated with key developments. Personnel work independently, earning fees for the business and sharing expertise on a case basis. BH2's reputation, and therefore future business growth, is predicated on acceptance of their view about the past, present and future of the City marketplace, which they seek to construct through on-going dialogue with investors, suppliers and users of property. Environmental issues are part of this dialogue, but only as part of a hierarchy of wider concerns. As another real-estate agent puts it:

> 'Yeah, there is a feeling that it's good to keep the cost down and because energy is quite a large section of service charge costs it's seen that there is an advantage of doing that, but purely a money economic benefit of doing it. It's not because it's environmentally friendly.'

While strongly diverging in terms of vision and strategy, all real-estate actors share in the process of translating environmental concerns into the priorities of urban development. Seen this way, opportunities for environmental innovation are embedded within the changing contexts of property provision.

Changing strategies of property development

> The environment is important not only for conservation and health, but also a key marketplace influence and purchasing factor. Consumers are genuinely concerned about the environment. In short business can't afford not to design and upgrade their buildings to protect the environment and tenants which occupy them.
>
> (Fedrizzi, 1995: 35)

Given the diversity of organisational worlds that real-estate actors inhabit, and the often conflicting priorities that characterise their strategies, it is perhaps surprising that development occurs at all. In order to understand this process, and subsequently to identify opportunities for environmental innovation, we must recognise how diverse property interests are linked through the practice of designing and developing buildings. In seeking to extract their particular forms of value for the development process, each real-estate actor follows a strategy that refers to a past, present and possible future. Architects seek to extend the continuum of a design ethos. Developers aim to establish new packages of land, funding and occupation. Investors strive to establish more accurate readings of risk and return. Occupiers attempt to secure more appropriate space. And agents endeavour to steer market dynamics. Building design is continuously shaped through a series complex negotiations between real-estate actors, in the context of wider technical, legal and commercial constraints, as they each attempt to extract value from development activity. The design specification represents the material outcome of this process. However, not all viewpoints will necessarily be represented in the development proposal. Depending upon market conditions, some real-estate actors will have more power to influence the process than other actors.

For example, in the 1980s, the British market was strongly controlled by investment concerns (Guy, 1998). The choices of designers and occupiers were framed by the demands of large investors who desired highly specified buildings in order to maximise both their potential market and their rental return. This was underpinned by a market in which demand far outstripped supply, a lease structure which gave total security to landlords, and a huge volume of available capital for speculative development. Occupiers and ecological architects had little power to influence this process. Consequently, decisions about the installation of complex systems of air-conditioning, raised floors, suspended ceilings, the provision of power-load capabilities and floor-loading capacities, resulted in a specification that far outstripped the actual needs of occupiers who had to bear the cost of energy-intensive buildings. With energy costs and CO_2 emissions some 50 per cent higher in air-conditioned offices (Harris, 1993), the environmental implications of this process are clear. As property agents used these lavish buildings as a com-parative benchmark for valuation purposes, so a conventional script (a transferable specification protocol) emerged that framed subsequent office design. For instance, real-estate actors interested in constructing a naturally-ventilated office would be strongly advised by property agents that it would fail to compete with 'higher' specified buildings, with the consequent risk of lower rental values. One architect comments:

'. . . there is a list of 50 things your building must have and these 50 things range from VAV (variable air volume) air-conditioning, 2.7 metre floor to floor ceiling heights, three lifts that allow 30 seconds travel or waiting time. All these things are absolutes as far as (agents) are concerned because they are selling it to their counterpart in another office and it's a circular thing.'

Even development for owner occupation or pre-let development was not immune from these pressures. The increasing volatility of the global market-place was such that all building owners and occupiers had to view office space as a competitive disposable asset subject to market pressures. As another architect commented:

'Our own experience in UK work is that many estate agents, developers and (behind them) institutional pension-fund managers consistently act irresponsibly in denying experimentation and demand inefficient building solutions that rely on high-energy environmental control installations.

Even when circumstances do not demand it, agents usually insist on air-
conditioning installations in order to achieve established market rental
criteria.'

Driven by this design script, similarly designed office buildings, fully air-
conditioned, powered and loaded, appeared in the Thames Valley, Bristol,
Manchester and Edinburgh. Figure 4.1 highlights the materialisation of an
institutional specification during the 1980s.

However, this conflict between the suppliers and users of buildings is not
a static relationship. The relative power and strategic interests of real-estate
actors is conditioned by the dynamic ebb and flow of the market, with
occupiers' voices drowned in circumstances of under-supply and attended to
in conditions of over-supply. The 1990s has seen a re-balancing of control of
the British property market, from suppliers to occupiers. The background to
this was the collapse of the financial markets on the infamous 'Black
Monday'. There was a subsequent deterioration in the domestic and world
economy, rising finance costs, falling rents, mounting competition and
diminishing demand. All this led to bankruptcy for many property companies, serious over-exposure to property debt in the banking sector, and a
general loss in confidence in the property business. Against this commercial
background, the 1990s has seen a whole series of shifts across the social,
economic, legal, regulatory, cultural and technical landscape of property
development practice.

Users have greater opportunities to negotiate about the kinds of space
they are occupying. With lease structures becoming more flexible and rents
dropping, the costs-in-use of buildings have become apparent. With the
UK's Department of Trade and Industry producing specification guidelines
that recommend stringent energy conservation and the avoidance of air-
conditioning wherever possible in Government buildings, property agents
are beginning to recognise the commercial potential of efficient, non air-
conditioned space. Developers have become equally concerned with expenditure. While investment values and rental income decline, all real-estate
actors are keen to foster greater sensitivity to actual occupational requirements in the design of office specifications. A developer comments:

'Change is happening now . . . not just because people are becoming
more environmentally aware, but because the development equation
doesn't stack up at the moment. So it's a commercial business objective
that's actually bringing about lower specification buildings . . . but
that's good if it also brings about environmentally sensitive buildings.'

There is of course great reluctance to be the first to modify specification
levels. Aversion to market exposure is enhanced in periods of development
slump. However, there are signs of a collective will at work. The British
Council for Offices, a diverse amalgam of interested property professionals,

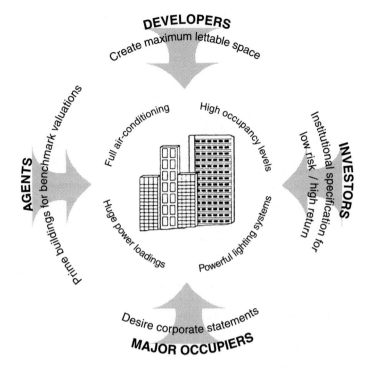

Figure 4.1 Institutional specification of property in the 1980s.

are producing a recommended 'appropriate' or 'realistic' specification for the 1990s. Similarly, the Building Services Research and Information Association (BISRIA) are composing an environmental code of practice for building services. Aimed at designers, surveyors, owners and occupiers, these manifestos seek to stimulate enhanced working conditions, minimise waste and promote the use of renewable resources. Energy efficiency is a central plank of this strategy.

Figure 3 provides an overview of the shift in context currently reconfiguring development processes.

A wholesale shake-up of the conventions governing property practices has been instigated by this fundamental shift in relations of building provision and use. It is possible to detect an alternative approach to the British property market evolving which, while market-driven, is potentially environmentally benign. It takes as its focus the search for 'appropriate' offices which more precisely match space and specification to occupiers' needs. In particular, there is increased awareness of the value of the workplace, both as a financial cost and a source of organisational benefit (Laing and Crisp, 1992). Rigorous standards of commercial efficiency are being directed towards building costs, with levels of energy efficiency related to overall

Table 4.2 Changing social organisation of property development in the 1990s

1980s	Signals	1990s
Investors/developers	Market power	Occupiers
Exchange	Focus on value	Use
Trophy	Building image	Tool
Empty space	Product	Serviced space
Rent and forget	Culture	Let and love
Adversarial	Actor relationships	Collaborative
25 years	Lease terms	Flexible
Upward only	Rent reviews	Negotiable
Letability	Valuation	Usability
Overhead	Balance-sheet	Asset
Occupiers	Maintenance costs	Landlords
Standardised	Design	Customised
Maximised	Specification	Appropriate
Fully variable air volume	Air conditioning	Mix-mode/natural
Intensive	Resource use	Conscious

business performance. In this sense, the market is 'leading us to sustainable development practices' (Chaffin, 1998: ix). Figure 4.2 highlights this new social organisation of property interests.

In order to extract 'value' in this new development landscape, each actor has had to re-think their strategy: architects are better able to offer highly efficient designs which evoke a sense of place; developers are seeking to cut development cost by trimming specifications and providing alternatives to full environmental control; occupiers are looking to exploit opportunities for procuring efficient, healthy workplaces; investors are attempting to identify market-friendly buildings that provide both utility and flexibility; and agents are looking to understand and capitalise on new occupier trends.

In sum, 'if the tenant is prepared to help reduce risk, time and effort, the developers can happily reduce the price. He can create a better building which meets specific occupier requirements more closely' (Freeman, 1997: p146). As a developer argued, through this general interrogation of the economic priorities of the property development, 'businesses are becoming more environmentally conscious at a commercial level'. Under the rubric of financial efficiency, attention is being sharply focused on the uses and abuses of costly resources. These commercial contexts provide the background to emerging social innovations fashioning alternative development practices. With cultural, organisational and technical change altering patterns of demand, energy performance is now located within a wider set of concerns, encouraging the emergence of a range of new design priorities that relate to environmental innovation; new working practices that emphasise efficient use of space; new investment strategies that reduce risk though enhanced predictive power rather than on the pursuit of 'prime' specifications; new

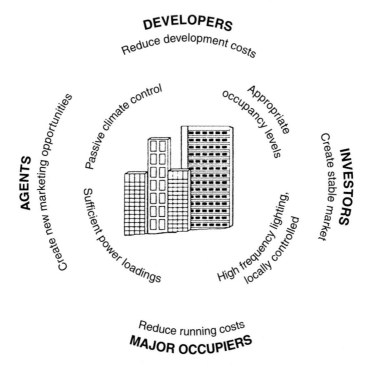

Figure 4.2 Social organisation of property interests in the 1990s.

development priorities for appropriate design geared to user need; new design principles that prioritise energy efficiency and healthy workplaces; and new forms of property provision which offer flexible patterns of use. A developer again comments:

> Well yes, after the recession they [occupiers] are looking for ways to save costs. They are looking at running costs from a hard nosed commercial perspective, they are not looking at a link between running costs and environmental costs necessarily.

New environments of innovation

> A quiet revolution is taking place in architecture which could transform our relationship with the elements and experience of the workplace, and it is being propelled by a return to an old principle – windows that open . . . Air-conditioning may soon be a thing of the past as modernist and classicist architects move towards a more energy conscious and less combative approach to the elements and help satisfy the cravings of workers for more natural light.
>
> (Pilkington, 1995: 2)

The move to a more demand-oriented, cost conscious market-place has challenged the resource intensive design specification script of the 1980s. New desires and concerns are emerging to re-shape the design of office space. A new form of office space which provides a flexible, healthy workplace, which takes into account the desires of its inhabitants and their concern for wider environmental issues, and which avoids ostentatious statements which evoke a culture of excess, is being increasingly demanded. As an agent comments, 'people are more aware about energy and the planet and because of fitness they are prepared to walk'. This shift in the desires of the 'market' opens up a new world of choice for designers, from pursuing naturally ventilated designs, to specifying energy efficient lighting, reduced power loadings and less energy intensive lifts. 'Less is more' seems to be the defining principle, reflected in the British Council for Offices'[2] 'best practice' guide to office specification. As an occupier put it; 'the interesting thing about this is that you are utilising assets and using resources in a very environmentally very beneficial way'.

This shift in the context of property development has led to a re-alignment of local development practices. The design and development of office buildings studied during the research illustrate how new configurations of real-estate actors, working in a 'demand-led' market, are re-interpreting environmental concern to co-produce new forms of environmental and commercial value. While the development strategy of each building was shaped by a commercial context, the designs employed nevertheless bear the impression of a changed specification script that is providing fresh opportunities for more environmentally conscious design.

Typical is the IBM building at Bedfont Lakes. Acting both as a developer and occupier, IBM wanted to create a customised space that would enable them to use their new 'SMART' space utilisation techniques. MEPC (the developers) were also keen to develop, but wanted to avoid exposure to an uncertain marketplace. A collaborative venture was instigated on a reclaimed industrial site. Issues of human comfort were addresses at design meetings with all IBM staff in which a consensus approach shaped the design principles. Two architects were commissioned to distinguish between the IBM and the speculative office spaces. Their brief was to respond to the natural surroundings and provide internal and external 'social spaces' for staff to mingle and relax; also alternative forms of work space such as 'drop-in' centres to facilitate mobile workers. Space utilisation studies were undertaken to avoid wasted space or use of unnecessary resources. Lighting was energy efficient throughout and IBM insisted on a new form of modular air-conditioning which could be locally controlled. While none of these design features were motivated by a pure environmental agenda, the benefits are clear.

A more explicit environmental agenda was followed by the property arm of British Gas when developing the Thames Valley Park Building. The aim was to produce an energy efficient building that acknowledged the natural surroundings and relied mainly on natural ventilation and lighting. The building also had to be designed to facilitate different configurations of occupation and, critically, to be commercially viable in the event of British Gas vacating the property. The Foster design was in shallow plan, utilising natural, sustainable materials with a finger-like design, directing the gaze of occupants out over the lake. The entrance was located at the back of the building along with the services, a rejection of the 1980s emphasis on building as status symbol. The building gained a high environmental rating[3] (36 out of 42 credits) and reduced energy consumption to half the rate of a conventional air-conditioned office building. Vital to the success of the project was the community of interests established around a green design. A mix of design, cost, occupancy and marketing objectives framed the form and specification of the building, which looks forward to the new, more environmentally conscious, millennium.

More environmentally radical, the Groundwork Trust building was designed to provide the organisation, a charitable environmental trust, with both a headquarters building and a living demonstration model of sustainability in action. Critically, the building also had to provide a rental income from the letting of office space. The aim, therefore, was to build a commercially viable, but explicitly green, office building. The design strived for (and almost achieved) self-sufficiency in resource generation and waste disposal through the use of wind and solar power, and composting toilets. Recycled and renewable materials were used throughout and environmental art constructed from disused materials is widely featured. The development mix of a committed client, environmental architect and innovative agent meant that the building has been successfully let and received wide publicity, including a green building-of-the-year award.

The development of these innovative designs is presenting fresh opportunities for environmental innovation, as new groupings of property interests seek to create complementary forms of commercial value. As the culture of the market ebbs and flows, real-estate actors selectively assimilate green issues by translating them into new business concerns, allowing commercial and environmental interests, at least temporarily, to coincide. However, this does not mean real-estate actors are simply picking up on, and implementing, a pre-defined notion of environmentalism. In tracing processes of design innovation we must be sensitive to the ways in which the notion of the 'environment' has been broken up and re-interpreted by real-estate actors as they pursue new property strategies. Instead:

> Green real-estate development has more than a single face. For one project, the most visible 'green' feature might be energy performance; for another, restoration of eco-systems; for yet another, the fostering of community cohesion and reduced dependence on the automobile.
>
> (Wilson, 1998: 4)

Each logic of environmental innovation relates to a different form of social or commercial value, and derives from a distinct, though related, source of environmental concern, with its own history and constituency of advocates. Different issues of concern tend to encourage a particular design strategy (Guy and Farmer, 2000). Different design logics may place particular emphasis on either the efficient use of resources, social cohesion, health, a closeness to nature or minimising the environmental footprint of buildings. Each of these design logics has very particular implications for office specification, mobilising biases in and out of the specification brief, and thereby shaping the subsequent development strategy. These logics rarely surface in isolation. In the design of any particular development, particular environmental logics may collide, merge or co-inhabit during debates about form, design and specification. As real-estate actors mobilise around partic- ular design logics, the conventions of form and specification start to be refashioned. That is, as the strategies of real-estate actors change, new conventions of design and specification begin to crystallise, and the scripts governing 'good', or best practice design specification begin to alter.

In thinking about environmental innovation we must, therefore, become sensitive to the range of possible logic of innovation which may surface in new buildings, and locate these design logics in the gradual reconfiguring of the institutional norms of commercial real-estate development. A logic of resource efficiency is by now recognisable by all real-estate actors, and has almost gained industry acceptance as good business sense. Similarly, the logic of healthy design is gaining increasing recognition as a component of best commercial practice. In the process of reframing commercial design, we can also begin to identify elements of a more aesthetic and community- minded design logic emerging, alongside an increased concern for reducing the environmental footprint of development.

Promoting greener buildings

> The key to good design and public policy is to go beyond our common
> assumptions – such as the notion that economic and environmental goals
> are inherently opposed – and to look instead for creative solutions that
> achieve a range of objectives simultaneously or over time.
>
> (Long and Long, 1994: 9)

By untangling the changing business strategies of real-estate actors, this chapter has revealed a range of new design priorities that relate to environ- mental innovation. These include: new working practices that emphasise efficient use of space; new investment strategies that reduce risk through enhanced predictive power rather than on the pursuit of 'prime' specific- ations; new development priorities for appropriate design geared to user need; new design principles that prioritise energy efficiency and healthy workplaces; and new forms of property provision which offer flexible patterns of use. Alternative environmental concerns are emerging from a set of issues that extend beyond ecology. These include: the need for organisational flexibility; the desire to visually symbolise more 'caring' values; concern over sick buildings; and the requirement for less alienating office spaces. The emergence of new design priorities is enabling the 'co-production' of commercial and environmental value, producing design specifications that act as material inscriptions of different logics of environmental concern. From this standpoint, we cannot view buildings simply as technical structures, the design quality of which can be simply related to an external definition of accepted environmental standards. Rather, the chapter suggests we can begin to locate opportunities for environmental innovation by identifying how these new design priorities take root in changing development practices.

From such a standpoint, current policy strategies for promoting greener buildings appear largely ineffectual. Regulatory issues rarely figured either in interviews or in design discussions conducted in this research. 'Best practice' design guidance tended to be quickly discarded, while promotional material was regarded as disconnected from the realities of the marketplace. The most powerful policy effect was that of 'anticipatory regulation' in which the property business is trying to anticipate future, mainly European, regulatory measures which they feel may adversely affect the value of current and future property assets. Rather than simply focusing policy instruments on either key decision-makers (through promotional campaigns), or the market (through regulatory sanctions), policy-makers need to develop a more relational framework for both understanding and shaping development processes. If the aim is to 'search for a management solution and associated property regime which will enhance environmental quality and avoid degradation' (Rydin, 1997: 6), then policy-makers need to alter their way of seeing the property process.

The chapter first points to the need for policy-makers to loosen their dependency on static, economic models of the development process, such as the division between speculative and owner-occupied buildings. The property 'market' needs to be viewed as a cultural entity, which is constantly being refashioned by a host of related social, legal, organisational, technological and economic processes. Social maps of this changing development landscape need to be constructed, monitored and constantly updated in order to provide a greater understanding of the inter-linkages between the actions of development professionals and the organisational contexts which frame their strategies.

The chapter then points to the need for policy-makers to alter their own identity, and relationship to development practices. Rather than view themselves as positioned 'outside' the property industry, policy-makers should consider themselves as part of the network of interests shaping, design and development, and seek to connect themselves to internal industry debates, which relate to issues both within and beyond conventional notions of environmental concern. Examples here include: (i) the concern of property professionals with the calculation of 'worth' or 'value' (Mallinson, 1997); (ii) debates about office specification and construction materials[s] ('British Council of Offices, 1997); (iii) debates about the future of working practices and the 'office' space itself[4]; (iv) the development of new forms of collaborative professional practice and education (Latham, 1995); (v) future regulatory frameworks. The involvement of industry representatives in the reformation of the building regulations is perhaps one model of this approach (see Raman and Shove, Chapter 8 this volume).

In this way we might develop a policy framework which connects environmental objectives with the changing objectives of development practice. Refocusing policy interventions away from key individuals and towards organisational actors, whose changing interests must be monitored and mapped, we might better connect policy strategies to professional debates about the future of the office, appropriate design specifications, collaborative working and professional education. At the same time, the notion of 'attitudes', that frames the current policy view of environmental innovation, would become situated in relation to both function and context, and thereby be better able to explain variability in design and development choices. As Potter and Wetherall suggest, this 'shifts the focus from a search for underlying entities – attitudes – which generate talk and behaviour, to a detailed examination of how evaluative expressions are produced' in specific contexts (Potter and Wetherall, 1987: 55). Rather than presume the 'character of human reasoning and rationality' to be 'uniform', 'corresponding to a model of individual, rationalist self-interest' (Shackley, et al., 1996: 215), we should begin to map the framing of the environmental choices of real-estate actors as they relate to the changing market contexts of building design, development, investment and use.

Notes

1   This chapter is based upon a research project, 'Developing Alternatives: Environmental Innovation and the Property Business', funded by the Economic and Social Research Council under the Global Environmental Change Programme.
2   The British Council for Offices (BCO) was formed in 1990 as a forum for property occupiers, owners and developers.
3   Utilising the Building Research Establishment Environmental Assessment Method (BREEAM).[2]
4   RIBA strategic studies (offices).

References

Ahrne, G. (1994) *Social Organisations*. London: Sage.
Akrich, M. (1992) The de-scription of technical objects. In W. E. Bijker and J. Law *Shaping Technology/Building Society*. London: MIT Press.
Behling, S. and Behling, S. (1996) *Sol Power. The Evolution of Solar Architecture*. London: Prestel.
British Council for Offices (1997a) *Good Practice in the Specification of Offices*. London: BCO.
—— (1997b) *Good Practice in the Selection of Construction Materials*. London: BCO.
Building Research Establishment *Energy Consumption Guide 19*: BRE (no date).
Burr, V. (1995) *An Introduction to Social Constructionism*, London: Routledge.

Chaffin, J. (1998) 'Foreword. In A. Wilson (ed.) *Green Development: Integrating Ecology and Real-estate*. Chichester: John Wiley and Sons.

Environment Committee (1993) *Fourth Report – Energy Efficiency in Buildings*. London: HMSO.

Fedrizzi, S. R. (1995) 'Going green: the advent of better buildings'. *ASHRAE Journal*, December: 35–37.

Freeman, P. (1997) 'From adversaries to partners'. *Estates Gazette*, February 8: 145–147.

Guy, S. (1998) Developing alternatives: Energy, offices and the environment. *International Journal of Urban and Regional Research*, 22 (2), 264–282.

Guy, S. and Farmer, S. (2000) Contested constructions: The competing logics of green buildings'. In W. Fox (ed.) *The Ethics of the Built Environment*. London: Routledge.

Hajer, M. (1995) *The Politics of Environmental Discourse: Ecological Modernisation and the Policy Process*. Oxford: Oxford University Press.

Halliday, S. (1996) *Environmental Code of Practice for Building and their Services – Case Studies,* Vol.1, April. The Building Services Research and Information Association (BSRIA).

Harris, D. (1993) 'How to cut office energy costs'. *The Times*, 20th October: 33.

Hawkes, D. (1996) *The Environmental Tradition: Studies in the Architecture of the Environment*. London: EandFN Spon.

Healey, P. (1991) Models of the development process: A review. *Journal of Property Research,* 8, 219–238.

Laing, A. and Crisp, V. (1992) *The Responsible Workplace*, London: Butterworth Architecture.

Latham, M. (1995) *Constructing the Team*. London: Department of the Environment.

Lees, A. (1992) *Overview of Environmental Issues facing the Property Industry, The Response of the Property Industry to Environmental Change*, Society of Property Researchers, RICS.

Long, N. and Long, A. (eds) (1994) *Battlefields of Knowledge*. London: Routledge.

Luithlen, L. (1994) *Office Development and Capital Accumulation in the UK*. Aldershot, Aveber.

Mallinson, M. (1997) *Calculation of Worth: An Information Research*. RICS.

Myerson, G. and Rydin, Y. (1996) *The Language of the Environment: A New Rhetoric*. London: UCL Press.

Pilkington, E. (1995) Buildings of future returning to nature. *The Guardian*, 1 April p. 2.

Potter, J. and Wetherell, M. (1987) *Discourse and Social Psychology: Beyond Attitudes and Behaviour*. London: Sages.

Rydin,Y. (1992) Environmental impacts and the property market. In M. J. Breheny (ed.) *Sustainable Development and Built Form*. Pion.

—— (1997) Planning, property and the environment. *Planning Practice and Research,* 12 (1), 5–7.

Shackley, S., Wynne, B. and Waterton, C. (1996) Imagine complexity: the past, present and future of complex thinking. *Futures*, 28(3), 201–255.

Sudjic, D. (1996) A house in the country, *The Guardian,* 2 June, p. 7.

Timmermans, S. and Berg, M. (1997) Standardisation in action: Achieving local universality through medical protocols. *Social Studies of Science*, 27, 273–305.

Vale, B. and Vale, R. (1991). *Green Architecture. Design for a Sustainable Future.*, London: RIBA.

Weir, F. (1990) *Towards Ozone Friendly Buildings*. London: Friends of the Earth.

Wilson, A. (ed.) (1998) *Green Development: Integrating Ecology and Real-estate*. Chichester: John Wiley and Sons.

Woods, C. G. (1992) 'A philosophy of an organic architecture'. In C. G. Woods and M. Wels, *Designing Your Natural House*. Amsterdam: Van Nostrand Reinhold.

5 Banking on the environment
Risk and rationality

Andrea Coulson

'UK Banks first became involved with environmental risk assessment in the early 1990s following the Environmental Protection Act 1990, which raised fears of banks becoming liable for pollution caused by their customers. The banks were anxious not to follow the example of the US where lenders faced liability under the Superfund legislation. The liability debate continues, as does the British Bankers' Association's role in lobbying on behalf of the industry. In more recent times, however, there has been a shift in emphasis away from liability issues. Reputational risk is the new environmental issue – an issue for both banks and our customers working together.'

During the 1990s much has been written on the fears of financial lenders about environmental liability. As environmental legislation has developed, lenders have been concerned that they may become directly responsible for environmental damage to property taken as security on a debt, or face loss of repayment where a borrower's solvency has been jeopardised by increased environmental liabilities. In recognition of these risks, lenders have created environmental management policies and have incorporated risk assessments in their lending practice. Now, an additional fear, indicated in the statement above from a senior bank official, is one of reputational risk through association with a polluter.

There has been research within the banking sector on its environmental management activities and lender practice (UNEP, 1992; EDR, 1994; Smith, 1994; UNEP and Salomon Brothers Inc., 1995; Coulson, 1997; Delphi and Ecologic, 1997; Hill *et al.*, 1997; PricewaterhouseCoopers, 1999). However, an in-depth examination of corporate environmental assessment by a single bank lender has not been undertaken. To redress this imbalance, a detailed case study was conducted with a major UK bank, Lloyds TSB. The study examined environmental assessment within its commercial lending function.

This chapter details the research process and findings of the case study. The central question posed is – how is environmental risk perceived and its associated management rationalised, by bank lending officers? Risk, in the case study, is conceptualised as a social construct. Emphasis is placed on examining risk representations and the influence of communication mechanisms on risk perception. The rhetoric of 'environmental risk' in banks is important and may indicate a more fundamental change in environmental values – but expressed in banker's language. Environmental issues are translated into terms such as 'credit risks'. But what exactly does this mean? How is it constructed and used by banking professionals?

The chapter begins by outlining details of the case method. It is framed by a description of the public face of Lloyds TSB with respect to risk representation and environmental management. This is followed by a depiction of the bank's internal environmental policy and procedural framework, its development and deployment. Emphasis is placed on examining lending officers' shared mental models of risk assessment. The final part of the chapter brings together examples of risk assessment from two hypothetical lending decisions taken by a group of the bank's lending officers. The chapter concludes by outlining the typical influences on environmental risk perception and assessment, and some of the wider implications of the study.

The case

The study was conducted between October 1997 and October 1999, during which time Lloyds and TSB were in the process of operational merger and undergoing a period of pronounced institutional change. This provided an opportunity to witness new policy development and confirmation. The key case contact was Head of Group Environment Risk, Richard Cooper. Richard had prime responsibility for environmental policy making and day-to-day operational environmental management within the Group; in particular, environmental credit risk-assessment. His title and role highlight the fact that environmental issues are considered primarily from a risk perspective. It was necessary to seek formal research access to bank documentation and personnel through research negotiations with Group Environment Risk (GER).[1]

The case study was conducted in three stages. The first stage was an examination of the Group's public environmental policy and its interface with environmental policies and procedural guidelines with respect to credit-risk assessment. The examination also involved documentary review, a series of interviews and focus group meetings with GER members, and observations at environmental training workshops.

The second stage was a questionnaire survey of lending officers across the Group. The objective of the survey was to gain an initial impression of the level of environmental consideration taking place within the commercial lending process, as well as lenders' awareness of, and views on, bank policy and procedural guidance. The questionnaire was piloted in two regional bank offices. The process included interviews with local lending officers to elicit their wider comments on environmental risk assessment. Questionnaires were issued to 2000 lending officers across the Group, to embrace all commercial banking offices in the UK and a sample of business banking offices. A satisfactory response rate of just over 25 per cent was achieved.

The final stage of research was a detailed examination of two hypothetical lending cases through interviews and focus groups with bank officers based in the north east of England. The lending cases were derived from two real situations, part of the bank's work during the prior financial period. Case one was the provision of finance to support a housing development on a potentially contaminated site. Case two involved a request to finance the expansion of a metal plating works. Further case details are highlighted later in the chapter.

The lending-case files, including financial statements, valuation reports and environmental consultants' reports, were provided by the bank in an anonymous form. During the course of case examination, officers were provided with an initial case outline. Additional information, such as that noted previously, was provided on request to simulate a 'real' lending process. To supplement the case studies a week was spent observing help-line operations and specialist case reviews by GER officers.

Examining the public face of Lloyds TSB

Before introducing case findings drawn from Lloyds TSB Group internal operations, it is important to examine the Group's public posture on the environment. Throughout the period of study, Lloyds TSB presented its environmental commitment in the form of an environmental policy statement within an information pack entitled 'Lloyds TSB Group: The Community and our Business'. The statement included a promise to 'continue to provide detailed guidelines to lending officials which will help them identify environmental risks in the UK and abroad'. It clearly focused on 'risk' as a central lending issue (Lloyds TSB, 1997a). The policy statement and subsequent procedural guidelines were an amalgam of the former Lloyds and TSB policy statements and their environmental-risk assessment procedures.

Further commitments to environmental risk had been made through signature to the United Nations Environment Programme (UNEP) statement by financial institutions on the environment and sustainable development. As a corporate signatory, Lloyds TSB had explicitly recognised 'that environmental risks should be part of the normal process of risk assessment and management' (UNEP, 1997).[2] The bank had also made a general endorsement to the International Chamber of Commerce Business Charter for Sustainable Development.

As a steering committee member of the UNEP Financial Institutions Initiative, Richard Cooper, noted previously as head of GER, had taken an active role in promoting the environmental risk agenda of the banking community. At a local level he had helped shape the British Bankers' Association (BBA) position on the environment and chaired the BBA Environmental Issues Advisory Panel. The panel was established in 1992 by the BBA's Risk Management Committee and has been actively involved in government liaison and acknowledgement of special lender circumstances regarding environmental liability, in particular the development and introduction of the UK Environment Act 1995 (BBA, 1993; 1995). Prior to his position as head of GER for Lloyds TSB, Richard was head of environment risk with TSB; so he brought to his various roles considerable experience in bank-lending practice.

Given the uncertainty surrounding the interpretation of environmental legislation, and resultant liability risk, members of the UK (and international) banking community have shared their lending experiences to develop a common defence. This, additionally, serves to reduce some of the competition between banks on environmental matters. But, as confidence in environmental risk-assessment has developed, a number of banks have sought investment opportunities in 'sustainable' companies. One example of this is a series of green products offered to small and medium sized enterprises under a European Investment Bank initiative (Coulson, 1999). At the time of the study, Lloyds TSB had not offered a dedicated 'environmental loan' but, as noted by Richard Cooper, 'in Lloyds TSB we consider environment issues as an integral part of commercial performance. One of the major considerations in pricing lending is quality of management, and good environmental management is usually a sign of good all round management.'

Like an increasing number of other European banks, Lloyds TSB produce an annual environmental report on their environmental performance and future environmental objectives (Hill *et al.*, 1997; PriceWaterhouseCoopers, 1999). Some argue that such reporting represents transparency and public accountability. Others suggest it is more a public relations exercise. However, Lloyds TSB's report does not take the form of a separate, glossy, brochure. It is part of a more comprehensive Group information pack, available on request to interested parties. It has not been the subject of an extensive advertising campaign (Coulson and Monks, 1999). Such a conservative communication stance is typical of a number of UK banks in the initial stages of reporting, fearful of reputational risk (Nicholson *et al.* 1995; Coulson and Monks, 1999).

The Group's first report was issued in 1997 (Lloyds TSB, 1997b), a practical document outlining key environmental management activities and corresponding objectives for the following year. In 1998, environmental performance was reviewed against this commitment, and new objectives for 1999 were established (Lloyds TSB, 1998).

Specific objectives for lending included:

- Objective for 1998 – to complete the training of business lending officers and similar training and awareness raising exercises for other

Group lending companies. Reported achievement – over 120 environmental workshops were attended by 1300 lending officers and a distance learning workbook and video had been distributed to those not able to attend the workshop;

- Objective for 1998 – to continue to develop the Environmental Risk Handbook launched in 1997 to help our lending officers identify environmental risks and work with our customers to promote environmental good practice. Reported achievement – in particular, sectoral business issues were addressed in more detail and an internal help-line established in 1997 had provided advice on over 1800 individual lending cases during 1998; and

- Objective for 1999 – to promote awareness of environmental risks and environmental management among our small and medium-sized business customers. This objective remains to be reported on. However, as part of a British Bankers' Association initiative, Lloyds TSB have issued leaflets to their commercial and business customers explaining their environmental lending position and the value of environmental management.

Internal policy and procedural frameworks

The Lloyds TSB public statements and reported commitments, noted previously, form one representation of policy and environmental management activities within the Group. Risk perception and its management appears as a central policy issue within the bank. This policy is translated into procedural guidelines, primarily through an environmental risk handbook, a programme of training, and a distance learning workbook and video. Anxiety about environmental liabilities underline such actions, 'the primary drivers of environmental assessment within our lending function'. Indeed, policy documentation and procedural 'tools' such as these are clearly one representation of the banking community's fears about the environmental consequences, or inheritance, of their loans (Barrett, 1994).

Policy development and deployment

Group lending officers are given discretionary powers to make decisions based on authorised financial lending limits. Beyond this, cases are referred for approval up the bank hierarchy (Berry *et al.*, 1993a,b). An individual officer's position is justified on the strength of their credit expertise and on the expectation that they will follow bank policy guidelines in making their lending decisions. Inherent in such a social structure is a formal referral process – which provides one means of verifying policy applications. Another method of policy scrutiny is a Group-wide internal audit. Most lenders involved in the research were long familiar with the banking and loan culture, having been with Lloyds or TSB since leaving school, many working in the same, or neighbouring, branch office.

GER are the Group's environmental lending experts and environmental policy makers. In fulfilling these roles and responsibilities, the GER team aimed to provide ongoing support to enable lending officers to respond effectively to environmental change and, ultimately, make sound credit decisions. This was achieved primarily through the provision of a central help-line facility offering lender support in evaluating an environmental credit risk. They acted when lending officers felt 'an environmental risk may exist and wish to explore environmental risk assessment options'. A regular GER newsletter provided legal and technical updates.

Advisers within GER were all experienced Lloyds or TSB bank officers who had been retrained in environmental management. Their environmental-lending expertise was honed through dealings with case referrals. They had close links with various external advisers should additional support be required. In particular, their role included specialist consultation with the Group's established panel of environmental consultants who were commissioned to carry out what one GER adviser termed, 'scientific environmental risk assessments such as phase one or phase two reviews'.

The panel of consultants could have considerable influence on the environmental-risk perceptions held by GER advisers and lenders. It should be noted, however, that the consultants were not credit experts: the power to interpret risk and act accordingly rested with '*expert*' lenders.

GER had designed an environmental credit-risk assessment policy which provided a skeletal framework for assessment. Lending officers layered case details on to this framework and then interpreted case 'facts' according to their own lending experiences. As described by a senior advisor in GER: 'the assessment of environmental risk is a systematic approach, bank policy and procedures allow sufficient flexibility for the lender to respond to the individual issues facing them at any one time'.

An examination of environmental/credit policy implementation was not, therefore, purely an issue of establishing policy awareness, control verification and testing. Putting into operation Group and functional environmental policy required judgemental application within each lending situation, resulting in a narrower or wider interpretation of environmental credit risks – depending on the perceived risk inherent within individual lending situations.

In responding to the research questionnaire, 87 per cent of lending officers claimed to conduct environmental-risk assessment and 81 per cent believed the incorporation of environmental-risk assessments within lending decisions is a generally accepted practice within the bank. Putting environmental-risk assessment into perspective, one lender noted that 'the environmental issue is one of many considerations in lending money'. And another lender asserted: 'environmental issues should be considered by all owners and occupiers'.

Some 97 per cent of respondents were aware of the Group's environmental policy statement, but a number of lending officers specifically noted that 'environmental-risk assessment is in reaction to perceived environmental risk attached to individual lending circumstances as opposed to policy requirements'. A number of questionnaire responses focused on lender-liability issues; in particular, one lender noted: 'European directives will not allow this [environmental risk assessment] to go away. Especially if losses are incurred'.

In comparing questionnaire commentaries by lending officers, it was clear that perceptions of environmental risk and level of assessment varied considerably, according to nature of individual lending portfolios. As one lender claimed, environmental-risk exposure within lending portfolios is perceived 'as a function of borrower size, industry and location'. This is further illustrated by lender comments noted below:

> 'I am aware of environmental issues, but at the level I deal with borrowing and account-size, it is inappropriate in most cases. This however does not mean it is not an extremely important issue', in contrast to 'the size of my customers means they are inherently risky'.

> 'the nature of my portfolio tends to be safe/clean industries', as opposed to 'I have a mixture. Environmental assessment is not necessarily applicable in all sectors – retail, nursing homes are generally low risk compared to high-risk industries such as petrol stations and farming'; and

> 'I operate broadly in an area of relatively low risk – but we cannot be complacent.' 'Our area is generally contaminated and we have to accept this'. 'A lot of land in my area would be an unsatisfactory risk due to deposits of mine waste (including arsenic) and emissions of Radon gas'.

Shared 'mental models'

Many respondents to the case questionnaire described how they would deviate from specific environmental lending-policy and procedural guidelines. They would adopt a partial, or informal, 'mental' assessment of environmental credit risk. One lender noted 'a mental assessment is always undertaken but a paper based document completed only in a few cases – obviously the most relevant'. Another lender noted, 'I am getting into *thinking of this*'.

Similar findings have resulted from a number of studies of general lending procedures where experienced lenders were found to rely on 'mental models' for guiding their assessment procedures. Formal guidance tools are more likely to be used by new, inexperienced, lending officers. Such tools are used for 'first considerations' and awareness raising; either establishing standard credit issues with new lending officers or new credit issues. They are consistent with a 'workbook' style regulation in bank policy and practice (Barrett, 1994).

The lending-case examples offer a more detailed insight into the way mental models and guidance materials were handled. On first reviewing the hypothetical lending cases, officers identified largely the same key issues, perceiving the same environmental risks for assessment. Those who elaborated most on potential risk issues, did so with reference to experience of similar lending situations and/or potential pollution issues. The specific details of environmental credit-risk assessment procedures will be reviewed in the next section; here I will explore mental modelling.

In terms of environmental credit-risk assessment, procedural guidelines were seen to provide a framework for assessment upon which lending officers layer case details and interpret results according to their lending experience. As noted previously, GER policy-makers recognised that 'guidance documentation had been purposefully designed to be abstractions applicable to a wide range of lending situations according to lending officer interpretation and expertise'.

For those lending to high-to-medium-risk industries, and/or in locations where there is a higher level of environmental-credit-risk, risk assessment was automatic. In such instances, assessment was conducted as a matter of course without direct reference to policy or procedural guidance materials. However, reliance was placed on the same principles as those who made explicit reference to formal guidelines. Thus, it is proposed that once environmental credit-risk assessment becomes a habitual practice, the guidance framework becomes internalised as a mental model. Lending officers did not need to consult the environmental handbook for each lending case as procedures were familiar, 'in the same way credit training manuals are not consulted for every lending case'.

Working with groups of lending officers of varying grades within the same office, revealed how a 'bank' risk perception and rationality for risk assessment was formed. Lending officers frequently drew on their colleagues' expertise, both during formal case referral outside of discretionary lending limits *and* in informally ruminating on case issues. They would share case experience and tips on how to work through the environmental risk handbook and supporting workbook. This sharing of risk perception extended to 'GER's expert environmental credit risk advisers'.

Many lenders justified their method of environmental risk assessment in organisational cultural terms – 'it's the way we do things around here' and 'bank ways and policy'. How procedures are established and perceived to work is an issue of 'cultural' acceptance for the lending officer. Policy-makers view reference to procedural documentation as a way of socialising officers and coding procedures that are generally accepted as adequate.

The negotiation of environmental-risk standards and procedures, both between policy-makers and lending officers, and officers up and down the lending hierarchy, was not free from conflict and resistance to change. In particular, lending officers voiced concerns about the required levels of assessment, 'too much paper work', and associated time commitments.

Procedural acceptance involved a common-sense approach that operated through the production, rather than presumption, of knowledge. Ratifying acceptances was largely the responsibility of senior lending officers. They provided expert assurance that practicalities of cost and timeliness had been accounted for.

Environmental credit risk-assessment

'The management of risk is not new to banks. It is the overall assessment and quantification of risk that determines whether the bank wishes to lend, the price of borrowing, the requirement for security and so on. Risk assessment is about recognising the risk issues, assessing the impact these may have on the bank and the customer and most importantly measuring the likelihood of any potential risk actually occurring. Environmental risk has introduced an entirely new set of risk criteria and if a lender is to reach a sound decision these new risks must be successfully factored into the overall credit decision.'

(Senior Manager, GER)

Environmental risk assessment was typically carried out in three stages. The first two standard stages fall in line with the lending process in general: (i) desk-top review of the application to gain an initial impression of risk; and (ii) an interview and, where possible, site visit, with a borrower to confirm initial expectations.

In each lending case, environmental assessment by a lender was essentially a high level review, seeking to highlight the risks associated with the customer's task activities, land and management processes. The assessment was not an in-depth study. Lending officers see themselves as credit experts not environmental experts.

A third, more detailed, course of investigation may be required where a potential high environmental risk requires further investigation. This would involve the lender, and possibly GER, commissioning a specialist review from a member of the bank's panel of environmental consultants.

Lending case studies

Key features of the bank lending process (and environmental credit-risk assessment) emerged from the way lending officers reviewed each research case. During interviews, each case was considered in turn, but the results have been taken together to highlight commonalities within lending processes. The lending scenarios were each pursued in a staged form with lenders encouraged to talk through their normal environmental risk assessment process. To supplement introductory case data, information from the original lending files was, on request, provided to the lender.

Lending case studies

1. Housing Ltd

The proposed customer is a well-established house-building company. They have requested a facility to support a six-month build programme for a residential housing development in a rural location recognised for its mine workings. Following housing completion the site will be sold (currently under contract with buyer) and the debt repaid in full.

2. Metalplating Ltd

The proposed customer runs a well-established metal plating operation, in a traditional industrial location and requires finance to upgrade kit.

Both cases are new lends!

Stage one – desk-top review

The lender's first question was typically – what am I dealing with? Scenario assessment began with first impressions of the environmental risks of the customer's business (process) and location-sensitivity (e.g. land contamination). Who am I dealing with? Is this a new lend? Am I familiar with this customer, process and/or location?

Given that each hypothetical lending case was posed as a new-lend situation, company financial statements and more traditional financial performance indicators were required. The lender was likely to conduct a high level review of the financial position of a company and evaluate its position with respect to the nature of the business and its market location.

After reviewing the financial statements of each case, lenders found some comfort in that 'everything seemed in order'. No environmental costs and liabilities were obvious from a financial statement analysis. The case companies were depicted as profitable businesses with adequate cash-flow forecasts. In contrast, both cases, by their nature and location, were found to pose environmental risks. The environmental risk attached to the housing development case was, clearly, from siting residential property and gardens on old mine workings. In the case of the metal-coating company, the risk was handling hazardous chemicals used in the cleaning and coating process, and siting on already contaminated land. However, lenders proposed that, if the businesses were 'well managed', potential risk should not be realised. As noted by one lending officer, and reiterated time and time again by others: 'we are in the business of lending, we do not want to turn away profitable business, we need to adopt a sensible and practicable attitude to environmental risk'.

This point was echoed by Richard Cooper, GER: 'Lloyds TSB does not consider it appropriate to exclude specific industries on the basis of environmental risk. However, failing to recognise a risk issue, or worst of all simply ignoring it, will be as detrimental to a business as over-reacting to it. In considering the wider environmental risk issues, we can work with our customers to pursue potential opportunities offered by environmental management'.

Some lenders were familiar with the nature of the business and/or the location and drew upon past experience to elaborate on potential risks and their management – best and worst practice. Reference was also made to the relevant experience of lending colleagues within the bank, in particular those who had come across similar cases. Environmental risk assessment was high-lighted as a means of 'offering added value to the customers as opposed to a barrier to new propositions'. Lenders revealed considerable knowledge of lending-portfolio composition and lending responsibilities. Some even spoke of the environmental risks associated with their own branch office.

Where lenders were personally unfamiliar with either the borrower's process and/or location, they acquainted themselves with potential credit risks by reference to formal guidance documents: the Environment Risk Handbook, 'standard' industry and location checklists, and a risk classificatory matrix system.

Based on this initial process, an 'informed' perception of risk was derived. Subsequent assessment of that risk then varied according to the borrower's industrial activity/sector and geographical location. Prior research has shown that industrial-sector risk assessment is a common priority for lenders. Less has been said about location. Bank classificatory systems for industrial-sector risk analysis have been found to vary. Some catalogue a borrower according to a list of high-risk industries, such as extractive industries or chemical pro-cessors. More complex systems include specific reference to substances handled and particular manufacturing processes (Barrett, 1994; Coulson, 1997).

Stage two – simulation of interview and site visit

If the lender perceived that an environmental risk warranted further investig-ation, a second, more in-depth, review of risk would take place. This stage of assessment involved weighting risk potential against how well the customer managed the issues identified. From interviews and site visits, lenders familiarised themselves with the borrower's business and its management. With an established bank customer, existing file history is used as an indication of their 'track record'.

Interviews would normally be held on a borrower's premises, so providing an opportunity for a site review. Particular emphasis was placed on a borrower's ability to put together and defend the loan application, and to offer support for the quality of financial and environmental information provided. In the case of environmental – risk assessment, site visits provided an opportunity to identify signs of pollution and potential environmental liabilities. It also confirmed the existence and quality of assets. Furthermore, a site visit helped lending officers establish an environmental profile of the business, while reviewing the applicant's ability at work.

Having established the initial boundaries of the cases, the lenders' queries centred on one question – is the site contaminated? Lenders queried past land use, attending particularly to surface water and underground storage tanks. It was noted that borrowers should have considered any site contamination and sought to rectify any problems.

Site profiles were provided for review, including observations from the original lending officers:

Site profiles

Case 1:
Part of an old mining village. The site is situated 300 yards from the village centre including shops, school and housing. An estate road is under construction to the south of the site. To the north the site is separated from a carriageway by a retaining wall with 1960s' housing beyond. Housing also lies directly to the west and east of the site. The land is flat, sloping only slightly towards a stream that runs the length of the boundary. The land has been cleared for building.

Past use: agriculture.

Case 2:

The customer has occupied their existing site for some 10 years. The site is in an industrial area with engineering business surrounding, there are no residential areas nearby or evidence of surface water. Visual inspection proves positive, all areas seem clean and tidy. Stored chemicals are all bunded and appear in order. A formalised environmental management system (EMS) is evident.

Past site: light engineering activities.

Lenders sought to acquaint themselves with the borrowers' operations – from input, through construction and processing, to outputs and their disposal. Their findings were considered against legislative requirements on the borrower. In the light of these, the lender considered how well the customer managed risk. Live client files were used to reveal how environmental impacts were judged for similar cases, and what guidance was offered in the Environmental Risk Handbook and workbook.

Land quality in both cases was viewed as important from two aspects: first the value of any security taken after accounting for any contingent environmental liabilities; and secondly the effect on the financial position of the company after accounting for any potential clean-up liabilities. In both lending cases the companies were operating on potentially unstable sites. Housing Ltd faced the risk of old mine workings and Metalplating Ltd faced the legacy of industrial past use. Having established that contamination may exist, the question became: is any potential contamination likely to cause harm, taking into consideration the proposition at hand and the neighbouring property?

For Housing Ltd, the potential for contamination was regarded as very high. The proposed construction of residential housing and gardens and proximity to the local population raised issues of potential public safety. This risk was enhanced by the fact that run-off from local mine workings could contaminate local water supplies. One lender noted a newspaper story in which residents of a housing estate had 'woken up to craters emerging in their back gardens where old mine workings had collapsed'. Lenders believed that construction operations could disturb any mine workings present, but felt that the presence of council road-building in the area gave an indication that the site was 'safe'. With this in mind they checked that appropriate planning permission had been obtained by the builder and that the bank had evidence of this.

The primary fear of lenders with respect to Housing Ltd was their own reputational risk through association with a developer 'who could build such a property' – more so than 'what would be the liability of the bank'? Regarding reputation, a number of lenders noted that the potential borrower was a 'well-established' house building company who had a reputation for good management and good quality housing. Furthermore, the housing was being carried out under contract with a buyer, further guaranteeing income towards repayment. Taking these considerations together, lenders felt that their risk fears were slightly reduced. Two courses of standard action were proposed: consult GER for advice; and/or commission an environmental audit.

For Metalplating Ltd, assessment of land quality centred on the environmental sensitivity of potential pollutants. Despite the high environmental risks posed by metal plating, file notes for Metalplating Ltd revealed the borrower as having a good understanding of these risks. Notes from the site visit clearly indicated the presence of an environmental management system. This was viewed as particularly significant when considering repayment ability, indirect lender liability, and the influence of environmental legislation on such risk-sensitive borrowers. A number of lenders expressed confidence that Metalplating Ltd could 'continue to win business based on the high quality of their environmental management'. In addition, contamination potential was mitigated by the fact that there was no neighbouring residential site or evidence of surface water.

As a secondary check on the companies, lenders requested that waste-transfer notes would be required to check the legality of the companies' waste management procedures (e.g. with licensed operators). In addition, a number of lenders said that they would check that there had been no illegal emissions attributed to the company. However, given the specialist nature of metal plating, few lenders were prepared to assume that the site was well managed and free from significant environmental risk. They wanted further advice from GER experts, including environmental-risk assessments.

Lenders appeared to have made only limited use of financial information to establish environmental risk, preferring to judge the company according to its awareness of environmental issues and its management response to these issues. A number of banks have noted problems with the financial quantification of risks, especially given the lack of standardisation of environmental accounting information and different notions of environmental value (Coulson, 1997).

To supplement their own analysis, copies of site valuation reports were requested by lenders, valuations were requested to specifically include environmental considerations. If necessary, these would be provided by specially commissioned consultants. As noted by one lender and echoed by others: 'standard practice of valuers is to offers their opinions with a disclaimer attached on environmental liability identification'.

To the surprise of lending officers, the valuation report for Housing Ltd raised the issue that 'an unexplained smell of diesel was present at the site on inspection and should be investigated further'. The valuation report for Metalplating Ltd provided no indication of any environmental liabilities being present.

Based on the lenders' findings, GER advisers recommended that the lender responsible for Housing Ltd discuss with the potential borrower the possibility of commissioning an environmental consultant to carry out an environmental site survey. The new fear of GER and the lender was that an underground storage tank, possibly used to store agricultural fuels, was present and unstable. A scientific survey of the site was therefore necessary. GER advised that the issue be raised as a customer-service point, recommending liability recognition.

Given the environmental-management competence demonstrated by Metalplating Ltd, it was felt that no further environmental risk assessment was necessary. Thus finance could be provided, as long as other lending criteria had been satisfied.

Stage three – specialist environmental assessment

In the case of Housing Ltd, negotiations with the customer revealed that an environmental site survey had, prior to bank contact, already been conducted. The survey had involved extensive soil sampling and testing, and site profiling. Findings from the survey revealed that 'everything was in order, any soil contaminants were well below statutory levels'. The consultant's report was reviewed to establish its credentials.

Finally, lending officers agreed to provide finance to both applicants on the basis of established environmental risk and management practice. Lending officers documented their own conclusions from environmental assessments and scientific examinations, all placed in the context of wider credit considerations. These were then integrated with general lending criteria to support the final lending decisions. In summary, environmental issues were only one feature of many management considerations. As stressed by Peter Waite, GER, 'environmental risk could have both a positive or negative impact on financial performance depending on its management'. Once such loans had been established they were monitored through the bank's standard annual review process.

Conclusion

This chapter provides one representation of 'banking on the environment' and an initial insight into the social construction of a lending officer's rationality for environmental management. The case findings show that environmental-risk assessment is becoming a day-to-day reality for some banks' lending officers and their borrowers. But, as stressed by the British Bankers' Association (BBA, 1993), lending officers try not to cast themselves in the role of environmental experts, but as financial specialists aware of best, and worst, environmental business practice. In practice, this becomes a debatable distinction.

Traditionally, the lending situation has been viewed as one in which a lender balances the financial risk of a borrower defaulting on repayment against financial return. Accordingly, a lender's role in society is to support economic development. Underpinning the lending process is a recognition that the banking community is vulnerable to the (mis)behaviour of their borrowers and economic contingencies. The lender thus absorbs credit risk on the basis that a risk premium will be charged and, where appropriate, insurance may be taken in the form of security.

Holding a lender liable for the environment risk of their borrower, or their inherited environmental legacy, establishes lenders not only as credit experts but, *de facto*, as environmental experts with legitimate power of authority to police corporate environmental performance. In a society in which banks are competing for resources and influence with other banks, their legitimate power over their borrowers should be questioned, and thus their individual influence on corporate environmental management behaviour questioned. However, taken together, a position on the environment by the banking community could have a powerful impact. In the UK, through the British Bankers' Association, banks have begun an active process of effecting a community role with governments, and sharing experience of environmental risk and assessment methods.

The case described in this chapter provides an example of how environmental considerations now influence the level of financial support available for economic development and environmental management. The foundation for environmental considerations within bank-lending processes is viewed partially as a response to concerns regarding a lender's potential liability for the environment, and partially in response to risk to bank reputation through association with a polluter. However, as one lender noted 'where environmental issues are apparent, we as lenders then have a duty as individuals, to the bank, our customers and the environment, to bottom these issues out before proceeding'. Officers guard against the risks of lender liability for the environment, while pursuing lending opportunities with companies whose management seek financial and environmental benefits through sustainable activities. The resulting value is to the bank (usually first) and then their customers and society.

The Lloyds TSB example shows that sharing lending experiences and developing lending processes based on industry, customer and regional specialisation contribute significantly to improving environmental awareness and management, not only within the bank but also within the wider bank community. Given environmental and legal uncertainty surrounding risk assessment, environmentally-related procedures and routines become institutionalised within the bank through a process of negotiation and consensus formation.

The question of how environmental risk assessment techniques work, and procedures are perceived to work, is portrayed as an issue of institutional and, to an extent, cultural agreement. Learning becomes the subject of social positioning. Credibility for a lender's view of how 'the environment' will react is secured by the commitment of a bank's membership to their institution. Emphasis is placed on environmental policy development, and communication among bank associations and within individual bank organisations, to support a 'bank' rationality for environmental-risk management within the lending process. Environmental considerations appear as an integral part of their lending decisions in reaction to perceived environmental risk attached to individual lending circumstances.

Risk preferences within banks are an indication of how environmental considerations now influence the level of financial support available for economic development and environmental management. As bank policy-makers and lending officers successfully capture environmental issues within their existing economic frameworks, companies seeking finance from the bank can expect to be questioned on their environmental policy and management practices. This is a trend which will continue.

Notes

1 Publication restrictions have been applied to maintain bank confidentiality and the bank has approved the release of case finding.

2 The statement was launched in May 1992 in response to the Kyoto Protocol, as a statement recognising the need for *banks*, along with governments, businesses, and individuals, to acknowledge their social environmental responsibility. It has since been modified to represent the increasing range of *financial institutions* now involved in traditional banking activities. The original statement by banks made specific reference to lending activities with signatories that 'as part of . . . credit risk assessment, we

recommend when appropriate environmental impact assessment'. At the time of merger, only Lloyds Bank was a signatory. Richard Cooper, on behalf of the newly formed Lloyds TSB Group, reaffirmed operational commitment to the statement principles in 1999 at the Fourth Roundtable Meeting of the UNEP Financial Institutions Initiative, in Chicago.

References

Barrett, J. (1994) Weighing up the risks. *Certified Accountant*, October, 42–44.
BBA (1993) *Position Statement: Banks and the Environment*. London: British Bankers' Association.
—— (1995) *The Environment Bill: Lender Liability*. British Bankers' Association Issues Brief, March. London: British Bankers' Association.
Berry, A. J., Faulkner, S., Hughes, M., and Jarvis, R. (1993a) Financial information, the banker and the small business. *British Accounting Review*, 25, 131–150.
Berry, R. H., Crum, R. E., and A. Waring (1993b) *Corporate Performance Evaluation in Bank Lending Decisions*. Chartered Institute of Management Accountants, Research Studies. London: Chartered Institute of Management Accountants.
Coulson, A. B. (1997) 'Corporate Environmental Performance Considerations within Bank Lending Processes: the Social Construction of Risk Perception'. PhD Thesis, University of Durham, Business School.
—— (1999) 'Capital Market Risk'. Workshop report of the ESRC Financial Sector Environment Forum, No. 3. Glasgow: University of Strathclyde.
Coulson, A. B. and Monks, V. (1999) Corporate environmental performance considerations within bank lending decisions. *Eco-management and Auditing*, 6, 1–10.
Delphi International Ltd and Ecologic GMBH (1997) 'The Role of the Financial Institutions in Achieving Sustainable Development'. Report to the European Commission, November. London: Delphi International Ltd and Ecologic (CMBH).
EDR (1994) *Second Annual Financial Institution Environmental Survey*. Conducted by Dun and Bradstreet Information Services and Environmental Data Resources, Inc. June. Connecticut: Environmental Data Resources.
Hill, J., Fedrigo, D., and Marshall, I. (1997) *Banking on the Future: A Survey of Implementation of the UNEP Statement by Banks on the Environment and Sustainable Development*. London: Green Alliance.
Lloyds TSB Group (1997a) *The Community and our Business: Environmental Policy Statement*. Birmingham: Lloyds TSB.
—— (1997b) *Environmental Report*. Birmingham: Lloyds TSB.
—— (1998) *Environmental Report*. Birmingham: Lloyds TSB.
Nicholson, Graham and Jones (1995) *Bank Liable for Environmental Clean-up*. Banknotes, Property. London: Nicholson, Graham and Jones.
PricewaterhouseCoopers (1999) UNEP Financial Institutions Initiative 1998 Survey. London: Pricewaterhouse Coopers.
Smith, D. R. (1994) 'Environmental Risk: Credit Approaches and Opportunities, an Interim Report'. Prepared for the UNEP Roundtable on Commercial Banks and the Environment, 26–27 September, Geneva.
UNEP (1992) *Banking and the Environment: A Statement by Banks on the Environment and Sustainable Development*, Foreword. Geneva: United Nations Environment Programme.
—— (1997) *Banking and the Environment: A Statement by Financial Institutions on the Environment and Sustainable Development*, Foreword. Geneva: United Nations Environment Programme.
UNEP and Salomon Brothers Inc. (1995) *Banks Foresee Growing Opportunities and Importance of Environment in First Global Survey*. Geneva: United Nations Environment Programme.

Part 2

Regulating

6 Being a regulator

Stephen Fineman

There is little doubt that, for large corporations especially, mandatory environmental regulation is now a fact of industrial life. In Western Europe and North America, sophisticated legislative regimes have developed to regulate the management of a range of hazardous substances and industrial waste. Generally speaking, regulatory philosophy seeks initially to encourage industry to put its own house in order, but then applies sanctions such as prosecutions, fines and withdrawal of permits to operate, if they fail or default.

Typically, environmental regulation has been observed in 'input–output' form. Regulatory pressure is applied to an industry or company (the input) and this creates an output effect – such as reduction in pollution incidents, changes in factory emissions, cleaner watercourses, different forms of waste management, and so forth (Fischer and Schot, 1991; Smith, 1993). But environmental regulation, like any other legal instrument, does not operate in a social vacuum. It is only as good as those who apply and police it, and it is unlikely that industrial managers will be passive recipients of even legally enforceable requirements. Indeed, we know that environmental regulation is often resisted or diluted by some corporations (e.g. Howard, 1997; Fineman and Clarke, 1996), while others are spurred by regulation to be 'greener than the rest' and gain competitive advantage (e.g. Brown *et al.*, 1998; Sanchez, 1998; Gouldson and Murphy, 1998). Crucially, though, it is what happens *between* the regulator and the regulated where the viability of environmental regulation lies. While environmental law provides the scaffold for regulatory conduct, it is the actors, both the regulator and the regulated, inspector and inspected, who breathe life into this scaffold, shaping regulatory standards and control (e.g. see Gould). It is this process, and some of its policy implications, that is the focus of the present chapter.

Street-level bureaucrats

In addressing this issue, I conceptualise environmental inspectors as street-level bureaucrats (Lipsky, 1980; Fineman, 1998). Street-level bureaucrats, typically, work for legislatively defined agencies of social control and have face-to-face contact with those they regulate. The environmental inspector, in this view, is similar to the police officer, customs-and-excise official, social worker or health-and-safety inspector; people who interpret the law to make it workable. The precise nature of regulation is open to the officer's interpretations, assumptions and political preferences, as well as being susceptible to tacit negotiation between the parties involved. Indeed, much of UK environmental law is specified in ways that require some flexibility of this sort, despite its monolithic appearance (Bell, 1997).

Casting environmental regulation in this form shifts it from a dispassionate, mechanical process to one that is infused with active reality construction as the parties 'trade' their mutual positions, present and save face, test out and exercise their power. Environmental standards are likely to be more malleable than they appear, be culturally and sub-culturally influenced, and not always applied evenly. The perception of what an environmental problem 'is' may be far from uncontentious, nicely illustrated by Lowe *et al.*'s (1997) study of farm pollution. For traditional diary farmers in the UK, farm waste has typically been regarded as 'natural', literally absorbed within the seasonal cycle of farming. They are, therefore, puzzled by the environmental inspector's view that such waste is now 'pollution' and subject to special controls.

In attempting to make regulation work, the environmental inspector sits, often uneasily, at the intersection of a number of different interests – economic, industrial, environmental and governmental. These are not always in tune with one another. For example, to enforce environmental compliance on an organisation may risk its economic viability. To prosecute a company to show that the government is 'tough on polluters' may draw the inspector into expensive and protracted legal proceedings. To accommodate industry's requirements reinforces a collaborative atmosphere, but can be also be seen as appeasing polluters.

Against this backcloth, we may ask some important questions:

- What actually happens when regulator meets regulated?
- How are regulatory standards formed and deals done?
- What are the implications for regulatory policy and practice?

These questions will be addressed through a qualitative study of the work of a major environmental regulatory agency – the Environment Agency of England and Wales.

The Agency

The Environment Agency of England and Wales regulates some 2000 industrial processes on waste disposal, water quality and industrial emissions, each area defined formally according to dedicated legislation. The Agency is mandated to promote sustainable development (itself a not

uncontentious concept – see Beckerman, 1994) and to collaborate sympath-
etically with various public interest groups. It employs approximately 9500
people, organized in three tiers – head office, eight regions and 26 sub-
regions or areas. It reports to national Government and is subject to
changing ministerial priorities. It operates amongst a policy network of
environmental stakeholders, some of whom try to radicalise its policies and
actions (such as green activists) while others are keen to blunt its influences
(such as more conservative industry groups and trade associations). The
Agency's work, therefore, is not straightforward or uncontested.

Area offices are located throughout England and Wales where local
managers co-ordinate the daily activities of field inspectors – the main focus
of this chapter. Most inspectors have advanced technical backgrounds – such
as in environmental science, chemistry, physics, geology, hydrology, nuclear
engineering, or agriculture. Some, especially in waste management, have
been recruited for their confrontation-management skills.

The inspectors visit industrial sites, sometimes unannounced, sometimes by
appointment as part of a routine licensing process. Companies must pay a fee
for the licenses and associated technical tests. The kinds of industry vary
according to the region of the country, but can include water companies,
chemical works, power stations, hospitals, waste treatment centres, engineering factories and farms. Inspectors tend to specialise in one of three areas: river
and groundwater pollution, waste disposal, or integrated pollution control.
Integrated pollution control (IPC) has its own legally 'prescribed' processes –
chemicals or emissions that are deemed sufficiently dangerous to require tight
mandatory control. The exact technical manner of control is decided according
to the 'best practicable environmental option' for the control or disposal of a
pollutant, through the 'best available techniques not entailing excessive cost',
BATNEEC. These rubrics are enshrined in environmental legislation.

The inspectors

The focal sample in this study was a cross-section of 82 Agency staff, the
bulk of whom were front-line field inspectors and their immediate managers
in six different area offices. Twenty inspectors were involved with IPC regulation, 22 with water quality and 22 with waste regulation. They represented
the full range of age and experience within the Agency. The remaining
participants were regional and head office managers.

Two methods of inquiry were employed – individual interviews and work
shadowing. Individual interviews took place with all participants. These
were confidential, semi-structured discussions, exploring: the dynamics of
the regulatory encounter; how regulatory standards were determined in the
field; how regulation was policed; and the sources of pressures and demands
on the individual inspector. All interviews were tape recorded and analysed
thematically. Work shadowing took place with 14 field inspectors, who
together represented water, waste and integrated pollution control. I accom-

panied inspectors on their normal site visits. Some visits took place by appointment, often with a single site manager with environmental responsibility, but sometimes with a senior management team. Others were unannounced spot-checks. Before each visit I was briefed by the inspector on his or her expectations and on the history of the 'case'. After a visit there was a discussion about what had happened. During inspections I would record my impressions of the site and the processes being regulated, including verbatim quotes on what was being said, how it was said, and how the parties were influencing each other.

Inside regulation

What picture do we get of regulatory inspectors and inspections? Here are two contrasting examples.

Don

Don is a waste inspector in his early 50s. He is an ex-policeman, a burly, chain-smoking, man. He works at the rough, tough, end of waste regulation, with some rough, tough, operators – or so he wished to present them. Today's visit to a landfill site is to be surprise one. As we drive to the site he talks about the difficulties of prosecution because of ambiguities or 'stupidities' in waste regulation law, 'which defence solicitors exploit' . . .

> Last week I interviewed the director of a landfill site – after an official caution and three months of reminders. We use an interview room – a bit like a police station. He came with his solicitor, saying, in mitigation, he can't afford the improvements we are asking for. So do we close him down or keep the wheels of industry turning? In one breath the Agency is asking us to up our prosecutions; in the other that we should help industry. In the last resort I'll stand my ground; there are some awkward bastards. Now and again I'll pull them into line; crack the whip. In conflict situations one of my younger colleagues will come with me because lawyers will try and discredit us as individuals, and the evidence. Then there's the magistrates' courts – they're a farce! It's 'does your face fit'.

Don has little patience for procedural offences 'like not having a sign on a licensed site. "Ah, an offence!" It carries 6 months imprisonment under the Environment Protection Act – for not having a bloody piece of wood! If it were harming health or the environment that would be different'. And (later), during our site visit, Don would point mockingly to likely procedural offences – such as the angle of waste storage being incorrect, or a fence being not quite right.

Generally, he says, he is left to his own devices as to whom he inspects and when. Complaints from the public receive priority, such as fly tipping. Often he has to come between neighbours in disputes . . .

. . . more likely out in the sticks than in the town. Mr Towny moves into the countryside and converts an old barn or something. Then his idyll is shattered when a local farmer starts burning pig shit. I sometimes have to say, 'that's what they do in the countryside'.

We pay our unannounced visit to the landfill site. It is in a flat area of the countryside, alongside a busy motorway. Don describes it as a licensed enterprise, but 'Mafia backed in the States – allegedly Mafia money'. The site is also a stone quarry some five years old. There are huge 'active' open excavations besides old excavations, 'cells', filled with household garbage. It is bleak. Dust swirls and loose rubbish blows around. There is a pervasive, foetid smell. The filled cells are eventually restored to grazing land, but, as the waste rots, methane gas is produced. This is vented, either directly to the atmosphere, or to fuel power generators on the site that produce electricity which is sold to the national grid.

In the middle of the site is what resembles a giant's cricket-practice net. A massive, box-frame of netting, open at one end. It was built at Don's insistence (and a condition of the license) to prevent loose rubbish blowing over adjacent fields and farmland. It is a very windy site and this often bursts the net, as it has done now. Also deer and rabbit poachers have found the netting useful for their trade: they cut bits off. Don is aware of all the defects but insists that the important thing is that the company is prepared to respond in some way to his environmental demands, so he will take no further action: 'It's image. Show you're doing something'.

We drive onto the site to find Phil, the site manager, in his shed-cum-office. Don, on several occasions, refers to the man's youth and skinhead appearance with thinly disguised prejudice – but also comments that he 'has the formal qualifications to do the job'.

Don's style is bullish, open and personal. He jousts with Phil. Phil appears to be keen to collaborate with Don, but cautiously. Formally, no regulatory work seems to be happening, but there is a sense that both men are quietly keeping an eye on each other, while Don explores various areas of the business and some of the environmental precautions on the site. On our way out of the site Don is keen to describe how he can adapt his regulatory style:

> I tailor my support differently to different people. You've got to get to the level of the person. It's no good going in to this sort of place with a suit and tie, 'Good morning Mr . . .' approach. I can put on the hoi-polloi if necessary. It's getting to their level.

Amy

Amy is a water quality inspector. She is visiting an electro-plating works which is on a high-risk environmental site – a chalk aquifer which is vulnerable to water contamination. Heavy industry in the area has, for years, 'been slopping solvents about'. Her last visits were 'very cooperative', although her first one, some three years ago, revealed illegal discharges of chemicals into drains. But her hands are partly tied by the law: 'If a farmer has a leaking oil tank I can enforce bunding [a seal around the tank]. If it happens in any other industry, like this one, I can only *advise* bunding. It's nuts!'. She is concerned about how the chemicals are stored. Some are highly toxic and very dangerous if they reach the watercourses.

We are to meet the Quality Control Manager – someone Amy does not know. We find him in a modest office amongst a ramshackle collection of old, single-storey, buildings. There is a maze of passageways that lead in and out of shed-like workshops where metals and chemicals meet. The air is acrid. There is debris – rusting, redundant, machinery latticed with ivy and brambles growing through cracks in the walls. There are open vats of chemicals with waste outflows draining to unprotected channels on the floor. 'Welcome to hell' whispers Amy, 'not exactly an environmental showpiece'.

Amy runs through a list of requirements she sent to the company after her last visit. The manager appears nervous, but it is camouflaged with jokes and exaggerated reassurances. He occasionally evokes cost considerations as a reason why a particular improvement has not taken place. Amy listens attentively and quietly takes notes. She gradually takes control of the agenda . . .

> I need to look round the plant. I'll write a letter to you after, especially on anything which is urgent or illegal.

We walk the plant. Amy resists being led by the manager, frequently backtracking, spotting outflow pipes, slurry, unlabelled containers, quizzing the manager on what they were or did. When were they going to fix it? What about the cracked flooring near the chemical baths? What is that sink connected to? Rusting old transformers containing highly toxic coolants, a huge potential hazard. She was eagle eyed. The manager responded with a mix of reassurance and cautious defensiveness: 'Yes, we'll be doing that during our Christmas maintenance.' 'I'll have to talk to the boss about that one'. 'We'll have to wait for more pounds in bank to tackle that'.

Amy's responses varied, sometimes non-committal, sometimes gently insistent, sometimes praising, depending on the issue in hand. When the manager was obviously uncomfortable she would back off, but she had the last word. All this was performed through a veil of smiles and surface good humour.

After the visit she commented:

> The floors are really awful so there could be contaminated ground; a spillage could knock out the local water treatment system. I will be issuing them a legal order to put that right. But, believe it or not, it's not as scary as the first time I visited them; they've done a lot. He could be bullshitting, but there's definitely progress.

The working rules of regulation

In these accounts, there are themes that can be found in other regulatory encounters in the study. A key one is that the *working rules* of regulation are very much tied to what the inspector considers environmentally reasonable or unreasonable in the circumstances. Don is scathing about 'trivial' legislative requirements, so chooses to ignore them. Even major environmental requirements are not too closely scrutinised if the operator shows willing. Amy is similarly charitable about incremental improvements to what appears to be a fairly dire situation. But she decides to get tougher (by letter) about issues where she knows she has a firmer legal footing and which seem, potentially, to be very dangerous.

Enacting such rules could be subtle process. At one level it compensated, or substituted, for weak legislation and imprecise standards – which left regulatory outcomes and standards open to negotiation. Inspectors, however, were loath to reveal as much to industrial operators as it weakened their power base. So some would resort to bluff – giving the impression that standards were set and unmovable. This was especially so for IPC inspectors who were expected to apply the BATNEEC principle, the 'best available techniques not entailing excessive cost', in deciding a suitable best form of pollution control. While there were some Agency guidance notes on BATNEECs, they were far from comprehensive or foolproof:

> It's like balancing apples and pears. How much do certain measurable emissions actually damage the environment? Does x million pounds spent result in x million pound environmental improvement?

But bluff had it limits. Some industrial managers were as knowledgeable as the inspector about the imprecision or elusiveness of BATNEECs, so negotiations were, perforce, more balanced. This left inspectors vulnerable to challenge or compromise. Technical disputes could sometimes be heated, each party claiming authority over the meaning of risk or danger. Generally, inspectors were prepared to negotiate, but from a position of strength. If they felt unduly threatened they would pull rank, disengage from the interaction and/or follow it up with other symbols of authority – such as official letters and warnings, in terse, legalistic, language.

Collaboration and collusion

Predominantly, inspectors favoured a collaborative approach – to 'build a relationship', 'keep talking', 'never dig holes they or you cannot get out of'. Or, more poignantly, in the words of one inspector:

> You can turn the regulatory screw and make life hell for them, but that's rarely necessary. It requires sitting down and talking; chats over lunch.

Doing things in this manner had a number of advantages. It eased successive inspection visits; it fitted with official Agency philosophy to assist an operator to become more environmentally sustainable; and it helped to create rules of practice that both inspector and inspected found more-or-less acceptable. This last point was especially important as it addressed one of the contradictions of the inspector's role: they have the authority of the law, but need industry's consent to make it real.

What of the inspector's independence and impartiality in such circumstances? When does collaboration become collusion? There were three different patterns of response to this. One group of inspectors denied that good regulation was ever compromised; they knew where to draw the line and were unhappy about colleagues who, in their view, got too close to industry. Their own environmental interests were informed mainly by their professional background rather than being industry-led, such as in conserving river fauna and flora and preserving biodiversity. The second group was less firm: some partiality was inevitable as fairness was always a matter of negotiation. A degree of *mutual* capture was seen as a necessary feature of good regulation because inspectors and inspected needed to 'speak the same language'. Indeed, it was not uncommon for these inspectors to have once held senior posts in the industries they were now regulating; they were strongly pro-industry. The third group was fatalistic: powerful companies, especially, had superior professional and technical resources and always achieved a better regulatory deal. Such companies were effective at mustering support for their own agenda and were influential at lobbying senior managers within the Agency.

The extent of collaboration or collusion could be gauged by how much 'free' advice an inspector was prepared to offer. Recommendations on BATNEECs, pollution abatement plans, Agency formalities, technical specifications and so forth, could smooth regulatory transactions and contribute to good relations between industry and the Agency. It also dovetailed with Agency policy to help industry help itself. But, confusingly, the Agency also required that the burden of proof for environmental actions and improvements remained with the operator. The Agency should not be legally compromised, so advice should be supplied sparingly; staff should not act as consultants.

The issue was resolved idiosyncratically:

> I give as much advice as possible. Don't see why I can't give them the sort of advice they get from a consultant. It's part of my job. Consultants often exploit people.
>
> (Waste inspector)

> We mustn't be free consultants; it's not what the public expects. Doesn't leave our hands free for enforcement.
>
> (Waste inspector)

The company doesn't really need to employ a consultant. The inspector knows the processes well and together we can identify the things that need to be done.

(IPC inspector)

Moral orders – and getting tough

Cutting across these predilections was the way inspectors classified different industrial operators. They created their own moral order of their 'customers', capturing their feelings towards them from their past experiences. There were the 'obvious villains', the 'bullshitters', the 'cute', the 'clever', the 'co-operative', the 'genuine' and the 'trustworthy'. There were operators who were 'persistent offenders', 'recalcitrant', 'blatant polluters', or 'dangerous'. The inspectors applied these labels, in different measure, to stereotypical 'fly tippers', 'Gypsies', 'small farmers', or 'powerful industrialists'. While inspectors were keen to present a rationalistic, expert, view of themselves, 'knowledgeably green', this sober image did not prevent some extreme feelings. Frustration, anger, even rage was reserved for operators who were blatantly obstructive or physically threatening. Rarely were these emotions given free-reign during inspection visits, but they could play a not insignificant part in the toughness or leniency of subsequent regulatory conditions laid down by the inspector.

Inspectors could get especially tough with errant operators by issuing an enforcement notice. This would prohibit a particular polluting process or related industrial activity. Should the company fail to meet the conditions of enforcement, or breach the requirements of an Agency permit, then they could be prosecuted, risking a fine or greater punishment. Such was the sharp edge of mandatory regulation, to be meted out to the most 'deserving' on the inspector's list of offenders. But prosecution, regardless of reason, was a complex decision of the inspector. At heart, it was regarded as a breakdown in collaboration, thus a failure properly to regulate:

I regard prosecution as failure, both on our part and on those we're regulating. There's much table thumping, sabre rattling, letters, minded-to-send notices, all sorts of documents; but prosecution is very rare.

Threatening gestures were an important part of the regulatory ritual, a key feature of making regulation visible to both the operator and (in formal reports) to the inspector's superiors. But to instigate legal proceedings was a mark of professional defeat. Thus calls from the Agency's senior managers for more prosecutions to create a public image of a strong, non-compromising approach to polluters were contrary to what many field officers regarded as effective regulation. This was complicated by a shift towards 'the consumer' amongst UK public services. The Agency was publicly promoting a less-bureaucratic, more accessible, customer ethos. But for inspectors, the notion of industry as its customer was an uncomfortable notion, threatening to undermine the inspector's authority:

> So we are supposed to treat them [industrial operators] as customers, but what kinds of customers can you prosecute, or demand entry to their premises?

Prosecution undermined goodwill, leaving a 'prickly', if not openly obstructive, legacy for future inspections. Preferably, therefore, it was to be avoided. It also seemed a futile gesture when inspectors were convinced that an operator had few funds with which to pay a fine. Inspectors were often conscious of the social costs and benefits of prosecution. Their interpretation of the circumstances and the status of 'the accused' could make a marked difference to the outcome. This is exemplified in the machinations of one water quality inspector, reflecting on whether or not to prosecute an elderly farmer whose diesel oil had polluted a nearby river:

> Well, is it in the public interest in this particular case? Debatable. Will a prosecution succeed? Probably not. Will prosecuting an 85–year-old look good to the Agency? No. We'll put in a large charging bill and he will take it to his insurers. We need his cooperation in the clean up, so getting tough is counterproductive. I'm here to protect the environment as an environmental biologist; I don't want to shock the man into a heart attack. We rely on public support. We could spend thousands of pounds taking him to court and he will be given a conditional discharge. Bad PR for us. People in his village would not have helped me if they knew I'd prosecute. But I guess we're bending the rules. If it had been a young bolshie farmer we might have prosecuted.

Where prosecution was inevitable, the inspector was vulnerable in other ways. Despite legal support within the Agency, the inspector was often the key person to collect and collate evidence of an infraction, to be presented and defended in a court of law. This was not always a happy, or successful, experience. The inspector could be cross-examined by a skilful lawyer and confronted by expert witnesses hired by the company. The magistrate or judge did not necessarily share the Agency's concern about environmental protection. In the inspectors' eyes, the size of fines or other sanctions often diminished the true extent of the transgression, and larger fines were easily absorbed into the profits of major corporations.

Negotiating

Despite their sometimes-superior legal resources, industrial managers would tacitly connive with the inspectors to avoid prosecution. A lawsuit was a hassle for them, and a potential source of public embarrassment. It was often fodder for journalists and green activist groups who could inflict reputational damage to a company – especially one that claimed green credentials. Knowing this, inspectors could exert more pressure on an operator than would be suggested by the actual sanctions of law. On the other hand, an Agency-wise operator was aware of the inspector's preference for a negotiated agreement, so saw little merit in alienating the inspector or Agency.

Witnessing this negotiative process revealed each party testing out the other to gain ground or concessions. The inspector often wanted more environmental commitment than an operator was prepared to give; the industrial manager wanted to minimise expenditure and not be overburdened with Agency demands. Between them they needed to find a workable position and not lose face. The process was not always a peaceful one. Observe, for example, the following exchange between Martin, an IPC inspector, and Douglas, a plant manager of a multimillion-pound manufacturer of plastic pipes and gutters.

Martin had received complaints about dust blowing around the local neighbourhood, which he traced to open covers on the top of tall storage silos inside Douglas's works. During a previous visit he had instructed Douglas to correct the problem because the dust contained dangerous levels of lead. However, during the present, unannounced, visit, he found that the silos were still not properly sealed. Douglas is embarrassed and annoyed about the discovery. Back in his office he picks up the phone and delivers a very curt reprimand to an operator . . . 'I left instructions to ensure the top of the silos are clean, and they're not!' he barks down the phone. Douglas now turns on Martin, unleashing suppressed resentment. He's disgruntled that Martin can appear at any time for an inspection without someone 'competent in charge being around, who can explain what's happening'. Martin shrugs. There then follows a terse exchange.

DOUGLAS (firmly, staring at Martin): 'I'd like to flag a few more things up. When we've taken all our tests we are well below the danger levels! We feel aggrieved to pay you £3,600 a year for such low levels.' (He waves the test sheets at Martin).

MARTIN (coolly): 'I agree. But it's accidental releases that are the problem; fugitive releases.'

DOUGLAS (peeved): 'So if everything's bang-on we're not qualified for exception?'

MARTIN (calmly): 'Because of the legislation and your volume and escape points you cannot get automatic exemption. The onus is on you to prove it doesn't cause harm.'

DOUGLAS (exasperated): 'We've checked the blood levels of operators. There's no danger from lead in any of them!'

MARTIN: 'It's also the housing outside.'

DOUGLAS: 'That's false! Even there it's well below danger levels.'

MARTIN (backing off): 'I work on the current legislation. There is scope for debate when you get near the edge.'

DOUGLAS: 'OK. It's a grey area. I agree there's a small amount of powder . . .'

MARTIN: 'A kilo or two!'

DOUGLAS: 'But people are handling compounds in tonne boxes. That's more worrying than loose spills.'

MARTIN (disengaging): 'OK. It's an ongoing debate. I can't take it further today. You can apply for exemption any time. You can get a second opinion and appeal . . .'

DOUGLAS (rattled): 'Appeals don't work! I get exactly the same letter that you write to me, but this time signed by your boss.'

MARTIN (appeasing, looking uncomfortable): 'We have been working towards exemption. It's not impossible. We must go . . .'

In the car afterwards Martin looks ready to fight on. 'A tough company to visit! They try and bully you.'

In this interaction we witness a tense contest for control, with undulating boundaries. It is emotionally charged with dramatic postures, ploys and technical disputation. As the inspector presses his points home, hitherto hidden grievances of the plant manager are exposed. The inspector tries to retrieve his 'professional' front by becoming legalistic and bureaucratic – which largely fails to impress the manager. The inspector retreats, leaving the manager with a hint of accommodation to come. The relationship is preserved – just.

Regulating the environment is plainly more than reading off legal prescriptions. It is a process of technical and social ritual embedded in particular political contexts, where personal and professional reputations are on the line. Indeed, the testing of professional knowledge was a central feature of many of the inspections, where both inspector and inspected claimed expertise on environmental risk and dangers. On some occasions it appeared that the inspector was outflanked by the industrial manager, but the manager was unwilling to risk his licence to operate by insisting his own view prevailed. As one manager (professionally qualified in chemistry) confided to me during a break in a site inspection:

> I have to say we want to cooperate, we want to get the licence. But it's really irritating to have a technical conversation with somebody about parts per billion and parts per trillion and what the chemical make-up of this material is, when they don't know themselves and when the guidance is ambiguous. Additionally, I think we both believe that, at the end of the day, we're way below any real danger level.

Green pressures

As earlier noted, the work of the Agency and its inspectors takes place amongst a wide constituency of voices on environmental protection. Such voices, especially those of green pressure groups, are ones that the Agency is expected to attend to, if not consult. Green pressure groups vary considerably in form and intent. Some are temporary gatherings of citizens promoting local environmental causes, such as resisting a road development or objecting to plans for an out-of-town supermarket. More permanent, national and international organisations, such as Friends of the Earth, Greenpeace, Worldwide Fund for Nature and English Nature, bring more sustained pressure on the Agency and, separately, on some of the industries it regulates.

Notionally, Agency employees and green pressure groups share a common goal – environmental protection. But beneath the green veil are many differences and tensions. For a start, the organisational culture of the Agency itself was not a comfortable home for green ideologues. Inspectors who were perceived to be 'too green' were marginalised by their colleagues because they 'put people off', 'the kind of person who goes about cleaning rivers in his or her spare time'. Any green fervour had to be muted and expressed, if at all, in a *technical* discourse. The environment and its protection were matters of discipline – the discipline of science, the discipline of rationally weighing-up costs and benefits. While inspectors were well aware that these were not unproblematic concepts in environmental control, they provided a more acceptable way of proceeding than one based on ethical claims or 'emotions'. Sustainable development, a concept core to the mission of the Agency and to the concerns of green activists, was regarded with suspicion by inspectors – because of its insufficient rigour or plausibility:

> Sustainability is today's flavour, isn't it. Ultimately, it's an awful question to ask of any business; like their responsibility for all global events. It's such a massive task that I'm not sure how you start going about it.

> Well, you dig a hole in the ground, line it, put some rubbish in and wait for it to degrade. But we will not know until 50 years has passed whether we're doing the right thing or not. Is that sustainability? Who knows.

In regulatory fieldwork, therefore, inspectors would rarely speak openly of sustainability. They feared rejection from industry if sustainability was presented as a main reason for pollution control – because it was too readily associated with the extreme and 'airy' ideas of green activists.

Amidst such caution, however, inspectors were divided on how green pressure groups should influence regulatory policy and practice: there were those who were rejecting and cynical, those who were charitable, and those who were welcoming.

The rejecting and cynical inspectors were mostly IPC. They resented the incursion of the 'hysterical', 'extreme' and 'irrational' voices of green pressure groups. Green pressure groups were seen mainly in undifferentiated terms; they were people who threatened the inspector's control and authority. They did not reflect the 'balanced' and 'carefully researched' perspective that was 'fundamental' to the inspector's way of operating. In public meetings 'all they do is shout and howl us down'.

The charitable inspectors were mainly amongst those specialising in water quality and waste control. Green groups posed no serious threat; 'their heart is in the right place' and they were sometimes 'worth listening to'. The main concern was not be 'taken over' by them.

The inspectors who welcomed green groups found much to admire in their conduct. Green groups featured in the public clamour about environmental damage that helped instigate and legitimise the Agency, 'so we should be indebted to them'. They represented a voice of conscience, looking over the shoulder of the inspector, so to speak: 'Best thing that ever happened! They're a pressure on the Agency to make sure we are clean and green and doing our job properly.' Green groups were able to bring direct pressure to bear on polluting companies, such as through a campaign or via media attention. In this way they could reinforce the inspector's actions, sometimes achieving superior results: 'They can do things we can't. We are so prepossessed with the legal aspects of what we do that sometimes we can't say what we want to say to a polluting company.'

Regulatory realities and futures

Mandatory regulation does much to bring about incremental changes in the way industry approaches environmental problems. However, the present chapter reveals that the process is more fragile than it appears. Neither the statute book nor the bold claims of the Environment Agency (or indeed other such agencies) hint at the considerable interpersonal work and, often, improvisation that goes into sustaining the regulatory regime.

The environmental inspectors' street-level bureaucracy is one of making regulatory guidelines real and appropriate for the kind of people they meet. They will invent routines and rules where no suitable ones exist. Fairness, in these circumstances, is not treating everybody alike, because they are (in the inspector's eyes) often not alike. It is recognising that:

(a) many environmental infringements are 'procedural' and do not deserve much regulatory attention
(b) some operators are close to the edge commercially, so harsh regulation is unproductive, other than for 'obvious' criminals
(c) the intentions, trustworthiness and deference of the industrial manager are relevant considerations
(d) maintaining a collaborative, and sometimes slightly deceptive, stance can reinforce rather than undermine the inspector's influence
(e) actual prosecution generally hinders the regulatory task, but to imply prosecution is a powerful signal
(f) deals are sometimes done less for the sake of environmental security than for technical compromise

(g) the regulator and the regulated are mutually interdependent and a degree of collusion is necessary to get the job done; but

(h) it should not appear that way: it is important for public confidence that the myth of the independent regulator is not punctured. This is achieved through reassuring Agency public relations about tough action on polluters. It is reinforced, cautiously, by the inspector who can transform a collaborative regulatory chat into a stiff confrontation and formal warning.

Through these processes the greenness of regulation looks a little pale. Regulation poses few questions about the way the market economy and its consumerism may be part of our environmental problems – and most inspectors are content not to raise such issues. Indeed, in this manner inspectors fit more comfortably into the Agency's culture. In *regulating* existing environmental conduct, the agents are not in the business of transformational change.

If the findings of this study can be generalised, there are clear limits to what mandatory environmental regulation can achieve in a pluralistic economy. Much of the inspector's energy is devoted to the *political sustainability* of their position, within the contradictions of their role and power arrangements:

• they dislike treating industrial operators as customers, yet are unwilling to take industry out of its own commercial market

• they are manifestly concerned with reducing pollution, but a significant proportion of them resist the incursion of environmental groups who share this aim

• they have the authority of the law behind them, but are relatively powerless without industry's consent

• they represent their own employer who wants unequivocal evidence of regulatory success, yet are uncomfortable with the most tangible form – prosecution

• they are required to support and encourage voluntary, greener, action, while also holding a prosecutory stick

• claims of impartiality require distance from those regulated, yet the variability of different regulatory encounters necessitates a fair degree of intimacy and capture.

Given these tensions we might regard field regulators as doing a valiant job in the circumstances, often skilfully steering a path between many contradictory demands. Some of these contradictions may be smoothed by a better alignment between what an agency formally expects of its officers and what they can actually achieve or deliver. But the efficacy of regulation is also circumscribed by social and political institutions which shape the whole endeavour:

the British approach to pollution control tends to be fairly pragmatic and involves a great deal of discretion. This discretion is normally exercised by specialist regulatory agencies . . . An important point is that this discretion is exercised on grounds that are not restricted to environmental factors. There is a traditionally close connection in British environmental regulation between social, political and economic factors and decisions on environmental protection'.

(Bell, 1997: 23)

Bell's portrayal of regulation resonates with the findings of this study, especially the discretion of regulatory agents. Regulating the environment is not just 'about the environment'. The environment, and damage to it, are politically contested constructions that reflect a range of institutional and stakeholder interests – government, legislature, political parties, industry, citizens groups, insurers, regulatory agencies, environmental scientists. Some will prevail more than others in the forming and re-framing of regulatory policy. Even in less-discretionary regulatory climates, such as the USA, the meanings of environmental damage are well politicised. For example, the virulent industry backlash to environmental protection groups has been shown to be a potent force in diluting environmental legislation and deflecting the intentions of the US Environmental Protection Agency (Rowell, 1996; Helvarg, 1997). Where industries insist on regarding pollution as an externality, and therefore none of their business, then a regulator can exercise tough controls to remind them otherwise. Compulsion, however, also fuels resistance and a tendency toward escalating control, where the 'deeper' virtues of greening can be well obscured. Better, perhaps, that other, independent, interventions, especially high profile educational programmes, should complement the regulator's efforts.

The loose drafting of environmental law clearly serves discretion and negotiation. Yet more tightly defined legal instruments would doubtless spare regulatory agents some of the ambiguities of control. Indeed, there were 'old hands' amongst the present sample of inspectors who declared that the existing statutes were so unhelpful and inconsistent that they were guided far more by their common sense than the wording of the Environment Act and its various amendments. The challenge, it seems, is to achieve legal clarity that is useful and supportive to the regulator, but that does not provoke industry resistance to the point where the regulator's role becomes untenable.

But whatever balance is hammered out between the various protagonists, it occurs in political environments where industry's muscle is likely to be substantial in relation to that of the green lobby and the (pro-industry?) predilections of the government of the day. Indeed, in ostensibly entrepreneurial societies, governments tread a delicate path between public concern about environmental degradation and the wealth-generating potential of industry which, inevitably, has environmental impact. Examples are rare of modern governments prepared to challenge the shibboleths of profit and growth in favour of a more radical index of social and environmental well being. But maybe they should.

References

Beckerman, W. (1994) 'Sustainable development': Is it a useful concept? *Environmental Values*, 3, 191–209.

Bell, S. (1997) *Environmental Law*. London: Blackstone Press.

Brown, R. L., Dean, T. J. and Douglas, T. J. (1998) Environmental regulation and competitive advantage: new insights into entry effects and industry structural characteristics. In J. Post (ed.) *Research in Corporate Social Performance and Policy*. Stamford, CT: JAI Press.

Fineman, S. (1998) Street level bureaucrats and the social construction of environmental control. *Organisation Studies*, 19 (6), 953–974.

Fineman, S. and Clarke, K. (1996) Green stakeholders: industry interpretations and response. *Journal of Management Studies*, 33 (6), 715–730.

Fischer, K. and J. Schot, J. (eds), (1991) *Environmental Strategies for Industry*. Washington, DC: Island Press.

Gouldson, A. and Murphy, J. (1998) *Regulatory Realities*. London: Earthscan.

Helvarg, D. (1997) *The War Against the Greens*. San Francisco: Sierra Club Books.

Howard, N. (1997) 'The protection of the environment'. London: Institute of Directors.

Lipsky, M. (1980) *Street-level Bureaucracy*. New York: Russell Sage Foundation.

Lowe, P., Clark, J., Seymour, S. and Ward, N. (1997) *Moralizing the Environment*. London: UCL Press.

Rowell, A. (1996) *Green Backlash*. London: Routledge.

Sanchez, C. M. (1998) The impact of regulation on the adoption of innovation: how electric utilities responded to the clean air act amendments of 1990. In J. Post (ed.) *Research in Corporate Social Performance and Policy*. Stamford, CT: JAI Press.

Smith, D. (1993) *Business and the Environment*. London: Paul Chapman.

7 Regulation matters

Global environmental discourse and business response

Jane Hunt and Sujatha Raman[1]

From a focus on localised problems such as pollution of air or water, the scope of environmentalism has steadily expanded to take on the globe. Following the identification of ozone depletion and the greenhouse effect, the relevance of specifically *global* environmental change has come to be implanted in the public consciousness in the 1990s. An explosion of international environmental agreements such as the 1987 Montreal Protocol (which set targets for phasing out chlorofluorocarbons or CFCs, held responsible for depletion of the ozone layer) and the 1992 Climate Change Convention in Rio (which set national targets for reducing emissions of CO_2, the main contributor to global warming) is one illustration of this phenomenon. The flurry of activity at all levels on the environmental front has, in turn, generated a growing academic interest, testified to by this book, in business responses to the environment. However, much of this literature pays little attention to systematic variations within the categories 'business' and 'environment'. Further, the role of government in this context appears to be either that of the policeman with the proverbial stick, or, lately, a mere provider of environmental information that is supposed to promote voluntary action.

On the one hand, various studies proclaim the importance of environmental awareness amongst businesses, and chronicle the development of environmental management strategies (Schmidheiny, 1992; Shrivastava, 1992; Welford and Gouldson, 1993: Elkington, 1994). These tend to focus on the extent to which environmental management systems have been adopted and/or new technologies put in place. On the other hand, there is tremendous interest in the plethora of government strategies for the voluntary 'greening of business' developed in light of arguments made since the 1980s that so-called 'command-and-control' regulation has failed. These take the form of exhortations to businesses to become more environmentally conscious, supplemented by various information campaigns on how business practices might be improved and how a few leading champions have successfully done so (e.g. British Printing Industries Federation, 1990; Energy Efficiency Office, 1992). Generic indicators are then totted up on the extent to which various sectors are on track; these are meant to pinpoint areas in which campaigns may need to be stepped up and the 'best practices' of the champions emulated.

Critical responses to this proliferation of environmental policy initiatives and management strategies generally tend to dismiss them altogether as representative of a merely 'cosmetic environmentalism' or 'symbolic politics' (Cahn, 1995; Gare, 1995). The argument goes as follows: fundamental challenges to present social and economic arrangements have been diluted by these efforts and absorbed into the mainstream in order to preserve the appearance of 'doing something'. While we do not deny that contradictions are rife in much environmental policy discourse, we argue that a more fine-grained analysis is needed. Both the proponents of the 'greening of business' and the critics of mainstream environmentalism share a flawed homogenised view of what the environment is and of how business and policy might interface with it.

In elaborating on this argument, this chapter draws on research carried out in two different projects funded by the Economic and Social Research Council's Global Environmental Change Programme.[2] The projects had in common the belief that variations in environmentally relevant action across sectors or across companies cannot simply be treated as distortions from a singular trajectory of greening. Instead, greening must be seen as something that takes its shape and meaning from the interpretations and actions of a host of heterogeneous actors in business and government. Differences in the organisation of particular industrial sectors are crucial for understanding not just variation in the capacity for action, but also in the nature and location of such actions, especially as they relate to the newly global construction of the environment. Relevant organisational features include the nature of different products and business processes, intra-business relationships within markets for production and distribution, and the malleability of the technological base of a sector.

The first part of the chapter elaborates on these differences in the case of four business sectors: baking, building construction, printing and refrigeration. Having taken these differences on board, we then seek to explore the extent to which the global environment has seeped into each of the four sectors, as suggested by how key players make (or, more revealingly, do not make) connections between global change and their sector's own business practices. As the current policy platform for alleviation of climate change, *energy efficiency* is a common globally-relevant theme across these sectors. The phase-out of CFCs in light of ozone depletion is a second theme derived from a concern with global environmental change; it is most directly relevant in the refrigeration industry, although the widespread use of cooling means that there are implications in each of the other industries.

In brief, we find that global environmental discourse has, indeed, been translated into sector-specific understanding of relevant practices in the cases of refrigeration and building. The roles of particular refrigerants in damaging the ozone layer, and of energy use in the refrigeration process which contributes to global warming, are both recognised by key players. Likewise, in construction, the idea that certain features of buildings erected today will determine the extent to which occupants may minimise their energy consumption tomorrow has largely been accepted. In baking and printing, on the other hand, we find a general awareness of global environmental change issues, but little connection made to the activities performed in these sectors themselves. The question we address in the second part of the chapter is therefore: what accounts for the significant difference in the practical translation of global environmental discourse in these four sectors?

That different sectors show different levels of 'absorption' of green messages is not in itself surprising. Rather, we are interested in exploring what might account for the difference. This question takes us from the study of individual sectors on their own terms to a cross-sectoral comparison which may be expected to yield an understanding of certain *patterns* of greening impact. That is, we may expect to find systematic similarities as well as differences when we consider business neither as a monolithic category, nor as composed of irreducibly unique sectors that may only be understood on a case-by-case basis. An identification of common patterns could then help generate more measured recommendations on what might be done in those sectors that appear to be lagging behind.

In this chapter, we argue that the development of *mandatory* environmental regulation makes a significant difference to a business sector's capacity to translate the generic informational messages and exhortations that constitute government policy to *voluntary* action. An elaboration of this point requires a move beyond traditional arguments for and against regulation, both of which are equally simplistic. While deregulation has not since been pursued with the same fervour as it was in the 1980s, the notion of regulation as an inherently inefficient instrument that is imposed by government on industry has managed to endure. Voluntary greening measures have therefore come to be seen as better substitutes for regulatory instruments. On the other hand, pro-regulation arguments have tended to treat regulation in purely technical terms. So long as standards are set correctly and the right conditions exist, regulation – simply, by force of mandate – will work as intended. Either way, regulatory standards are placed in a do-or-die situation if they are solely evaluated in terms of standard indicators of environmental impact that may not be capable of detecting more subtle, but crucial changes.

In conjunction with the technical approach, mandatory regulation needs to be understood and recognised as a *cultural* force, whose environmental impacts may not be simple and obvious, but may, nevertheless, be central to institutional transformation. It is such a view of regulation that we would like to offer and expand upon in this chapter.

We begin by mapping the ways in which baking, building construction, printing, and refrigeration interface with the environment and with environmental policy by virtue of their specific organisational features.

The nexus between industrial organisation, the environment and voluntary greening initiatives

The greening of business has come to be framed in terms of older debates about factors that influence business capacity for innovation more generally (Porter, 1990; Wallace, 1995). In the context of greening, 'innovation' refers to the development or the adoption of technologies which, apart from being novel, are also better from an environmental standpoint (depending on how this is defined). A few management scholars (e.g. Porter) argue that mandatory environmental regulation can actually stimulate innovation by prompting businesses to explore new ways of compliance which simultaneously reduce their costs and make them more competitive. Proponents of voluntary campaigns and initiatives, however, tend to see regulation as stifling innovation while arguing that their own proposals can help create the right kind of incentives for change. In either case, 'business' is treated in fairly undifferentiated terms.

Political economists and scholars of industrial organisation have long argued that the notion of a business firm used in textbook economic equilibrium models, as well as some varieties of business management, simply does not stand up to scrutiny. Businesses come in different sizes, employ a plethora of technologies and management procedures, and connect with a variety of markets that have different conventions. Further, sectors delivering different products or services exhibit different sets of relationships between businesses along the supply chain. In this context, a company's capacity to respond to green exhortations is inevitably shaped by its position within a network of other companies. In turn, a whole sector's capacity for 'green' innovation is a product of its history as well as the way in which its materials, technologies, companies, and consumers are linked together.

In this section, we examine four important differences in the organisation of our sectors – company size, product/process relationships, market relationships, and technological base – and the way in which each of these shape the sector's linkage with 'the global environment' and thereby, with voluntary greening initiatives.

Firm size

A long-standing debate in innovation studies is the relationship between the size of firms and their propensity to innovate: one school argues that only small firms have the flexibility and low levels of bureaucracy required for rapid transformation of new ideas from shop-floor to market, while the critics state that only large businesses have the resources and level of organisation to invest in innovation. Empirical evidence, skewed towards high-tech sectors, has yielded little consensus to date. Nevertheless, these debates on innovation and firm size provide some important pointers for our analysis.

The first is that innovation cannot be seen solely at the level of the individual firm or company, nor from the perspective of new technology. As we will see in the discussion to follow on market relationships, firms function within a network of other organisations and their capacity for environmental action is mediated by these relationships. Second, environmental improvements may have as much to do with changes to business practices, such as quality control, as with the adoption of new technologies *per se*. On the other hand, firm size, and *perceptions* about small and medium-sized enterprises (or SMEs as they are commonly known) do make a difference in terms of the interface between environmental campaigns and industry sector. It is therefore worth considering the distribution between SMEs and large organisations in each of our four sectors.

The printing industry is dominated by small and very small businesses against a few large players; the number of high street printing chains has also taken off in recent years. In baking, the demise of the independent high street baker is a product of the enormous increase in supermarket sales of baked products. This, in turn, encouraged the growth of medium-sized bakeries that supply supermarkets, and sometimes have their own small chains of shops. A few large 'industrial' bakeries also exist. Refrigeration divides into large and very large firms selling to retailers for the domestic market, and medium sized businesses supplying the commercial market with cooling systems (for both refrigeration of goods and air-conditioning of space). Small companies dominate non-contracted system maintenance and servicing. The building industry is notorious for its fragmentation and the number of 'cowboy' contractors. In the wake of massive industry-wide restructuring in the 1970s and 1980s, housebuilding gained a significant share of volume-builders (Ball, 1988), while the industry as a whole remains a mix of enterprises of different sizes and doing different kinds of work: roofing, glazing, design, plumbing, etc.

Greening campaigns face a number of hurdles in connecting with small businesses which tend to be geographically scattered, some living outside the net of formal databases and information systems. On the other hand, larger companies tend to be better organised for collective negotiations and to dominate industry trade associations. Voluntary agreements between government and business are therefore likely to be skewed towards those who can make it to the table. Even where small business owners are part of local business networks, their participation may be irregular or such associations may be inadequately linked up with national representatives. Indeed, in some cases, their sources of information may be their suppliers or clients rather than the association that represents them. For example, wholesalers are often the ones to inform bakers and printers about potential new inputs and other innovations.

The internal structure of small companies also constrains the potential for explicit and organised responses to green campaigns. Large organisations are simply more able to afford to create job roles tailored to environmental issues. On the other hand, smallness can be an advantage in the implement-ation of environmental decisions, once these have been taken. Finally, greening campaigns often fail to take into account the various idiosyncrasies of business practice at the SME level and the issues that really govern their decision-making.

Yet, in the end, generalisations about the impact of divisions between SMEs and large corporations can only be pushed so far. For instance, in our exploration of market relationships below, we discuss how capacity for environmental action is especially constrained in the case of larger companies in the housebuilding sector, owing to the highly structured nature of their relationships with their suppliers. More generally, *perceptions* about SMEs may be especially influential in maintaining the realities of their practices. Thus, deeply held beliefs about the inherently conservative nature or limited room for manoeuvre of small firms may be as much a problem as the neglect by policy-makers of constraints faced by SMEs. For example, in the building sector, the image of the jobbing builder has long served as the yardstick against which the possibility of stiffening building standards has been explored. The idea that the regulations can 'only go so far' (or else the standards they demand would be beyond the reach of the average builder) has, until recently, been a crucial brake on the scope of regulatory action (see Raman and Shove, Chapter 8).

Product and process relationships

Although energy consumption represents an environmental problem that cuts across all businesses, it intersects differently with the activities of different sectors, depending on the kind of product they make and for what market. (Note that our examples do not include service sectors). For example, in the case of baking and printing, it is the energy consumed in the manufacturing *process* that is of concern. The proliferation of product varieties (baking) and of new uses for old products (printing) do have environmental impacts in-so-far as they represent yet more uses of energy. Thus, the rise in fast food consumption and of new lifestyles has gone hand in hand with the increasing production of take-away food products by bakers, as well as 'fancy' breads meant for re-baking in the home. Likewise, printers produce an enormous range of goods and print onto an even greater range of all kinds of products from beer mats and pens to packages and books. However, in-so-far as these changes are perceived to be due to demand in other sectors in the economy, baking and printing are only indirectly implicated in these dispersed instances of energy use. On the other hand, if energy efficiency of their own production processes is the main issue, this depends on the manufacturing equipment (ovens and printers) supplied by other companies down the line. Bakers' and printers' capacities to respond to campaigns for voluntary greening are therefore constrained by this context.

In the refrigeration and construction sectors, the manufacturing of fridges and the erection of buildings obviously consume energy. However, the products are themselves major consumers of energy – and in the case of fridges, users of CFCs – with buildings accounting for half of the nation's CO_2 emissions and end-use of energy, and refrigeration the largest user of energy in the home after heating. Hence, their manufacture to efficient standards has been especially highlighted.[3] Refrigeration divides into domestic and commercial suppliers, one producing the ubiquitous fridges and freezers, the other supplying refrigeration systems as well as free-standing cabinets largely to food and drink retailers.[4] In the discussion of market relationships that follows, we will see how linkages between commercial suppliers and their clients have helped reinforce the association between commercial refrigeration systems and global environmental impacts. On the other hand, as stand-alone items, domestic fridges have been successfully targeted for energy-efficiency labelling, although the extent to which such labels actually influence consumer choice depends on the practices adopted by retailers.

Buildings, on the other hand, are unique as 'products' even just in terms of the sheer number of elements that combine to make them up. Constructing them for the purpose of minimising the energy that occupants may be expected to use could be framed in many different ways in-so-far as there are several products within the product that might be targeted. So, one option for energy-efficiency campaigns is to focus on specific elements, such as walls, roofs, floors or windows, and provide information on how best to construct them to maximise their insulating capacity. Yet, the amount of energy used is dependent on the way in which different elements – both inside and on the envelope of the house – *interact*. Such a perspective would take into account the efficiency of building services such as lights and heating systems as well as the insulating capacity of external elements. In the 1990s, the UK government therefore attempted to promote home energy-labels which are framed in terms of the expected energy performance of the building as a whole. By providing energy-efficiency information, such labels are meant to stimulate home-buyers to voluntarily make environmentally better choices. However, as we see below, such voluntary action appears to be true of only a handful of consumers.

Market relationships

A dominant theme in debates on innovation is the extent to which the impetus for new products and practices are demand or supply driven. Our research finds that customer influence varies significantly depending on the relationship between suppliers, producers, distributors and customers that is itself different in different markets for goods and services. In this context, it is worth pointing out that many businesses are intermediate producers, that is, they sell to other businesses rather than to individual consumers; 'customers' could therefore be from either group, or from government or non-profit organisations.

In the baking and printing sectors, the suppliers of manufacturing equipment are often larger than their customers and have enough market clout that the individual baker or printer is able to exert little influence on product design (although some specifications may be negotiable). On the other hand, many medium-sized bakers are themselves suppliers to other businesses; indeed, their growth has been spawned by the growth in supermarkets. Some bakers in the medium-size category have attempted to match their small, high street counterparts by opening avenues to sell directly to the public, as well as to other businesses such as pubs, cafes and garage forecourts. In any case, bakers report that there is no environmental pressure from anyone from this range of customers whose concerns largely rest with food hygiene.

By contrast, supermarkets have been in the lead in driving environmental improvements in commercial refrigeration. Especially with their rapid expansion in the 1990s, supermarkets have become the major customer for refrigeration systems. Contractors in the business of design and supply of these systems report that supermarkets were very concerned that systems should be CFC free, even before this was strictly necessary. This was attributed to their 'need to be seen to be green' given the public visibility of the ozone depletion/CFC issue. However, this applied only to the 'Big 5' (Tesco, Sainsbury, Asda, Safeway and Waitrose), whose middle class customers are perceived to be environmentally conscious. By contrast, supermarket discounters were reportedly concerned primarily with price. Either way, since refrigeration accounts for the major proportion of a store's energy bill, the prospects for energy efficiency improvements are good. On the other hand, white-goods retailers play a key role in the domestic refrigeration market. Being the mediators between producers (their suppliers) and individual consumers (their customers), these big retailers and their sales practices ultimately influence consumer capacity to make energy efficient choices (Winward *et al.*, 1998).

The market structure of printing reflects the enormous diversity within this large industry. Small general printers supply individuals and other small businesses, some specialising in products such as labels. Larger firms (though still small in terms of numbers of employees) may focus on a specific area such as fine art or books, or be generalists. Other specific sub-sectors, each with their own networks of production and distribution, include newspaper printing and printing onto a variety of containers. One of the printing industry's largest customers is the government. The scope for customer pressure on printers to be energy efficient consequently varies across these groups.

In house building, volume builders and materials suppliers have traditionally been locked into relationships of mutual dependence. National head offices of building companies negotiate prices with suppliers and strike deals over bulk discounts. Suppliers also serve as mediators and, often, as *de facto* decision-makers for their builder clients when questions of compliance with new energy-efficiency standards, whether voluntary or mandatory, arise. In this context, the individual volume builder's room for manoeuvre is that much more limited. On the other hand, the link between house builders and homebuyers is much more fragmented and insufficiently subject to controls. Campaigns for making sellers supply more information on energy efficiency in the form of energy-labels, and thereby help customers make environmental choices, appear to have had little success. Homebuyers are said to be interested in 'location, location, and location' alone, which means that builders make little attempt to market homes on the basis of energy efficiency. While lack of interest may be a self-substantiating myth, builders have little incentive to supply the kind of information promoted by the government, let alone make the appropriate improvements in the first place.

In the world of commercial property building, rising energy consumption is associated with the boom in air-conditioned offices which have become the norm in a market whose cyclical nature puts special pressures on profit-making in the short term. The potential for re-fashioning design specifications in environmentally innovative ways is mediated by a complex set of relationships between investors, architects, developers, estate agents and occupiers, and the different ways in which they see the property market (see Guy, 1998 and Chapter 4 of this volume for a more detailed analysis).

Technological base

The possibilities for and constraints on change are shaped by the specific *combination* of production technologies used in a sector. The baking industry uses relatively simple technology and much of its equipment has long lifetimes (over 30 years) with obvious implications for the diffusion of new technologies. However, ovens – a major energy user – have always been designed with moderately high efficiency, and the conventions of use have traditionally been to minimise energy consumption.

Printing technology ranges from long-life (sometimes second-hand) mechanical printing machinery which can be serviced and maintained by the printer, through to cutting edge developments in electronic reproduction which is bought and used as a 'white box', the contents of which the printer cannot control, manipulate, or even understand. Although printing technology is a rapidly developing area, the high-tech nature of new machines provides little room for printers to shape their own practices of use in energy-efficient directions.

The picture in the refrigeration industry is almost the reverse. Until recently, refrigeration technology was more or less unchanged since at least the 1950s. Its stability became such a culturally embedded norm that even the colour of fridges could only be white! It is only with the introduction of environmental legislation that changes have had to be introduced, albeit against much resistance in the industry.

Buildings, of course, have the longest life amongst these products. Once erected, serious material constraints make improvements to energy efficiency that much harder. The poor quality of the majority of housing stock in this country in terms of their notorious 'leakiness' has led some to advocate large-scale new build programmes. On the other hand, many industry analysts also believe that significant energy efficiency achievements in new homes may never be possible so long as England and Wales are dominated by masonry construction and site-based assembly of brick and block components. Unless housebuilding is revamped along the lines of other industrial manufacturing processes, as has been the case in Japan and parts of Scandinavia, the industry will remain in the 'dark ages' – or so the argument goes. While this image of complete technological stasis is somewhat exaggerated (Ball, 1988), the fact remains that some of the difficulties cited in introducing energy efficiency improvements in a technological system that relies on site-assembly are plausible. Factors such as the lack of weather controls in the workplace, or the de-skilling of work in a cyclical industry, relate to broader issues of quality control, which in turn, have implications for energy use: draughts from gaps in floor edges, poorly installed insulation, or failures in double-glazing units are only a few examples from the litany of frequently cited problems.

So far, we have explored key variations in the organisation of industrial sectors and their interfaces with the global 'environment'. Using the cases of baking, building, printing, and refrigeration, we have illustrated the difference that the following factors make:

- *Firm size*: Sectors that are highly fragmented with a high proportion of small firms are difficult to tackle by means of campaigns for voluntary environmental change. This could be due to simple communication problems arising from a lack of representation of small firms in government–industry networks; decision-making constraints faced more commonly by some small firms; or just the perception that such businesses are resistant to change. With small firms making up the bulk of bakers and printers, while also being notoriously common in building construction, such difficulties beset greening initiatives in these sectors more so than in refrigeration.
- *Product and process relationships*: Generic exhortations to become environmentally conscious may fail to distinguish between product and process changes. In baking and printing, it is energy-efficient improvements in the manufacturing processes that are most relevant from the standpoint of global environmental change. However, such changes would require the supply of improved equipment, which depends on the actions of the relevant manufacturers rather than bakers and printers themselves. On the other hand, a case for manufacturing fridges and constructing buildings to energy-efficient standards can, in principle, be made directly to firms in these sectors.
- *Market relationships*: Once we recognise the relevance of process changes, we begin to consider businesses in relation to each other rather than as autonomous entities all equally receptive to greening campaigns. Influence

over environmentally-relevant decisions varies across suppliers, producers, distributors and customers in different sectors. For example, supermarkets (as customers) have been demanding energy-efficiency changes from their suppliers of commercial refrigeration systems. Likewise, materials suppliers and property developer clients are known to be especially influential in domestic and non-domestic building respectively. On the other hand, bakers and printers buy their equipment from significantly larger companies whose design standards they find difficult to influence.

- *Technological base*: Finally, the potential for environmental innovation is both enabled and constrained by the specific combination of technologies – and their lifetimes – that is the norm in each sector. Baking ovens tend to be in use for over 30 years, while buildings have much longer lives, making radical changes difficult to introduce at random. Printing technology, on the other hand, has recently seen a number of high-tech changes, while refrigeration technology has, after a long period of stability, taken up new refrigerants that are supposed to avoid harming the ozone layer.

The picture so far offers a good reminder of organisational and technological differences that are unique to specific sectors and that therefore shape their interface with the global environment differently. Yet, our interviews with representatives of each of these sectors show that, *despite* these differences, global environmental 'storylines' have been systematically more successful in both refrigeration and building, considered in relation to the printing and baking industries. Businesses or their representatives in all four sectors show a general familiarity with problems of ozone depletion and global warming; however, only those in refrigeration and building make the connection – sometimes, reluctantly – between these global problems and energy-consuming activities (and refrigerant choices) within their own control. In the rest of this chapter, we argue that the introduction of mandatory regulation in these two sectors has been crucial in generating the discourse that links the global and the local. In order to make this point, we first consider the ways in which the role of regulation is commonly understood.

Understanding the role of environmental regulation

In evaluating environmental regulation or other forms of public policy, scholars typically frame the relationship between policy, business, and the environment in either *instrumental* or *cultural* terms. The instrumental approach is characteristic of environmental economics (Pearce *et al.*, 1989) and some varieties of legal and political science discourse (Hillman and Bollard, 1985; Gray, 1995) where policy is treated as a governmental device for controlling business through mandatory regulation or channelling its activities through strategies of persuasion and information provision.

Despite fundamental differences in the *means* espoused by promoters of market versus regulatory instruments, both groups evaluate policy in terms of narrowly defined outcomes. Thus, for the pro-regulation group, regulation is akin to a big stick which can be successfully wielded to whip businesses into shape. Equally, for deregulationists, mandatory standards inevitably fail in that they try to 'command-and-control' businesses; they must therefore make way for the superior policy techniques of persuasion. Either way, since 'policy', 'business' and 'environment' are treated as independent categories, real interactions between these worlds remain unexplored and policy evaluation revolves around technical indicators of environmental impact, or around excessively bounded categories of policy 'formulation' and 'implementation'.

As we suggested at the beginning of this chapter, a cultural approach is needed to detect connections between the worlds of public policy, business and environment that extend beyond the confines of a policy's stated objectives. 'Policy' is commonly used to refer not simply to what governments do, but to the way in which 'diverse activities by different bodies are drawn together into stable and predictable patterns of action' (Colebatch, 1998). In this respect, it extends beyond decisions taken by political leaders to the programmes and procedures developed by administrative bodies in a particular domain such as, in our case, the environment. In turn, cultural interpretations of the way policy works focus on more than formal policy objectives. By looking at the culture of policy-making and implementation in an area, they bring to light the underlying assumptions that frame a policy programme as well as its blind-spots and unintended consequences. Below, we identify what we call 'thin' and 'thick' notions of policy culture, both of which have some validity but remain insufficiently attuned to the often invisible influence of regulatory policy.

One approach (e.g. Guy, 1998) finds that regulation and other forms of environmental policy fail to engage with the realities of business cultures, and thereby end up imposing a framework that sits in uneasy tension with the meanings and practices of everyday activities in the business world. For example, Guy argues that environmental policy frameworks related to the commercial property industry have pre-judged notions of what counts as environmental strategy and why such strategies have not been adopted. Rather, policy-makers should identify the often unconscious potential for environmental innovation that exists in practices not explicitly labelled as such, and explore ways of building on it. Instances of 'unconscious environmentalism' have also been identified in other industries (Purvis *et al.*, forthcoming): for example, bakers have begun to buy more energy efficient refrigerators because these have become the market norm. While such claims are perfectly valid on their own terms, it does not mean that *public* policy ought to simply follow and encourage existing business trends. Indeed such trends may themselves have been indirectly set in motion by prior policy frameworks that were in tension with business to begin with. Thus, this approach ultimately suffers from a too 'thin' notion of policy culture, where 'policy' and 'business' remain in different worlds.

A second argument appears to reject the potential of public policy altogether, seeing it as a normalising force that absorbs and minimises the impact of radical environmental ideas (Gorz, 1993; Grove-White, 1996). These scholars argue that the environmental threat has merely been 'managed' rather than tackled seriously. The cultural contradictions of modern societies and enduring beliefs in the validity of existing economic and political arrangements attest to the failure of policy, in their view. In other words, when fundamental value-systems have been left intact, the raft of environmental legislation is merely 'cosmetic' and representative of 'symbolic politics' rather than of significant change (Cahn, 1995; Gare, 1995). Again, there is some plausibility to such critiques of environmental policy, but they ultimately suffer from a too 'thick' notion of culture. Only cultural and value shifts are seen as indicative of genuine changes, a view which treats culture as an autonomous, non-material system rather than as embodied in concrete institutional practices.

We argue that a better cultural approach to policy, business and the environment would recognise that (a) environmental regulation (as one form of public policy) is negotiated and co-produced by a range of government, business and other actors, and (b) regulation is itself a cultural force which shapes business action in ways that extend beyond its specific technical content. While we draw from the insights of the 'thin' and 'thick' notions of policy culture, we move beyond both narrowly defined technical measures and equally narrow demarcations between 'culture' and 'policy' and suggest the following ways in which mandatory regulation can work.

Environmental regulation in baking, printing, refrigeration and building

We begin by reviewing the state of global environmental regulation in each of our four sectors. In both baking and printing, mandatory regulatory standards exist only in relation to (local) environmental health and safety; none have been introduced with the purpose of controlling energy consumption as it impinges on the global environment. By contrast, regulation has made significant headway in both refrigeration and building sectors, motivated partly by the high proportion of end-use of energy in these cases.

Citing damage to the ozone layer, the Montreal Protocol (1987) introduced a ban on the offending refrigerant agent known as CFCs. Initially, this ban only affected refrigerant producers rather than the makers of refrigeration systems. However, knock-on effects began to emerge since the adoption of CFC alternatives required changes in refrigeration technology.

Likewise, the requirements of the Rio Climate Change Convention (1992) have been translated into European and UK legislation for the refrigeration and building sectors. Domestic fridges must now carry an energy label designed to inform purchasers of the model's energy efficiency relative to other models. The minimum permitted efficiency for fridges is also to be progressively raised. Discussions on requiring similar labelling for commercial systems have foundered on the argument that non-standard products are not amenable to such an assessment of energy use, but have produced a voluntary, but widely used index of warming impact. Mandatory energy labelling has also been introduced in the case of new homes via revisions to the building regulations in 1995 (see Raman and Shove, Chapter 8 for further details). Their actual function in relation to home-buying remains problematic, especially in-so-far as ratings only need to be provided by builders to building control officers rather than to buyers themselves.

Despite the tensions in these policy shifts and the difficulties in tracing immediate environmental impacts, we argue that regulation does make a difference in the following ways.

Creating a discourse

In the 1990s, scholars of the policy process (Haas, 1992; Sabatier and Jenkins-Smith, 1993) have challenged the traditional focus on 'power' and 'interest groups' and begun to take seriously the role of ideas in influencing policy outcomes, or sometimes introducing radical shifts. Political and social systems are said to be capable of changing by 'learning', although the process is never straightforward. A raft of environmental legislation introduced in recent years has provided an empirical stimulus for studies in this vein.

For our purposes, we turn the ideas-and-policy question around and examine the role of policy (or more specifically, regulation) itself in generating new ideas or discourses. In the context of refrigeration and building, a shift in environmental discourse from localised health and safety issues to a more diffuse global change is particular striking. Baking and printing sectors, on the other hand, remain focused on local environmental issues alone, such as food hygiene and hazardous chemicals (both of which are regulated), and paper recycling (which has emphatically entered popular discourse). We argue that new regulations in the case of building and refrigeration have been instrumental in promoting this discursive shift.

A discourse may be defined as 'an ensemble of ideas, concepts, and categories through which meaning is given to phenomena' (Hajer, 1993: 45). Examining the response to acid rain in Britain, Hajer points out that by creating a specific vocabulary and highlighting a particular construction of the situation, discourses frame problems in one way rather than another. It is through the construction of discourses that institutional and material practices are interpreted and transformed. Discourses provide a certain story-line – in our case, scientific discourse about the global environment (global warming) has been translated into a pragmatic story that relates to actors at the sectoral level (how energy or refrigerant use by fridges and buildings makes the earth warmer). We argue further that regulation mediates

between the scientific and pragmatic levels, by providing institutional rein-
forcement of both discourses.

Thus, via the Montreal Protocol, and the Climate Change Convention, the
global environment has become embedded in the commercial refrigeration
industry. While ozone depletion is not explicitly discussed, it structures the
examination of various alternatives that have emerged in the light of
existing, as well as anticipated, controls. The Total Equivalent Warming
Index is the tangible manifestation of this phenomenon. This index aims to
assess a refrigeration system's total impact on the global environment as a
combination of the system's energy use and of refrigerant emissions, HCFCs
(hydrochlorofluorocarbons) and HFCs (hydrofluorocarbons) both being greenhouse gases. Since different refrigerants entail different levels of energy
consumption – thus, ozone-depleting CFCs are actually relatively efficient
users of energy – the relative pros and cons of different options are both
accounted for in the calculation. Whilst not wholeheartedly embraced by all
parties in commercial refrigeration, the Total Equivalent Warming Index
has, at least, become common currency.

Likewise, in the building industry, the global environment has permeated
through revisions in the building regulations to provide a new basis for energy
efficiency standards. In a sector where structural safety, fire hazards, sanitation
and health risks from condensation have been the basis of standard-setting
since the Victorian era (and dating back even earlier to the Great Fire of
London in 1666), the discourse of global change (i.e. as seen in actions taken in
the name of alleviating global warming) has been truly novel. Again, this shift
is not without its tensions, especially in terms of the conventions and norms
that implicitly regulate the inspection procedures of building control officers.

In this context, it is worth noting though that the creation of a common
discourse does not, in itself, constitute agreement across companies on who
exactly bears responsibility or what is to be done, nor that intelligible
measures of practical effectiveness are readily available for comparative evaluation. Indeed, refrigeration companies, housebuilders, commercial property
developers and air-conditioning manufacturers regularly put up a good deal
of resistance against government efforts to strengthen regulatory standards
that are claimed to adversely affect business in these areas. Also, as Hajer
points out, discursive shifts may not necessarily be accompanied by
institutional change. However, the fact that a particular storyline has become
embedded in two sectors and not the others, cannot be dismissed as a *merely*
discursive effect. This is because institutional change necessarily evolves
through the development of new constructs and arguments, some of which
may only be implicit or arguments by omission.

Creation of new networks

This refers to organisational rearrangements which may or may not accom-
pany the rise of new discourses. A number of studies have argued that

innovation depends on the strength of links between different companies or their representatives across the supply chain. This applies in a policy context as well, as some studies of policy networks indicate. On the one hand, government–business networks allow information to be exchanged and trust to be built up, both of which are essential for implementation of new agreements. On the other hand, governments can stimulate the development of new networks between businesses which might be expected to promote the creation and take-up of new practices. In the case of both refrigeration and building, we find that new networks between businesses and between government and business, have emerged from the introduction of new mandatory regulations.

In the refrigeration sector, new networks can be seen most obviously in the growth of groups interacting directly with government on matters of future policy development. Commercial refrigeration has learnt that it needs to watch the global environmental policy stage. By being aware of policies as they develop, they not only have a chance to influence regulation, but also to anticipate future regulation in their current decisions – as opposed to making wasteful capital investments which might fail to comply with potential future requirements. Although policy uncertainty is something about which businesses routinely complain, the new practice of looking to the future could have environmentally benign effects. However, it is worth noting that smaller businesses are much less likely to be participants in new government-business networks and relationships. None-the-less, as environmental policy becomes embodied in technological and institutional systems, such networks could widen and become more inclusive.

Networks between key businesses in particular sectors also exhibit changes. For instance, the commercial refrigeration industry has begun to anticipate the needs of their major supermarket customers who are now firmly perceived as being environmentally conscious. Thus, the energy efficiency of systems has come to be a crucial element of competition in the tendering process. On the other hand, since the management structure of supermarkets is internally fragmented, the global environment appears only in the activities of buyers of refrigeration systems. By contrast, buyers of baked goods for the same stores stick to environmental issues relating to food hygiene regulations and do not appear to raise energy efficiency matters with their suppliers.

Revisions in the building regulations and the introduction of energy performance standards have significantly re-aligned the policy network in building construction by bringing new players on board and stimulating the fragmented boiler industry to organise itself into a trade association. Rising participation from the non-domestic building industry has been especially critical in this regard. While some of these players – e.g., those from the air-conditioning sector – strongly resist the prospect of new regulation, others – e.g., building service professionals – have shaken up the policy process with pro-regulation arguments. Traditional complaints from the housebuilding and masonry sectors can no longer go unchallenged in this context. Such organisational changes have, more recently, allowed radical new questions to be posed about the future reach of regulation – for example, a possible extension from new build to existing buildings which, after all, are responsible for the bulk of energy consumption. More generally, the regulations provide the only common ground that allows networking between various parts of a highly diverse and fragmented industry.

New markets, technologies and standards

Finally, we come to one of the more commonly observed impacts of regulation, i.e., its role in the adoption of new technologies or standards and the subsequent generation of new business (Wallace, 1995). Rather than postulating a deterministic link between regulation and these impacts (as in an instrumental approach), we suggest that the cultural shifts previously discussed are constitutive of any such technical/market changes, should they take place.

In refrigeration, as already noted, the Montreal Protocol engendered the necessity to use alternative refrigerants. Some already existed at the time, and others have been developed as the market has opened up to new products. For instance, a large manufacturer of gases (Calor) started producing hydrocarbons for the refrigeration market, while other companies have developed blends of gases to replace CFCs. Likewise, the requirement for energy-labelling on domestic fridges has generated research and development on better insulants and door seals.

A second consequence of the Montreal Protocol was the new attention paid to refrigerant leakage. Pre-Montreal, CFCs were cheap and it was usual for a large proportion of the refrigerant in a system to leak out into the atmosphere and be replaced during routine servicing. Post-Montreal, the combination of a rise in refrigerant prices and the inflammability or toxicity of some CFC-substitutes has prompted the search for ways to minimise leakage. Further, since the CFC ban covers only new production and does not extend to its use in refrigeration systems already in existence, a new business sub-sector providing leak detection equipment and influencing the design of specific components such as pipe junctions has been created.

In building, the introduction of home energy ratings has spawned a new business service, namely, companies that provide approved ratings for building control purposes. Their long-term impact is yet to become clear. However, the building regulations for the conservation of fuel and power have clearly stimulated a market for the insulation industry, and the development of new materials – even in traditional brick-and-block construction – whose use is intended to satisfy rising energy efficiency requirements.

In baking, where no global-environmental regulation exists, technology is being driven by other factors. As noted earlier, supermarkets have taken over the lion's share of baked-goods retailing, and over the same period there has been a growth in 'fancy' breads which pose a challenge to the standard package of sliced bread. Current perceptions that the consumer wants 'fresh' bread have generated the uptake of 'bake-off', where goods are part baked at a central bakery, then often chilled, and transported to the point of sale where baking is completed. This increases the amount of energy required to bake any item, further illustrating the absence of a discourse of global climate change in this sector. The printing industry similarly ignores global concerns, efficiency being construed as the number of items printed per minute rather than anything to do with energy. Speed of production is a major driver, customers' expectations having risen to create ever-shortening periods between order and delivery, and leading to such energy intensive practices as the delivery of goods by air.

These examples of technological and market changes are mediated by the cultural force of mandatory regulation that encompasses but goes beyond its technical specifications. Such specifications may be contrary to existing business practice, but may well stimulate new technological or process developments for the better. Likewise, the technical details may fall short of specifying broad-ranging requirements for industry to satisfy, but may yet unintentionally generate the impetus for such changes. It is for these reasons that neither the 'thin' nor the 'thick' notions of culture are sufficient to capture the dynamic interaction between policy, business and the environment.

Conclusion

We began this chapter by pointing to a significant gap between generic exhortations and campaigns for the greening of business and the uneven and complex realities of organisational practice in different sectors. We argued that policy initiatives for voluntary greening must engage with organisational factors – firm size, product and process differences, intra-business networks within markets, and technological base – that vary by industry. Taking four industries – baking, building construction, printing, refrigeration – as examples, we examined the different ways in which they interfaced with the 'global environment' in the first place, and thereby, with the new greening campaigns.

Global environmental impact is more readily highlighted in the refrigeration and building industries since they make products that account for a high proportion of the nation's energy consumption. By contrast, bakers and printers have relatively little capacity to respond to green campaigns since it is the energy consumed in the course of their production process – and thus, the efficiency of the equipment they use – that is of concern. We then turned to the question of a company's capacity to influence its suppliers or customers towards environmentally better choices. Again, this varied enormously, with small bakers and printers, for example, having little room for influencing the large suppliers of their manufacturing equipment, while large supermarkets have been able to make their refrigeration system suppliers compete on the basis of energy efficiency. This highlighted the importance of company size, with SMEs generally having less clout and being less connected up with information and trade networks. On the other hand, the barriers faced by SMEs can easily become a self-fulfilling myth for policy-making in some conservative domains. Finally, we pointed out that the technological base of a sector may be far less malleable in some cases than in others.

Stepping back from this sectoral diversity, we noticed that, despite the many contradictions and criticisms, the 'global environment' has become successfully embedded in the refrigeration and building sectors, but not in baking and printing. That is, connections between business practice in the specific sector and global change has been made in the former cases, but not in the latter. This, we argued, was an outcome of the cultural influence of environmental regulation which has remained tied to local issues in baking and printing, but been linked up with climate change and ozone depletion in building and refrigeration.

We then elaborated our perspective of regulation as a cultural force whose capacity to mediate between policy, business and the environment typically goes unnoticed in standard instrumentalist evaluations of policy. In contrast with other culturalist arguments that prioritise an autonomous domain of cultural values or of everyday business practices above policy, we argued that regulation can itself represent a broad-ranging cultural shift in a sector. By generating new discourses (in our case, from localised health-and-safety to global environment), enabling the formation of new networks between businesses and between business and government, and providing the institutional glue for technological or market changes in a sector, regulation can and does shape the domain for environmental action in subtle ways.

Notes

1 Authors listed in alphabetical order. No priority intended.
2 Sujatha Raman worked on one of these projects on building regulation, 'Constructing Regulation and Regulating for Energy Efficient Construction' (February 1996–January 1998, Award No: L320253223) with Elizabeth Shove at Lancaster University. Jane Hunt worked on the second project that examined the baking, printing and refrigeration sectors, 'Global Environmental Change and European Business' (May 1996–June 1998, Award No: L320253204) with Martin Purvis and Frances Drake at the University of Leeds.
3 Note that life-cycle measures of a product's *embodied* energy are meant to capture the energy consumed at various points in its supply chain process. In-so-far as energy-related policies in our four sectors do not yet incorporate such measures, product and process impacts are likely to be perceived of independently. In any case, end-use energy will remain important in the case of some products and not others.
4 A third sub-sector not covered in our study is that of industrial refrigeration, supplying cooling equipment, for example, to chemical manufacturing processes.

References

Ball, M. (1988) *Rebuilding Construction*. London: Routledge.
British Printing Industries Federation (1990) *How to Become a Greener Printer*. London: British Printing Industries Federation.

Cahn, M.A. (1995) *Environmental Deceptions*. Albany, NY: State University of New York Press.

Colebatch, H.K. (1998) *Policy*, Buckingham: Open University Press.

Elkington, J. (1994) 'Toward the sustainable corporation: win-win-win business strategies for sustainable development', *California Management Review*, Winter, 90–100.

Energy Efficiency Office (1992) *Practical Energy Saving Guide for Smaller Businesses: Save Money and Help the Environment*. London: Department of the Environment.

Gare, A.E. (1995) *Postmodernism and the Environmental Crisis*. London: Routledge.

Gorz, A. (1993) Political ecology: expertocracy versus self-limitation. *New Left Review*, 202 (Nov–Dec), 55–67.

Gray, T. (ed.) (1995) *UK Environmental Policy in the 1990s*. London: Macmillan.

Grove-White, R. (1996) 'Environmental Knowledge and Public Policy Needs'. In S. Lash, B. Szerszynski and B. Wynne (eds) *Risk, Environment and Modernity*. London: Sage.

Guy, S. (1998) 'Developing Alternatives: Environmental Innovation and the Property Business', End-of-Award Report to the Economic and Social Research Council's Global Environmental Change Programme.

Haas, P. (1992) Introduction: epistemic communities and international policy co-ordination. *International Organisation*, 46 (1), 1–35.

Hajer, M. (1993) Discourse coalitions and the institutionalization of practice: the case of acid rain in Britain. In F. Fischer and J. Forester (eds) *The Argumentative Turn in Policy Analysis and Planning*. Durham, NC: Duke University Press.

Hillman, M. and Bollard, A. (1985) *Less Fuel, More Jobs*. London: Policy Studies Institute.

Pearce, D., Markandya, A. and Barbier, E. B. (1989) *Blueprint for a Green Economy*. London: Earthscan.

Porter, M. (1990) *The Competitive Advantage of Nations*. New York: Free Press.

Purvis, M., Hunt, J. and Drake, F. (forthcoming) *Means, Ends and Attitudes: Ambiguities in the Greening of Business*.

Sabatier, P. and Jenkins-Smith, H. (1993) *Policy Change and Learning: An Advocacy-Coalition Approach*. Boulder: Westview Press.

Schmidheiny, S. (1992) *Changing Course: A Global Business Perspective on Development and the Environment*. Cambridge: MIT Press.

Shrivastava, P. (1992) Corporate self-greenewal: strategic responses to environmentalism. *Business Strategy and the Environment*, 1 (3), 9–21.

Wallace, D. (1995) *Environmental Policy and Industrial Innovation*. London: Earthscan.

Welford, R., and Gouldson, A. (1993) *Environmental Management and Business Strategy*. London: Pittman.

Winward, J., Schiellerup, P. and Boardman, B. (1998) *Cool Labels: The First Three Years of the European Energy Label*, Oxford: Environmental Change Unit, University of Oxford.

8 The business of building regulation

Sujatha Raman and Elizabeth Shove

> If you're doing a story on climate change (on television), how do you show it? Do you show it with someone whizzing past in a car, or perhaps, stills of traffic jams? Or do you show it with people sitting in shirt-sleeves in their homes in the winter?. . . . There's nothing nothing duller than somebody putting insulation into a loft as a picture.

With these remarks, a spokesperson for the insulation industry highlights the virtual invisibility of the humble building in high-profile environmental campaigning. The wider environmental implications of individual driving habits are far easier to dramatise, he suggests, than those of equally problematic actions such as turning up the heat (instead of putting on a jumper) or ignoring basic, but 'dull', advice about investing in better home insulation. In this context, *regulation* of building construction by government seems to be the natural, one-step solution. Without further stimulus, neither individual householders nor the construction industry are likely to take the actions required to reduce energy consumption in order to alleviate global warming. Government, on the other hand, can use its regulatory powers to compel builders to improve standards of energy efficiency and in that way guarantee significant environmental benefit. Or so the argument goes.

In this chapter, we examine the *making* of building regulations as a social and organisational process. When considering the relationship between business and the environment, we argue that regulation itself can usefully be seen as a business, the terms of which are themselves negotiated by a variety of public and private actors. This view is in contrast to the more conventional interpretation of regulation as a uni-directional instrument of policy – that is, as a stick wielded by government over business (Shove and Raman, 1996). Rather than seeing environmental standard-setting as some-thing which is invented and imposed, or which simply mirrors government commitment, we also argue that the potential for environmental regulation is situational, and must be understood with reference to the sector specific characteristics, histories and practices which constitute, in this case, the wider world of building construction.

As a case of environmental regulation, energy efficiency in buildings is crucial in its own right. Approximately half of the UK's total energy consumption, and an equivalent proportion of its energy-related CO_2 emissions, relates to the energy used in buildings (Henderson and Shorrock, 1990). Mundane activities such as the heating of water and space, lighting, artificial ventilation, and the use of numerous domestic appliances and items of office equipment have consequently acquired a new political significance, albeit one that has not yet hit the headlines, in the drive to increase efficiency and minimise the emission of greenhouse gases held responsible for global warming. Some end-uses are, of course, more significant than others, and some more susceptible to government influence and control. Energy consumption in the home, most of which relates to heating, accounts for 30 per cent of all energy used in the UK (Henderson and Shorrock, 1990). During the 1990s, the fastest growing area of energy consumption in the building sector related to the energy used in air-conditioning offices. For these reasons, domestic and non-domestic energy use represent potentially important targets for environmentally inspired regulation.

The Building Regulations of England and Wales are not an area normally associated with dramatic change. Given their roots in a localised system of Victorian by-laws introduced as part of the urban public health movement, the philosophy of building control remains grounded in matters such as structural and fire safety. Yet, the section of the regulations that deals with conservation of fuel and power (Part L), was significantly revised in 1995 with the expectation of producing a 20 per cent saving in energy and a 500,000 tonne reduction in CO_2 emissions. This step followed on the heels of the 1990 Environment White Paper which highlighted the contribution that building regulation could make – especially via the introduction of mandatory energy-labelling of newly constructed homes – to strategies for controlling global warming. Following the 1992 Rio Convention, the UK's Programme for CO_2 Emissions (Department of the Environment, 1992) reiterated this policy promise, and a new climate-change-inspired Part L came into existence in July 1995. Analysis of these revisions shows how arguments about global climate change have been used to legitimise new forms of government intervention.

All parts of the Building Regulations define standards that must be met at the time of construction. Those relating to energy conservation are intended to limit the energy consumed when the building is in use. In the past, building regulations were essentially prescriptive. In other words, they itemised elements of building structure and specified minimum levels of, for instance, insulation for external walls, roofs, floors and glazing. In this context, improving standards generally involved incrementally increasing required levels of insulation, all of which had immediate consequences for the sales of particular materials and the fortunes of the companies involved.

During the late 1980s, approaches toward building control (and other areas of regulation as well) began to shift from a prescriptive philosophy to a 'performance-based' approach. Performance-based systems, partly inspired by the fear that regulation might inhibit innovation, involve the specification of certain minimum requirements, in our case for energy efficiency, but do not determine the means by which those targets might be met. The commercial implications of performance-based regulations are not so obvious: depending on the routes actually taken, there could be benefits for the timber industry, or it could be the concrete-block makers who gain. More than that, the performance route implicitly extends the reach and scope of regulation, drawing in companies and organisations never previously interested in such matters. For example, the 1995 revisions allow housebuilders to demonstrate compliance by demonstrating that their building has a high energy rating as measured by the 'standard assessment procedure' or SAP. The factors which go into the making of this rating include much more than the building fabric or the details of wall, floor and roof construction. SAP ratings also reflect the type of heating system installed and the sort of fuel to be used. As a result, and for the first time, boiler makers began to have an interest in a regulatory system which previously focused on the durable elements of the building to the exclusion of shorter-lived systems and services.

By exploring the relationship between business, regulation and environmental policy in this sector we also have an opportunity to explore the practical implications of performance-based regulation. What new kinds of lobbying are involved in establishing, negotiating and implementing performance standards and how do modes of regulation modify the terms of government industry interaction? Again, the 1995 revisions to Part L provide an instructive case with which to reflect on the dynamics of consultation under these more open and uncertain conditions.

Finally, this case allows us to reflect on the fuzzy edges of regulation and the notion that mandatory standards are important not just in themselves, but for the effect they have on related, but unregulated practice. Since the turnover of building stock in the UK is relatively small, around 1–2 per cent annually, energy-related regulations that apply to new construction cannot be expected to make much contribution to environmental objectives in the short term. In fact it is precisely because buildings are long-lived that actions taken today are important in the long term from the environmental standpoint. Yet the revisions to the regulations, and in particular, the requirement that housebuilders supply an energy rating, was explicitly viewed as a means of kick starting the use of energy-labelling in the much larger market of existing dwellings.

Some suspect that this sideways move toward the major environmental target of the existing stock represents the thin end of a future regulatory wedge. Might building regulations be used to extend the reach of energy related legislation to the entire property market? Radical ideas along these lines have been the subject of debate within the UK Department of the Environment, Transport and the Regions (DETR) and beyond since mid-1998 (Oscar Faber, 1998). Whatever happens, we can already see how environmental regulation might be designed and positioned to have an influence that reaches beyond the formal limits of implementation and control.

In sum, energy-related building control has gone from being a relatively mature or stable area of government activity to one that appears to be at the vortex of increasingly wide-ranging changes. Various factors come together to create a situation in which current trends in the substance and form of environmentally inspired policy are pushing the regulatory system to its limits. First, the need to reduce energy consumption appears to be more urgent than ever, and for this reason, regulatory initiatives have been introduced with reference to a novel environmental logic. Second, changes in the mode of regulation have increased uncertainty regarding the commercial implications of new standards and have drawn new organisations and interests into the regulatory framework. Third, building regulation is being more or less explicitly designed to influence a much wider range of practices and conventions than those subject to formal control.

All three considerations have implications for the terms on which government and industry interact and for the part which both had to play in shaping the revised standards. Having outlined some of the reasons why energy related building regulation deserves further analysis, we now say something about the benefits of developing a more sociological approach to studying the process of regulation.

Researching regulation in the making

Regulation is often viewed as a rather blunt instrument as compared with the 'softer' market mechanisms of policy (Shove, 1995). In the 1980s, arguments were made in the UK for deregulation along with a greater reliance on 'market instruments' – for instance, providing information to companies and consumers, removing market barriers, and promoting consumer awareness of the link between energy use and the environment. This rather clear cut dichotomy between regulatory and voluntary instruments of policy, a split which is also paralleled in much of the literature, ignores the fact that regulation itself contains 'soft' aspects rooted in the necessary negotiation of standards and their implementation by government and business actors. By focusing on the process of making regulation we hope to reveal something of the underlying philosophies, norms and practices which regulation and business have in common.

As Clark (1992) observes, 'real regulation' is context-sensitive. Its qualities and characteristics are not the mechanical product of environmental need translated into uniformly applied regulatory standards. Others have also made the point that regulatory frameworks are far from neutral. Instead, regulatory debate provides a focal point for sometimes 'furiously contested' struggles between multiple actors with opposed interests (Hancher and Moran, 1989). Equally, there are sectors (typically relatively mature ones in which relevant actors, linked through well-established networks, share a common history of mutual interaction) in which the regulatory process is much tamer and in which its stabilised boundaries are simply taken for granted. In either case, we argue that analysis of regulation and regulatory policy-making must be located within the social and organisational setting in which legal frameworks and/or technical standards are defined and interpreted (Hawkins and Thomas, 1989).

In the sections that follow we draw on research funded by the Economic and Social Research Council's Global Environmental Change Programme as a means of investigating the process of building regulation. This research involved detailed scrutiny of negotiations between government, industry and research in setting and implementing the 1995 revisions to the energy part of the building regulations. The Building Regulations Division of the (then) Department of the Environment provided access to minutes of advisory group meetings, consultation responses, and other internal documents related to the revisions. Analysis of this documentary material, and of a programme of interviews with key players in the process, generated insights into the world of 'real' regulation which confirm, counter and complicate some of the positions outlined in the literature.

We make use of four ideal-type models of how regulators, industry actors and scientific or expert knowledge interact in the making and implement-ation of new standards. We use these four conceptual models, first, of policy institutions, second, of policy interests, third, of policy networks and, finally, of policy systems, as a means of successively making sense of our research material and exploring the key dimensions of stability and change which characterise the tensions and dynamics of regulation in the making.

Regulatory institutions

Legal (Boyle, 1994), economic (Manners, 1995) and environmental advocacy (Hillman and Bollard, 1985) perspectives tend to treat regulation, business, and research as autonomous practices undertaken by quite distinct institu-tions. In this tri-partite model, regulation appears to be a linear process in which government (the regulator), with the aid of expert knowledge (from research organisations), controls the activities of business.

Up to a point, the linear model fits the case we have studied. The impetus for revising the building regulations stemmed from the government's commitment to reduce CO_2 emissions (HM Government, 1990). With advice from the Building Research Establishment and the Building Regulations Advisory Committee, the Building Regulations Division (part of the (then) Department of the Environment) prepared and distributed a consultation document outlining proposed changes. Industry responses helped iron out technical flaws and problems of interpretation. The revised amendments were passed by Parliament in 1994 and came into effect a year later. In short, government set the regulatory agenda in association with technical research institutions. Though included in the consultation process, industry's role was

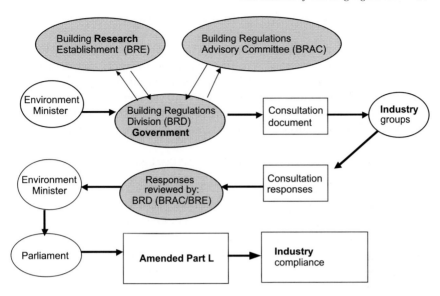

Figure 8.1 Mapping institutions.

to comply with the new standards. Figure 8.1 plots the main actors and shows how they might be positioned in such a linear model.

This description matches the 'official story' as related by our industry respondents. The builders we interviewed claimed, perhaps rather cynically, that government's distance from industry, and hence from the realities of home-buyers' expectations, explains the generation of what were viewed as unworkable or unrealistic standards. Respondents from the non-domestic sector went further, arguing that regulation made little difference to 'as-built' energy standards which were ultimately driven by industry practices, the norms of property rental agreements and client expectations. In both cases, clear distinctions were drawn between the intentions of 'government' and those of 'industry'.

As a 'model-in-use', that is as a model which reflects the discourse of key actors, this kind of institutional analysis is undoubtedly influential. Yet as a robust analytic framework, it fails to capture important features of government–industry interaction.

From institutions to interests

In recognition of the multiplication of lobby groups in modern political systems, political scientists have stressed the influence of industrial interests in the making of policy (Dahl and Lindblom, 1976). Instead of reviewing the role of homogeneous and rather abstract 'institutions', interests-based analyses show how actual organisations like industrial trade associations or professional associations interact with specific government agencies – in this case in order to influence legislative standards.

When applied to our case, this policy interests model allows us to hear the babble of voices represented in the consultation process thorough which the revised energy standards were refined and shaped. It also allows us to distinguish between established players and newcomers, and between perspectives within what we have so far referred to as 'industry' or 'government'. The following paragraphs outline just some of the positions involved in the 1995 revisions.

Established interests

Of those lobbying for higher energy standards, representatives of insulation companies stand out as being especially vociferous. Factions arguing most forcefully against the tightening of Part L included housebuilders, their opposition based on the fear that higher standards would increase costs and weaken the market for new as opposed to 'second hand' homes, and lightweight-concrete-block makers who stand to lose if construction practices change. Individuals representing these associations have been involved with the Building Regulations Division for a decade or more and their predictable rhetoric masks tacit acceptance of compromise and a well-worn familiarity with the rules of the game.

Changing interests

The National House Building Council (NHBC), the major provider of warranties for new homes in the UK, has traditionally opposed higher energy standards fearing more insurance claims if builders were 'forced' to fully-fill cavity walls. However, the NHBC's position changed significantly in the 1990s. In its relatively new role as an approved inspector (i.e. as a private organisation approved to compete with local authority building control officers for the work of inspecting compliance with building regulations) and provider of energy ratings, the NHBC has become, at least in principle, closer to the 'regulator' than to the 'regulated'.

Ambivalent interests

The case of the Royal Institute of British Architects (RIBA) illustrates a different aspect of representation. While the RIBA has always participated in the consultation process, it does not stand for any single, focused viewpoint. Individual members, firms or academics may have a special interest in green design, but the profession as a whole tends to balk at regulatory 'interference'. This ambivalence is reflected in the contrasting recommendations of the RIBA's Building Control Committee, which called for less detailed regulation, and its Energy and Environment Committee, which pressed for a sharp rise in energy standards.

The policy interests approach reminds us of the diversity of positions at stake. In this it raises a further question: how are these multiple interests evaluated and managed? The traditional answer is that the Building Regulations Division, together with its advisory committee's technical working party, 'sifts' commercial interests from technical evidence submitted by consultees. Like the main committee itself, this working party includes members from academia and industry (traditionally from the domestic sector) and therefore draws on expertise from different quarters. It is through this balancing of perspectives, combined with reference to independent scientific evidence (traditionally, but not exclusively, provided by the recently privatised Building Research Establishment) that proposals are developed, tested and evaluated.

The policy interests model allows us to see how industry and government interact well beyond the formalities of consultation. Representatives of housebuilding, in particular, occupy multiple roles: as members of expert advisory committees, informants, sparring partners and critics. However, the policy interests model does not easily recognise the diversity of interests *within* government – represented in our case by persistent tensions between sponsorship of the construction industry, on the one hand, and promotion of environmental regulation on the other. Nor is the interests model much help in analysing the dynamics of change and stability. For this we need to turn to theories of policy networks and policy systems.

From interests to networks

The concept of policy networks (see Rhodes, 1997 for an overview) has been developed partly in response to the fragmentation of governmental as well as private interests, and the transfer of several once-public responsibilities to the private sector. This approach highlights inter-dependencies between interest groups. The regulatory 'institution' now becomes a network consisting of constellations of public *and* private players, said to 'co-produce' the process and outcome of regulation.

Figure 8.2 represents some of the more important players in this expanded network. Square boxes surrounded by black lines indicate government departments, units or divisions; curved boxes indicate an advisory function, circles identify professional or private commercial interests.

The value of this approach is that it allows us to observe the proliferation of interested parties and the range of organisations with a stake in the regulatory process. In addition, it reveals divisions within the Department of the Environment, and between central and local government. We can now show how changes in the purpose, mode and scope of energy-related regulation shape and are at the same time shaped by just such alliances.

Purpose

The 1995 revisions introduced an environmental logic into a regulatory regime previously dominated by issues of health and safety and a national

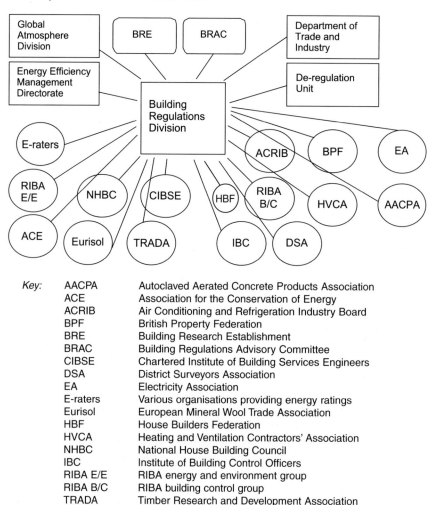

Key:

AACPA	Autoclaved Aerated Concrete Products Association
ACE	Association for the Conservation of Energy
ACRIB	Air Conditioning and Refrigeration Industry Board
BPF	British Property Federation
BRE	Building Research Establishment
BRAC	Building Regulations Advisory Committee
CIBSE	Chartered Institute of Building Services Engineers
DSA	District Surveyors Association
EA	Electricity Association
E-raters	Various organisations providing energy ratings
Eurisol	European Mineral Wool Trade Association
HBF	House Builders Federation
HVCA	Heating and Ventilation Contractors' Association
NHBC	National House Building Council
IBC	Institute of Building Control Officers
RIBA E/E	RIBA energy and environment group
RIBA B/C	RIBA building control group
TRADA	Timber Research and Development Association

Figure 8.2 Plotting the policy network.

economic interest in the conservation of fuel and power. Despite this new focus, established environmental lobby groups showed remarkably little interest in revising the energy part of the building regulations. Apart from submitting responses to the official consultation process, Greenpeace and Friends of the Earth did little to campaign for higher standards of energy efficiency in new buildings. Instead, environmental lobbying went on *within* government. The former Energy Efficiency Office (renamed the Energy Efficiency Management Directorate), together with the Global Atmosphere Division (both within the Department of the Environment) found themselves fostering and countering proposals developed by other divisions including the Building Regulations Division (also within the Department of Environment).

As we note below, the introduction of an environmental logic is important for the reach of future building regulation. In 1995, the specific focus on CO_2 emissions led to a corresponding focus on electricity consumption, the regulation of lighting, efforts to limit air-conditioning and mechanical ventilation, and the proposal to require energy ratings in the domestic sector. It also re-opened debate about ways of extending energy-related building regulation to the existing stock. As these points suggest, the introduction of an environmental rationale re-configured the range of interests with a stake in the process within government and industry.

Mode

In 1990, the statutory requirement of Part L was re-stated in functional terms (builders must make 'reasonable provision . . . for the conservation of fuel and power'). Two new methods of demonstrating compliance, both based on calculations of 'whole building' energy performance, were added as alternatives to the elemental method which prescribed specific U-values element by element and which had been the sole basis of the old deemed-to-satisfy system. The introduction of SAP energy ratings in 1995 as an additional method pushed the performance-based philosophy a stage further.

While all housebuilders have to provide a SAP rating, they are not required to meet any minimum threshold value. Instead, a SAP of 80–85 (depending on floor area) or more represents one amongst the three possible means of demonstrating compliance (Department of the Environment and the Welsh Office, 1995). By folding permanent (fabric-related), semi-permanent (heating/cooling systems-related) and fluctuating factors (fuel prices, though pegged to a three year average) into one index, the rating allows builders to trade between long term measures (like insulation), and those with a shorter life (like high efficiency boilers).

Uncertainty about how builders will actually react and what solutions they will in fact adopt introduces a further element of uncertainty about the technical risks, costs and commercial consequences of higher standards. This uncertainty blurs formerly predictable positions, creates new challenges for inspection and enforcement, and presents new problems for regulatory research. Opposition to the use of energy ratings in the regulatory process itself illustrates the potential for new and unlikely industry alliances to form. Though ultimately unsuccessful, efforts to keep the rating out of the regulatory framework generated unusual coalitions. For instance, insulation manufacturers (opposing the rating mechanism for fear that builders would exploit new opportunities for trade-offs) found themselves in agreement with their traditional rivals, the housebuilders (who disliked the idea of having to declare energy performance up front, and the extra cost of doing the necessary calculation). At the same time, boiler makers, who had little previous involvement in the building regulations, began to organise themselves in order to 'speak' with the regulators.

As this example from the domestic sector suggests, performance-based modes of regulation modify previously predictable relationships. It is not just that traditional actors are upstaged by rival interests. Rather, the point is that flexibility generates uncertainty, leading to transitory alliances and to a network of more complex but less stable relationships between government, research, and an ever more broadly defined industry (Raman, 1997).

Scope

As we have already noted, air conditioning represents one of the fastest growing end-uses of energy. Revision to the building regulations provided an opportunity to investigate ways in which the government might intervene to limit the escalating use of air conditioning in non-domestic (especially office) buildings. An initial proposal which would require designers to justify the use of air conditioning systems soon came to grief. The Building Regulation Division's first suggestions, developed in consultation with the Building Research Establishment, met with a swift and negative response from the air conditioning equipment manufacturers, property developers and electric utilities who together sought (and got) support from the Department of Trade and Industry and the Deregulation Unit. In reflecting on this process it is important to take note of silent as well as voluble voices. There are no organisational spokespersons to argue the case for passive cooling 'technologies'. Such design-based strategies do not involve the use of marketable commodities and so have no articulate interests to speak on their behalf. Again we see how the structure of the industry also structures regulatory discourse.

This example shows how closely the balance of argument relates to the organisation of commercial interests. The failure of those first proposals also revealed important gaps in the necessary web of government-industry relationships. In proposing to extend the technical scope of regulation, the Building Regulations Division over-shot the margins of its social reach. Having only a weak network and a limited history of interaction to build on in the non-domestic sector, the regulators had no foundation for effective negotiation.

The subsequent establishment of a non-domestic/air conditioning industry advisory group has had two functions. As intended, it has helped develop a pared-down index method for assessing the energy efficiency of air conditioning and mechanical ventilation systems (rather than evaluating the need for such systems as was at first proposed). Less obviously, the advisory group has helped the Division form working relationships with a largely unfamiliar sector whilst also organising an otherwise impossibly diverse array of interests. In this case, the regulators are actively involved in managing the networks on which regulation depends.

Reflecting on the building regulations in terms of *policy networks* allows us to identify patterns and relationships forming around, and contributing to, changes in the purpose, mode and scope of energy-related regulation.

Reference to the environment as a reason for conserving fuel and power increases the range of arguments and types of evidence deployed. Greater emphasis on performance targets has consequences across the regulatory system; requiring different methods of enforcement and increasing uncertainty about exactly which measures builders will adopt. It also presents new challenges for regulatory science and economics: what new knowledge is needed to set performance standards or long term targets, and what part could, or should, government research play in this process? Efforts to extend the scope of regulation draw in further unfamiliar interests and yet more conflicting priorities, again re-configuring the landscape of potential coalitions.

This network analysis suggests that the business of building control is becoming more uncertain and complex than ever before. At the same time, it is important to recognise that new relationships and arrangements have been developing within what remains a relatively enduring regulatory system.

From networks to systems

In this final section we highlight aspects of the regulatory system which frame and contain the developments outlined above. The first three points relate to the 'internal' world of building control.

Regulatory philosophy

For the most part, building regulation officials see their job as one of controlling 'laggards' rather than pushing the entire industry 'forward'. The emphasis is on 'doing what you know works [rather than] being subject to current fashions'. Although little systematic attention is paid to the real-life strategies of builders or to the constraints faced by inspectors, a general image of 'what the industry can stand' is critical. As our respondents explained, the strategy of 'going only for what the industry can cope with', is an important restraining feature. In this context, the notion of setting long term or as yet unachievable targets is both novel and alien. It is, however, quite common in other sectors, for instance, with respect to air quality in this country, and to building control in the Netherlands.

Forms of consultation

In meeting the mandatory requirement for consultation, the regulators have traditionally developed, and then sought comments on, detailed proposals. Though some take the opportunity to question the scope and underlying philosophy of energy related regulation, most responses are couched in comparably technical terms. This focus on technical detail has a stabilising effect on the character of regulatory debate. It is therefore important to acknowledge that the most recent round of consultation has deliberately invited more wide ranging and speculative comment. The changing environment of regulation raises new questions about the form and purpose of consultation and the need for contexts in which to address broader questions of legitimacy, mode, purpose and scope.

Inspection and enforcement

The possibilities of building control also relate to the cost and management of inspection. Local authority building control officers, like the private approved inspectors with whom they now compete, make tacit judgements about what requires direct checking either on site or on paper. Several respondents argued that building control was already stretched to the limit and that efforts to extend the scope, or change the mode of regulation would founder if attempted within the present framework of inspection.

Prevailing philosophies of regulation, conventions of consultation, and constraints of inspection link together to form the present regulatory system. Yet, there is no doubt that the system is under strain. Arrangements which have evolved in a more familiar and stable environment cannot handle the demands now made of them. Current discussions of self-certification, of long-term target setting, and of ways in which regulations might be extended to the existing stock (all of which form part of a new review announced in February 1998) suggest that regulatory theory and practice could be heading in new directions.

Possible new directions are, however, constrained by features relating not just to the system of regulation but also to the structure of the industry being regulated. Three examples illustrate the point.

Building methods

One is the extent to which traditional masonry construction practices are embedded in the organisational fabric of housebuilding. Our interview material and documentary data demonstrate the prevalence of the view that significant improvement in energy efficiency would require widespread adoption of timber frame construction or standardised industrial manufacturing processes. In other words, any significant advance in energy efficiency requires a paradigm shift in methods of construction, and as far as our housebuilding respondents could see, that was simply out of the question.

Organisational ties

Investment in normal ways of working has further stabilising consequences. Interviews with volume builders suggest that head offices frequently negotiate design packages and corresponding deals with materials suppliers which are then imposed on regional offices. In this, as in other cases, decisions about how to comply with regulation reflect conventions and commercial relationships linking builders and their networks of suppliers.

Consumer 'requirements'

Similar arguments about the social-cum-technological limits to change are advanced in the non-domestic sector. The escalation of energy demand is, for instance, explained in terms of the seemingly inexorable relationship between high rental value and high specification. If marketable properties now 'have to have' air conditioning then designers, contractors, systems installers and developers have no option but to work together to provide it whatever the environmental cost.

Given these ordering and stabilising features, the 'co-production' of regulation between government and industry is neither elastic nor unstructured. In practice, the uncertainties and flexibilities highlighted in the discussion of policy networks turn out to be regulated and ordered by a range of rather well established technological and organisational characteristics. It is for this reason that the Part L policy network needs to be situated within two ordering systems: the system of regulation and the system of building construction, both of which have their own habits, practices and interlocking anchors of inertia, as outlined above.

Regulation as business and business as regulator

In this chapter, we have made use of four models of policy analysis – moving from institutions to interests, interests to networks, and networks to systems – in an attempt to account for the relationships and practices involved in the revision of one important area of environmental policy making. In the process we have built up an increasingly complex picture of the ways in which government and industry interact in making and implementing energy-related building regulation.

This case highlights features common to other areas of environmental policy making. Greater emphasis on performance standards generates increasing uncertainty regarding the practical implications of new regulation for different parts of industry. No one knows exactly what the revised standards will mean for building construction or for the markets for key building materials. Re-defining the mode of regulation in performance terms also draws new actors into the debate and makes space for a more complex set of government–industry alliances. Boiler makers and air conditioning manufacturers have, for instance, added their voices to those of more familiar players involved in housebuilding or in the insulation industry. Widening the net in this way has consequences for the terms of regulatory debate as well as for the range of players involved. Confronted with the challenge of limiting the energy used in keeping office buildings cool, the government took the initiative to establish an unusually open and exploratory debate involving the manufacturers of air conditioning equipment, engineers, and property developers. Such pre-regulatory fora illustrate the potential for new models of government–industry interaction.

At the same time, we have underlined the stabilising implications of the fact that regulation is itself moderated by the way the construction industry works, and by taken-for-granted conventions of regulatory philosophy. In the case we have examined, and in others as well, regulation is seen as a back-stop: in the words of those we interviewed, it 'brings up the rear'. Viewing their job in this way, regulators argue that they cannot push industry too far or use their powers to stimulate the widespread adoption of novel or innovative practices. To do so would be to stretch systems of inspection and control to the limit and run the risk of failure on a catastrophic scale.

The implication is that if we are to understand the limits and possibilities of environmental regulation we have to take note of these and other sector-specific features. In our case, we have to acknowledge the traditions of industry practice including for instance, the technological 'log-jam' associated with continued reliance on conventional methods of masonry construction. As we explained above, relatively little more can be done to increase standards of energy efficiency within this technological paradigm. We also need to recognise the limits and possibilities afforded by the way the construction sector is organised. The fragmentation and interdependency which characterise relationships between builders, designers and suppliers is of real consequence for their ability to implement new standards of energy efficiency.

To summarise, performance-based approaches create the possibility for new forms of government and industry interaction. At the same time, the potential for 'real' regulation, that is regulation in practice, not regulation on paper, is defined by an array of sector-specific histories, relationships, technological conventions and economic priorities. Viewed in this way, the priorities and expectations of regulators still seem to differ markedly from those of industry and business.

On the other hand, we have also observed what appears to be an important trend in the blurring of regulatory and business practice. For example, we found the National House Building Council acting as both a representative of industry, and as an approved inspector charged with the task of ensuring that the industry complies with regulatory standards. Less directly, we have also seen the extent to which building materials suppliers take on the role of regulatory experts, providing advice and helping their clients keep up to date and meet new requirements. For instance, some offer 'free' energy ratings as part of a package deal also involving the supply of concrete blocks, insulation materials and so forth. More distantly but still crucially, regulators depend on business experience and an input of reliable business knowledge when framing proposals for the future and when assessing their viability. This is perhaps especially so in the more complex arena of non-domestic building, or when regulators attempt to influence equipment and services as well as the more standardised elements of building fabric.

Meanwhile, government regulators and inspectors are inhabiting an increasingly 'business like' world. Again starting with a simple case, local authorities compete with private companies (for example, approved inspectors like the National House Building Council) for the task of building control. We also see the devolution of regulatory responsibility in the proliferation of private companies offering energy rating services and so taking on some of the work involved in demonstrating and checking compliance. We observe similar tendencies within the standard-setting process itself. For example, responsibility for orchestrating the 'business' of consulting with industry has recently been sub-contracted to a firm of private consultants. In this case, government has enlisted business to organise and manage some of the labour involved in developing new regulations.

Discussion of environmental policy in other sectors suggests that these forms of crossing over between business and regulation are not unique to building construction (Irwin *et al.*, 1997). We are not in a position to assess the extent of such developments, nor even to say how novel they really are. However, we can say that they undoubtedly influence the ways in which government and business conceptualise and use regulation as an instrument of environmental policy.

In principle at least, recognising that regulation is co-produced makes it possible for government and industry to develop more radical proposals for the future. The move to performance-based regulation has already transformed the meaning of consultation. It is no longer a process of merely checking technical details but is now also one of establishing performance thresholds, and considering alternative means and modes of building control. Discussion of what might constitute acceptable and viable standards of energy efficiency in the longer run – that is, in 10 or 20 years' time – still lies beyond the margin of normal consultative debate. However, the opening up of consultation, the blurring of government and industry positions, and increasing environmental pressure makes it possible to imagine such a re-framing of regulatory discourse.

If this were to be the case, government might take on a new role in structuring and encouraging debate about really long term targets and in stimulating collective exploration of alternative routes towards those goals. Equally, we might expect business to play an even more active part as the co-designer of environmental policy. Though we have concentrated on the case of energy efficiency in buildings, and though this is an important sector in its own right, trends toward performance based standards and the blurring of business and regulation can be observed elsewhere. Having recognised the extent to which environmental policy is the outcome of tacit and sometimes explicit negotiation between government and industry, we must then acknowledge the power and the pull of distinctive, sometimes divisive histories of government–industry interaction across different sectors. Far from being a simple or inherently robust solution, the construction of environmental regulation requires the careful assembly of an often fragile, always contingent, and inevitably sector-specific edifice of inter-dependent relationships. Holding this structure together is what constitutes the real business of building regulation.

References

Boyle, A. (ed.) (1994) *Environmental Regulation and Economic Development.* Oxford: Clarendon Press.

Clark, G.L. (1992) Real regulation: the administrative state, *Environment and Planning A*, 27 (5), 615–627

Dahl, R. and Lindblom, C. (1976) *Politics, Economics and Welfare*, (2nd edn) Chicago: University of Chicago Press.

Department of the Environment (1992) *Climate Change: Our National Programme for CO_2 Emissions.* London: Department of the Environment.

Department of the Environment and the Welsh Office (1995) *The Building Regulations 1991: Approved Document L: Conservation of Fuel and Power.* London: HMSO.

Hancher, L. and Moran, M. (eds) (1989) *Capitalism, Culture, and Regulation.* Oxford: Clarendon Press.

Hawkins, K. and Thomas, J. M. (eds) (1989) *Making Regulatory Policy.* Pittsburgh: University of Pittsburgh Press.

Henderson, G. and Shorrock, L. (1990) Carbon dioxide emissions and energy efficiency in UK buildings. In American Council for an Energy Efficient Economy (ACEEE) *Energy Efficiency and the Environment: Forging the Link.* Washington, DC: ACEEE Press.

Hillman, M. and Bollard, A. (1985) *Less Fuel More Jobs: The Promotion of Energy Conservation in Buildings.* London: Policy Studies Institute.

HM Government (1990) *This Common Inheritance: Britain's Environmental Strategy.* London: HMSO.

Irwin, A., Rothstein, H., Yearley, S. and McCarthy, E. (1997) Regulatory science: towards a sociological framework. *Futures*, 29 (1), 17–31.

Manners, G. (199) Energy conservation policy. In T.Gray (ed.) *UK Environmental Policy in the 1990s.* London: Macmillan Press.

Oscar Faber (1998) 'A Review of the Energy Efficiency Requirements in the Building Regulations: Interim Paper', Prepared by Oscar Faber Consultants under contract to the Department of the Environment, Transport and the Regions (DETR).

Raman, S. (1997) Sizing up the policy information system for energy efficient construction. *Proceedings of the 1997 ECEEE Summer Study.* Copenhagen: European Council for an Energy-efficient Economy (ECEEE).

Rhodes, R. A. W. (1997) *Understanding Governance: Policy Networks, Governance, Reflexivity and Accountability.* Buckingham: Open University Press.

Shove, E. (1995) Constructing regulation and regulating for energy efficient construction. In T. S. Gray (ed.) *UK Environmental Policy in the 1990s.* Basingstoke: Macmillan.

Shove, E. and Raman, S. (1996) Big stick or bendy stick? Regulating for energy efficiency. I*Proceedings of the 1996 ACEEE Summer Study on Energy Efficiency in Buildings.* Washington, DC: American Council for an Energy-efficient Economy (ACEEE) Press.

Part 3

Learning and change

9 Smaller enterprises and the environment

Organisational learning potential?

Judith Petts

The idea that an organisational environmental culture might be an important attribute gained a significant level of acceptance during the 1990s. However, what it constitutes and how companies change culture to be environmentally friendly still awaits full description. Surveys of managers suggest that the environment has strong salience in business, not solely because they themselves have a passion for environmental protection, but because tangible (economic) benefits can be accrued. Recognising this economic imperative, government departments in Britain, for example, promote waste minimisation not as an environmentally sustainable activity but as a financial imperative.

There can be little doubt that 'the environment' is sufficiently nebulous an issue to provide a suitable banner for actions. To be able to claim to be 'environmentally-friendly' might be considered beneficial, but what it actually means would be open to debate let alone capable of being measured in terms of performance. It is a well recognised truism, for example, that companies who are accredited to the international environmental management standard ISO 14001, still make the lists of the major polluters. It is evident that in many big companies the environment has been institutionalised, but how far it has become embedded in the whole activity of production from product design through to sale – in the culture of the organisation – is debatable. The 'transcendent firm' espoused by the theoretical models of corporate greening still awaits clarity of definition let alone identification.

Whilst questioning of the real impact of formalising the environment within management systems is rife, it does serve to stress the key organisational components – communication, employee participation, training, relationships with external stakeholders, etc. – which should transform environmental initiatives from the purely technical. However, organisational theory, not least that which stresses the 'learning organisation', can sound good on paper, but can be more difficult to identify and analyse in practice. While the big organisations have begun to provide empirical evidence and the 'survey of managers' has become an almost academic and business ritual, our knowledge of the response and performance of smaller companies is poorer, including most importantly our understanding of the response of non-management — the employees who will be essential to the learning process.

Drawing on recent empirical research within small and medium-sized enterprises (SMEs) in Britain, this chapter examines the potential for organisational learning as suggested by the attitudes of management and non-management to the environment and environmental compliance. As background, the concepts of organisational greening and learning are critiqued. The survey results are presented in terms of individual attitudes to the environment, and the potential for these to be linked with the workplace and perceived management culture. Finally, the characteristics of the minority of SMEs who are taking some action in relation to the environment are examined — are these learning organisations?

Organisational greening

The 'green' business literature suggests a need for a significant shift in organisational cultures if sustainable environmental performance is to be achieved (Shrivastava, 1995). For the moment I leave open the key outstanding definitional questions which underlie much of the discussion in this book: i.e. what is 'greening' in the organisational context? can it be detected? and what is a sustainable environmental performance? Furthermore, to examine the underpinning of such questions we should explore the concept of the environment itself, for it is an easily used word but one encapsulating disciplinary-focused definitions — is it only the biophysical elements which support, life or does it include the social, cultural and economic elements around which human life is structured? is the state of the environment measured only by pollutant assimilative capacity, or also by the degree of individual and societal satisfaction with the relationship between humans and nature?

I adopt a simple view of greening which encapsulates strong environmental rhetoric within management and direct translation of this into corporate actions which find non-management support. These actions include compliance with environmental regulation (in itself a debatable point as we must question the relative environmental benefits of different legislation), and also a response to issues which have environmental salience externally, i.e. market and social resonance.

I deliberately avoid the concept of greening as a process of incremental change with a developing hierarchy of environmental strategies which in the greening spectrum ultimately produces the 'transcendent' firm (Welford, 1994; Dodge, 1997). The suggested gradation from externally-influenced greening (i.e. environmental compliance) to internally, culturally driven and supported change, appears to ignore a much closer interlinking of the external and internal factors (Eden, 1996).

Organisational learning

Whilst not necessarily incremental, greening does inherently require learning and adaptation. An organisation 'learns' if through the processing of information its range of behaviours changes (Huber, 1991), two different types of learning being characterised. Mechanistic learning involves response to error by individuals through modification of behaviour, but with no fundamental challenge to organisational assumptions. External triggers for environmental performance, not least regulatory, are often presented as being essential for organisational learning to begin – the bottom step of the greening ladder. The alternative view argues that external pressure alone will not bring about culture change, unless there is an internal capacity for response (Halme, 1997). The 'learning' organisation is characterised by a more reflexive process where underlying policies, aims and objectives are challenged and questioned resulting in a restructuring of organisational culture so that the company improves its potential to compete in a rapidly changing environment (Argyris and Schon, 1978).

A learning organisation is seen as essential to corporate greening (Post and Altman, 1994), being characterised by systems thinking which (a) gives individuals a shared responsibility for problems generated by the systems, (b) advances individuals as being equally as important as the management team, and (c) encourages corporate structures which support learning and reject functional divisions (Senge, 1990). In this context, learning is not limited to acquisition, but also distribution and interpretation of information and a fundamental change to the organisational memory (Gladwin, 1993).

In the top-down model of change, management takes the lead, identifying the environment as a relevant business issue, establishing an environmental policy and providing a structure by which this is disseminated down through the company with associated changes in business practice. Here, prescriptive strategies are unlikely to provide the employee participation which will lead to real individual commitment to environmental goals and provision of opportunity to play a full part within the workplace (Jones and Welford, 1997). The changes may be pushed down to the extent that employees may not feel the same commitment as management, only compulsion. Formal relationships dominate, and organisational culture can be instrumentally manipulated to fit corporate goals which in turn are indistinguishable from management goals.

By contrast the bottom-up approach is presented as involving changes in patterns of behaviour with people developing new values and beliefs from experience. Here change may be initiated in a small section or working area of the organisation as a result of the analysis of a specific problem, for example, apparently excessive packaging on products. Because the agents of changes at the bottom have less formal power, the manner of change promotion is more discursive and negotiative, although problems may arise if there is a subsequent lack of support from the top (Halme, 1997).

All of the models stress the importance of the individual. Personal experience and reactions to environmental issues are important not only in providing the trigger to action but in supporting and checking the learning process. Cognitive factors are important. If environmental beliefs are negative – for example, the environment is only a passing fad or it is only about compliance – then organisational learning will be impaired. Motivational barriers, such as feelings of uncertainty about an individual's job or challenge to developed and reassuring habits, are also important (Barrett and Murphy, 1995). Physical working conditions – i.e. the working environment – are inseparable from the 'green' environment. If the workplace is dirty, noisy, dusty, or dangerous, it will be difficult to promote a creative interest in the 'external environment' (Wolter *et al.*, 1995).

Therefore, it can be argued that similar to organisational safety culture (Pidgeon, 1991), a good environmental culture requires four main dimensions: (a) individuals who hold an attitude about the particular environmental issue being considered, (b) appreciation of the relevance of that attitude to their behaviour, (c) an organisational context and prevailing social norms which support and reinforce positive attitudes, (d) capacity for reflection upon practice (Petts *et al.*, 1998). This basic framework is used here as an argument for identifying management and non-management attitudes to the environment so as to enhance the description of environmental culture and the learning organisation. Drawing parallels with health and safety literature (e.g. Cox and Cox, 1996) which talks about the development of a safety culture as a process of 'winning hearts and minds', environmental response is dependent on choice – i.e. it is self-determined – as it is only by this means that people will be intrinsically motivated.

The evangelical tone of the culture change literature is beguiling, but, as it often lacks empirical evaluation of actual corporate responses and change processes, it provides us with less understanding of potential for, and barriers to, employee participation; i.e. what are the triggers, supporters and checkers? What are the diverse goals and values of individuals? Is the environment a strong component of employee concerns? Do employees value the environment? How do individuals define the environment? Is there a meaningful link between individual concerns and business operations? How is environmental information distributed and communicated within organisations? What are the management characteristics of organisations which appear to learn about greening more quickly than others?

SMEs and environmental learning

The empirical analysis here focuses on individuals within SMEs. SMEs are important. Some 38 per cent of all businesses in Britain are companies with 10–249 employees: 99 per cent of all businesses have 1–249 employees (the European Commission definition of SMEs as companies below 250 employees being used). Even if an individual activity could have a negligible environmental impact it is apparent that as a sector SMEs could have significant impacts.

The literature suggests that SMEs, in often having flat management structures, may be able to facilitate top-down and bottom-up change. However, most other indicators of potential seem to militate against SMEs becoming learning organisations in the environmental sense. They may be driven by the regulator and compliance rather than responding to customers, public opinion or other business sectors (Hillary, 1995). They may lack the resources (time, people, skills, funds) to monitor, anticipate and react to changes. Unlike large companies they may not be seeking to establish environmental leadership nor to influence the environmental agenda (Eden, 1996).

The survey

The empirical research method which provided the results discussed here is presented in detail elsewhere (Petts *et al.*, 1998, 1999; Petts, 2000a, 2000b). The distinctive features of the research were:

- A multi-method approach: face-to-face semi-structured interviews (57 in total); postal questionnaire (3090 posted, 389 respondents); and focus groups (50 participants), combining quantitative and qualitative analysis were used so as to counteract the deficiencies of individual techniques, to optimise access to the large and heterogeneous sector, and to ensure that both individual attitudes and corporate behaviour were identified. In total over 1000 individuals contributed to the research.
- Survey of both managers and non-management: a particularly good response from non-management was achieved, for example, representing 56 per cent of the questionnaire returns. The analysis revealed that non-management/management differences were the most significant, more significant than differences of response by industrial sector, location (rural, semi-urban or urban), size of company, sex or age. This suggests that the focus on SMEs in understanding attitudes to the environment may not be entirely appropriate or at least is inappropriately defined in terms of size alone. However, the research, in focusing on individuals, did not attempt to analyse actual organisational responses to the environment in detail and this may reveal greater size effects.

Individual attitudes to the environment

Public attitudes

We are interested first in the private views of individuals, management and non-management about the environment: i.e. their internalised views of the importance of environmentally friendly actions which might act as both triggers and supporters of environmental culture change. This stems from a reasonable assumption which characterises the public opinion research tradition, i.e. that environmental cognitions are the mainstay for environmentally friendly (or hostile) behaviours. The literature variably refers to environmental 'beliefs', 'concerns', 'attitudes', even 'paradigms' to refer to non-issue specific cognitive orientations. For ease here 'attitudes' are addressed.

Public concern about environmental issues relative to other issues of the day – fundamental policy issues such as health and social services, education, crime, unemployment, public transport – has been tracked in a series of surveys over a 10-year period (1986–1996/7) sponsored by the Department of the Environment, Transport and the Regions (DETR) (previously Department of the Environment). During the period there was an initial significant rise in the proportion of the population who viewed the environment as an important issue (8 per cent to 30 per cent between 1986–89), but thereafter the percentage has fallen back to 15 per cent (DETR, 1998). Having good personal health and a crime-free society are significantly more important to people than living in an agreeable environment.

However, as a specific personal issue rather than a comparative policy issue the environment generates considerable concern. Chemicals put into rivers and the sea record the highest concerns (63 per cent of people 'very worried'), toxic waste, radioactive waste, sewage and oil spills record scores between 52 per cent and 63 per cent. The next most significant issues are loss of wildlife, ozone layer depletion and traffic (40–45 per cent very worried). In general, responsibility for most of the global and national issues is placed with government (local or national). Industry's responsibilities are seen as primarily relating to pollution of rivers and to fumes and smoke from industrial processes

Surveys reveal different categories of problem which individuals identify: (a) the environment as a global issue, including global warming, loss of rainforests, loss of endangered species, issues which are remote from everyday life but which are perceived as having general societal and population impacts, (b) concern about the consequences of pollution for individual health, such as air pollution and asthma, (c) more local aesthetic issues to do with litter, road works, tree-planting, noise. However, in the national surveys the issues prompting comparatively least concern are the more local issues (in their effects and 'visibility') such as noise, vacant and derelict land, need for energy conservation and household waste disposal (<20 per cent very worried).

Attitudes predispose people to behave in a particular manner (Ajzen and Fishbein, 1977). However, the nature and extent of the relationship between attitudes and behaviour is complex. Attitudes and behaviour are affected by socio-demographic characteristics, including gender, education and family size (Stern and Dietz, 1994; Steel, 1996; National Consumers Council, 1997). Behaviour has been seen to be related to the ability to take action. Thus, whilst individuals perceive recycling to be beneficial this does not translate readily into personal actions without the support of structural factors such as accessible and easily usable recycling points. In the 1996/7 survey, 50 per cent of people reported separating paper for collection for recycling, most other materials being recycled less.

SME *attitudes*

Within the survey SMEs, the attitudes of both management and non-management were found to correlate closely with general public attitudes to the environment. Caution has to be expressed about any survey results in such an area, as people may regard it as socially unacceptable not to identify the environment as a concern. Nevertheless, 84 per cent of respondents to the questionnaire reported environmental concern. Air quality, the extinction of wildlife, water quality and traffic representing the most significant issues (Petts *et al.*, 1998), with no differences in levels of concern depending on whether people were in rural or urban locations.

Importantly, the views of management and non-management were largely the same. Only responses to 'global warming' and the 'extinction of wildlife' recorded any statistical difference between management and non-management, in both cases the latter recording a higher level of concern (for example 76 per cent of non-management were concerned about extinction of wildlife compared with 63 per cent of management).

In discussion, people often related their concerns to 'grounded' knowledge; for example, personal experience of declining fish stocks in a local river, incidence of asthma in their families, and loss of greenbelt around their town. Whilst people raised the full range of global, national and local environmental issues, there is no doubt that the latter found a more ready resonance than the national public surveys might suggest. Undoubtedly this was in part a reflection of the survey method. National surveys have a tendency to focus on policy-related issues, perhaps leading to an under-recording of local issues. If people are given the opportunity to talk about their concerns it is evident that the environment has both physical and aesthetic characteristics. As summarised by one employee – 'the environment is really everything around us – it is not one specific issue'.

People are concerned that the environment is not in good health, although the survey produced no overall agreement as to whether the state of the environment has improved or become worse, individuals using a range of indicators relating to personal experience. Given the broad dimensions of the environment which people referred to, it is possible that they actually found it difficult, or even irrelevant, to identify an 'overall condition' of the environment. Significantly, in support of other work on gender differences, female respondents were considerably more pessimistic about the state of the environment: 53 per cent considering that it had become worse compared with only 39 per cent of male respondents. Furthermore, the results indicated significant age differences in terms of concerns, younger people (under 25) expressing less concern than those over 55 years of age – 68 per cent expressing concerns in the former group compared with 93 per cent in the latter. In relation to communication within the workplace this may indicate a need to address the environment in different ways with different workers. It highlights a particular need to elicit people's concerns, interests and priorities as part of the communication process.

Discussion in the focus groups identified that elements of the environment which are of concern to people – such as noise, traffic pollution, and visual amenity – may not be directly regulated, therefore any corporate response will not be compliance driven but must rely on individuals' concerns and responses.

People found distinctions between the green environment and their work environment to be more practical than relevant, indeed, potentially confusing. As expressed by one non-management focus group attendee:

> I think that you tend to categorise into the living environment and the working environment, and the two do not necessarily mix at the same time. They should do . . . but what you think sometimes in the work environment, you contradict yourself when you are out of work . . . outside if you were honest with yourself you would say I should not do that because in the long term it is bad, inside work you might not bother.

Non-management in particular regarded a safe and clean working environment as a necessary precursor of organisational change in relation to the environment, in general. In one company, an arguably proactive management stance to the environment, was evident in a raw material purchasing policy, which focused on using timber from managed, sustainable forests. However, non-management could not conceive of this behaviour as being indicative of an environmentally positive culture as they considered the working conditions in the factory to be poor (fumes, sewage leaks, no provision of protective clothing being mentioned). When told that their company belonged to a major international environmental association, scepticism as to motive was voiced 'they must be being paid for being in it?' ' do they get a tax rebate for membership?' 'its probably the environmental manager who has joined, he has had to do everything on his own like that – the management are not interested'. This company illustrated the potential gulf between individual attitudes to the environment and the potential for environmental organisational learning if motivational and structural barriers are present.

Linking attitudes and workplace

Defining environmental responsibility

Both management and non-management believed that businesses have a social and moral responsibility to respond to the environment. People equated environmental responsibility with compliance with regulation, the majority defining the latter as a social and moral responsibility not merely an issue of avoiding prosecution. A pragmatic understanding that legislation could not provide for full environmental protection was linked to a view that environmental responsibility had broad dimensions. In the focus groups, issues of recycling and reduction of packaging; waste minimisation; consideration of transport use and change to diesel engines; the landscaping, general tidiness and look of a premises; the control of noise and smells within the workplace; maintaining a clean working environment, and generally being a 'good neighbour' were all connected with environmental responsibility. These issues matched closely with the personal definitions of the environment explored with individuals. In the main they are not issues subject to direct regulation. Clarification of what is important to people in terms of environmental policy focus within an organisation should help to define criteria of effective performance which have both corporate and individual salience.

Evidence of organisational learning

The elements of corporate culture relating to organisational learning – bottom-up as opposed to top-down management; sharing responsibility; building upon individual attitudes; open communication channels – were explored in the questionnaire through a set of mixed negative and positive scaled questions about the individual's own company.

In general, there was a positive attitude amongst individuals about their own companies in terms of management listening to individuals' ideas as to how to improve environmental performance. However, management were considerably more positive than non-management (66 per cent agreed that they listened to employees compared with 46 per cent of non-management). This was backed by the responses to a slightly different statement phrased in the negative mode 'my opinions cannot influence our company's impact on the environment' – 79 per cent of management disagreeing, 31 per cent of non-management. It was clear that managers perceived their organisational culture as a top-down mode of management, whereas most non-management were less supportive of this concept. Non-management employees referred to examples of their own suggestions – such as improving the recycling, storage and handling of oils; the reduction of packaging on products, and the use of recycled paper in the office – being taken up by management. However, these were explained as operation-focused issues as opposed to policy issues, the former perceived to be areas where it was easier for management to accept employee intervention than the latter.

Focus groups participants believed that employees are generally interested in environmental issues and amenable to changes to work practices and environmental initiatives:

'I think that the shopfloor are interested as people, as members of the human race, not specifically as an employee'

'I think that generally it is a very easy subject to raise support on'

'Its how you sell it – it has to be sold to the workforce'

'I think that they are interested but I do not see this as coming from the way that they work'

Although it was not evident that bottom-up initiatives were precluded, it was evident that the objectives of both management and employees needed to match and be supported by the organisational culture.

Although the majority of people were positive that their own company was aware of its environmental impact, there was a mixed response to whether individuals understood the environmental issues associated with their work and the ease with which it was possible to get people to understand the importance of environmental issues in their company. Difficulties were equated with:

(a) Communicating workplace relevance and promoting understanding of impact – e.g. 'we can't get people to understand the need to separate metal and paper in bins' (manager in an engineering firm); 'we need to be informed better about the ways in which we are polluting' (employee in a chemical company); 'many people do not understand what is meant by the environment, basic training is essential to help them to crystallise and develop personal attitudes in the business context' (engineering firm manager).

(b) The complexity of legislation – e.g. 'one negative aspect is the increasing volume and complexity of codes of practice/legislative, which are simply too difficult to interpret' (manager in textile company).

(c) The remoteness of the regulatory trigger from individual actions, particularly compared with health and safety legislation (Petts, 2000a) – e.g. 'health and safety in the main is more immediate and personal isn't it?' (textile company employee); 'the workers have been educated more about health and safety than environment – if something goes wrong the impact is immediate, not the same with the environment' (manager in chemical company).

(d) Changing long-established work practices – e.g. 'it's a habit-changing issue which is difficult when you have an older workforce' (employee in an engineering company); 'being concerned about the environment won't stop people tipping the bucket down the drain as usual' (employee in engineering firm);

(e) Pressures to change quickly – e.g. 'phased change is important, you achieve nothing by trying to thrust changes upon people' (a food company manager).

(f) Business competitive pressures which leave no time to identify how practices might change effectively – e.g. 'we are on piece-rate operations and speed of production is of the essence to the company, there isn't time to walk a bit further to a recycling bin' (textile company employee);

'being environmentally friendly does not always get the work out of the door' (engineering manager), 'if you have got pressure of work that will delay you taking any action' (engineering company employee).

In general SMEs are 'vulnerable' to non-compliance (Petts *et al.*, 1998) because of a lack of resources (time, skills, people, knowledge) and the pressures of business. Furthermore, other external triggers, particularly from customers in the supply chain, are not seen as being important as yet – only 32 per cent of managers agreed that customers were increasingly dictating performance.

Whilst management and non-management displayed few differences of opinion about the importance of the environment, the need for companies to respond, and the factors which may influence response, it appeared that the hypothesis that corporate responses may not reflect these individual attitudes was largely upheld. The survey portrayed a picture of relatively weak, or at least not fully developed, organisational learning amongst SMEs in general.

What makes proactive SMEs different?

This raises the question – what makes SMEs who are responding to the environment different? The research defined 'proactive' in terms of companies who were working towards implementation of an environmental management system – an overly simple criterion not least given the complexity of the concept of environmental responsibility that had been raised by the research, but one which made it relatively easy to identify companies. Whether it could be argued that these were organisations who had integrated concern and care for the environment into the firm's 'fundamental value system' (Roome, 1992; Welford, 1994) would require significantly greater organisation-specific analysis over time. Most importantly it would require specification of performance indicators which would allow for measurement, something currently missing from much of the business and the environment research.

The champion

The concept of 'the champion' – an individual who champions an environmental policy and its implementation – was introduced by both management and non-management and permeated the discussion in the proactive companies. In most cases the champion was a director or equivalent providing top management commitment, operationalised by adoption of an environmental policy. Most of the champions were still adopting a 'telling' leadership style (Hersey and Blanchard, 1988) with some beginning to move to a 'selling' style reflecting employee willingness to respond to the environment but a lack of full ability. The champion had to provide the starting point but then pass on the responsibility – 'the champion would say well I would like to see this covered, now go and discuss it with others and see what can be done' (comment by an engineering company employee).

The champion was important because the environment was not entirely a mainstream production issue, the environmental initiatives being followed not necessarily regulatory-focused – for example, energy consumption reduction programmes. We have to return here to the problem of defining environmental performance because it is clear that even in these firms it was not evident that they were fully compliant. Yet, should this debar a company from being defined as environmentally friendly? Major energy-reduction achievements might produce more tangible and measurable environmental benefits than compliance with regulations, for example, which require a company to use a registered carrier of waste.

Positive management attitude

The champions were not environmental specialists, all had acquired environmental responsibilities in addition to other functions. All were personally concerned about the environment but environmental performance was more than an ethical issue, it was being driven primarily by the market, the supply chain of six of the 12 companies being automotive manufacture. The environment was seen as having business benefits, potentially bringing direct financial spin-offs, a view which would vindicate government departments' approaches to encouraging waste minimisation for example.

Not once did discussions within the companies produce reference to sustainable development – the 'ultimate management vision' (Jones and Welford, 1997). For the research team it would have been extremely surprising if it had because, ignoring the definitional problems of the concept, the environment had not been discussed in such terms by any individual. Indeed the national survey of public attitudes (DETR, 1998) found that only 34 per cent of people had heard of the term and only 24 per cent thought that it was important to maintain the environment for future generations. Just as the language of sustainable development is not that of the public, so 'profits out, ethics in' is not the language of managers struggling to survive in competitive markets, with limited human and capital resources. Finding the direct business resonance of sustainable development concepts seemed difficult even for managers who had personal environmental concerns and even within companies whose environmental policies stressed 'care for our environment'. For these managers, environmental performance was primarily about reducing waste, increasing recycling and taking prompt action to comply with new legislation. It was highly pragmatic and directly business relevant, whilst still 'touching a nerve' (the comment of one managing director and champion) with personal attitudes.

Empowerment of employees

In the light of the motivational barriers identified earlier, the need to make the environment relevant to the workplace through the provision of requisite skills and knowledge and by appealing to employees' personal attitudes becomes paramount. SMEs have been perceived as lacking the capacity for environmental training (Hutchinson and Chaston, 1994). The meteoric rise in support and provision of information and training activities through national (e.g. Training and Enterprise Council) and European Regional Development Fund schemes has attempted to bridge the capacity gap. However, SMEs are often limited to local support networks (Bryson and Daniels, 1998) which may not offer quality training services.

The proactive SMEs had recognised the need for training, in one case all 100 employees attending external training provision (Petts *et al.*, 1998). Whilst the support to individual employees was important, with both personal (i.e. impact on people in their home life) and organisational learning evident, questions remained over longer-term development. The resources required to maintain training, including internalising it through in-house programmes and as part of individual employee development, were likely to be missing. One engineering company had extended their general training room to include environmental literature and learning material alongside what had been a primarily health and safety focus; however, this was the exception rather than the rule.

Empowerment requires not only knowledge but corporate structures to support the discursive and negotiative elements of the bottom-up approach. Flat management structures in 11 of the 12 companies had the potential to facilitate teamwork and management/non-management liaison, but this was equally true in most of the companies taking part in the research. In itself it will not provide support unless there is commitment to providing specific mechanisms for discussion. In the proactive companies regular team or cell briefings, a works forum, open-door management policies, company newsletters with environmental pages, were evident (Petts *et al.*, 1998). Joint health and safety and environment committees were also seen as important – as one employee commented 'this is really a genuine effort to get as much contribution from us as you do from the management. It is a joint effort . . . management respond to employee suggestions and explain why certain practices need to continue'. Such mechanisms provide for the movement of knowledge, information and ideas vertically and horizontally, actively through verbal communication, rather than passively through written means.

Conclusions

The research discussed here has gone some way to understanding management and non-management attitudes to the environment and environmental performance within SMEs. Positive personal environmental attitudes have the potential to act as both triggers and supporters of corporate response.

Individuals overwhelmingly support environmentally responsible actions, not just to meet regulatory imperatives but as an inherent component of modern responsible business practice. However, there is a need to define clearly what 'the environment' and 'environmental performance' encompasses, a premise that holds equally true for organisations, regulatory development and academic analysis. Certainly the terminology of sustainable development discussion does not seem to be an inherent part of individuals' language. This is not to suggest that it should be ignored, rather that effort will be needed to ensure that it resonates with personal attitudes and experience. Individual environmental concerns need to be elicited as part of developing corporate strategies. For example, the intertwining of the external green environment with the working environment in people's minds requires close attention. Failure to maintain a clean and safe working environment will act as a significant check upon potential external environmental initiatives in terms of employee support.

Environmental initiatives within businesses are triggered as much by market demands as by the regulator. Within organisations, barriers to, or checks upon, environmental performance are: (a) people-focused in terms of working habits and lack of understanding of environmental issues which are relevant to their work; (b) regulatory-focused in terms of complexity of legislation and the lack of individual responsibility compared with health and safety legislation; and (c) business-focused in terms of conflict with production and survival pressures.

The majority of SMEs would appear to have the first of the four dimensions of the learning organisation, i.e. individuals who hold positive attitudes about the environment. Many also have the capacity for reflection upon practice in that flat management structures should aid discourse. However, they appear to be some way from providing for employees and management to appreciate the relevance of their attitudes to their workplace functions and have as yet to develop an organisational context and prevailing social norms which support and reinforce positive attitudes.

Evidence of SMEs who are taking action to provide for the environment within their management structures points to the potential for organisational learning through environmental champions, positive perceptions of the business benefits of environmental performance and empowerment of managers and non-management through training, and opportunities for negotiation and discussion. SMEs often lack the functional divisions which act as a barrier to organisational learning; however, the barriers to environmental performance can serve to focus on the management team rather than advancing individuals unless there is genuine management support.

The environmental champion combined with (and supported by) a corporate culture which values the individual, devolves responsibility and supports knowledge acquisition and distribution, is not a reflection of size of company or sector of operation but inherently of culture. Regulation, or more likely market pressures, may drive a corporate response, even the appointment of a champion, but its success will ultimately be dependent upon the internal capacity for response.

Acknowledgements

The research was funded by the UK ESRC Global Environmental Change Research Programme (award reference no. L320353210) and conducted over the period December 1995–December 1997. The support of ESRC is acknowledged. The contribution of fellow members of the research team: Mr Andrew Herd (research associate responsible for much of the data gathering and analysis), Dr Simon Gerrard (now University of East Anglia), and Mr Chris Horne are also gratefully acknowledged.

References

Argyris, C. and Schon, D. (1978) *Organisational Learning: A Theory of Action Perspective*. London: Addison-Wesley.
Azjen, I. and Fishbein, M. (1977) Attitude–behaviour relations: a theoretical analysis and review of empirical research, *Psychological Bulletin*, 84, 888–918.
Barrett, S. and Murphy, D. (1995) The implications of the corporate environmental policy process for human resources management. *Greener Management International*, 10, 49–68.
Bryson, J. and Daniels, P.W. (1998) Busines link, string ties and the walls of silence: small and medium-sized enterprises and external business-service expertise. *Environment and Planning C: Government and Policy*, 16, 265–280
Cox, S.J. and Cox, T.R. (1996) *Safety Systems and People*. Oxford: Butterworth-Heinemann.
DETR (Department of the Environment, Transport and the Regions) (1998) *Digest of Environmental Protection and Water Statistics*, No. 20. London: HMSO.
Dodge, J. (1997) Reassesing culture and strategy: environmental improvement, structure, leadership and control. In R. Welford (ed.) *Corporate Environmental Management 2: Culture and Organisations*. London: Earthscan.
Eden, S. (1996) *Environmental Issues and Business: Implications of a Changing Agenda*. Chichester: John Wiley and Sons.
Gladwin, T.N. (1993) The meaning of greening: a plea for organisational theory. In K. Fischer and J. Schot (eds). *Environmental Strategies for Industry: International Perspectives on Research Needs and Policy Implications*, Washington DC: Island Press.
Halme, M. (1997) Developing an environmental culture through organisational change and learning. In R. Welford (ed.) *Corporate Environmental Management 2: Culture and Organisations*. London: Earthscan.
Hersey, P. and Blanchard, K.H. (1988) *Management of Organisational Behaviour: Utilising Human Resources* (5th edn). Engelwood Cliffs, NJ: Prentice Hall.
Hillary, R. (1995) *Small Firms and the Environment – A Groundwork Status Report*. Birmingham: Groundwork Foundation.
Huber, G.P. (1991) Organisational learning: the contributing processes and the literatures. *Organisation Science*, 2, 88–109.
Hutchinson, A. and Chaston, I. (1994) Environmental management in Devon and Cornwall's small and medium-sized enterprise sector. *Business Strategy and the Environment*, 3 1), 15–22.

Jones, D. and Welford, R. (1997) Culture change, pluralism and participation. In R. Welford (ed) *Corporate Environmental Management 2: Culture and Organisations*. London: Earthscan.

National Consumers Council (1997) *Consumers and the Environment*. London: National Consumers Council.

Petts, J. (2000a) The regulator-regulated relatioship and environmental protection: perceptions in small and medium-sized enterprises. *Environmental and Planning C: Government and Policy*, 18, 191–206.

—— (2000b) SMEs and environmental compliance: attitudes amongst management and non-management. In. R. Hillary (ed.) *Small and Medium-Sized Enterprises and the Environment*. Sheffield: Greenleaf Publishing.

Petts, J., Herd, A., and O'hEocha, M. (1998) Environmental responsiveness, individuals and organisational learning: SME experience' *Journal of Environmental Planning and Management*, 41(6), 711–730.

Petts, J., Herd, A., Gerrard, S., and Horne, C. (1999) The climate and culture of environmental compliance within SMEs, *Business Strategy and the Environment*, 8 (1), 14–30.

Pidgeon, N. (1991) Safety culture and risk management in organisations. *Journal of Cross-Cultural Psychology*, 22, 129–140.

Post, J. and Altman, B. (1994) Managing the environmental change process; barriers and opportunities. *Journal of Organisational Change Management*, 7 (4), 64–81.

Roome, N. (1992) Developing Environmental Management Strategies. *Business Strategy and the Environment,* 1 (1), 11–24.

Senge, P.M. (1990) *The Fifth Discipline: The Art and Practice of the Learning Organisation*. London: Doubleday.

Shrivastava, P. (1995) Ecocentric management for a risk society. *Academy of Management Review*, 20 (1), 118–137.

Stead, W.E. and Stead, J.E. (1992) *Management for a Small Planet*. Newbury Park: Sage Publications.

Steel, B.S. (1996) Thinking globally and acting locally? Environmental attitudes, behaviour and activism. *Journal of Environmental Management*, 47, 27–36.

Stern, R. and Dietz, T. (1994) The value basis of environmental concern. *Journal of Social Issues*, 50, 65–84.

Welford, R. (1992) Linking quality and the environment, a strategy for the implementation of environmental management systems. *Business Strategy and the Environment*, 1, 25–43.

—— (1994) *Environmental Strategy and Sustainable Development: The Corporate Challenge for the 21st Century*. London: Routledge.

Welford, R. and Gouldson, A. (1993) *Environmental Management and Business Strategy*. London: Pitman.

Wolter, T., Bouman, M. and Peeters, M. (1995) Environmental management and employment. *Greener Management International*, 11, 64–71

10 Agents of change in corporate 'greening'

Case studies in water and electricity utilities

Anja Schaefer and Brian Harvey

Central to most publications on business and the natural environment is the notion of change from current, largely unsustainable business practices to more environmentally responsible ones. This process is often called 'corporate greening'. But while the need for change is almost unanimously acknowledged, the means by which such change is to be achieved are less obvious or uncontroversial. Yet, these means of achieving the desired change are clearly important if progress in making human economic activity more ecologically sustainable is to be made.

Change in organisations in general is a major topic in strategic management, organisational development, corporate culture, organisational learning and other areas of management scholarship. A detailed discussion of this literature on organisational and strategic change would be beyond the scope of this chapter. Here we are focusing particularly on two questions: (1) where is the impetus for 'green' organisational change located and (2) who are the agents of such change? We examine these questions in water and electricity utilities.

Wilson (1992) suggests that there are three main levels at which organisational change can be located and analysed: (a) the individual member of an organisation, (b) the organisation as a holistic entity and (c) the wider social and economic context in which the organisation is embedded.

The tone of the literature on business and the environment is generally managerialist and voluntaristic, assuming that managers have discretion to change the strategic course of their companies if they so wish. This implies a relatively strong focus on individuals as agents of change, the importance of ecological vision and leadership by top managers (e.g. Steger, 1993; Shrivastava and Hart, 1995; Zeffane et al., 1995), and the role of environmental attitudes and/or actions of individual managers (Post and Altman, 1994; Stead and Stead, 1994; Gladwin et al, 1995; Fineman, 1996).

However, changes at the organisational and wider social and economic level are also considered. Thus, change at the organisational level features in many publications, including Roome (1992), Welford (1992), Gladwin (1993), Shrivastava (1994), Starik and Rands (1995), Zeffane et al. (1995), although this concern with the organisational level does not always include much analysis or theory on the way in which such organisational change would happen. Finally, wider institutional and socio-economic factors are frequently mentioned as drivers of organisational greening but only a relatively small number of publications make this a focus of their study (Starik and Rands, 1995; Garrod and Chadwick, 1996; Rennings *et al.*, 1997).

Methodology

The purpose of this research[1] was to give a detailed account of the strategic and organisational change processes by which a more comprehensive engagement with environmental issues is developed in six companies. For this purpose we used a comparative, qualitative case study methodology. Multiple case studies have the advantage of combining a relatively detailed understanding of the interpretations and perceptions of individual respondents and the processes within individual companies, with the opportunity to study the impact of forces outside the organisational boundaries through comparison between different companies and industries. The multiple case study methodology chosen here thus allowed us to study agents of change and change processes at all three levels identified above: (a) socio-economic and institutional; (b) organisational; and (c) individual.

The main data gathering method consisted of qualitative interviews with managers in different functions and at different levels in the company hierarchy.

Most interviews lasted between one and two hours and were carried out at the company's premises. The interviews followed a relatively loose semi-structured schedule. By this we ensured that topics that we considered to be important prima facie – such as the role of top management and the environmental function, employee involvement measures, interactions with external stakeholders and others – were covered in the interviews, but allowed sufficient flexibility for our respondents to talk about those issues that they considered important or relevant.

Most interviews were tape recorded and later fully transcribed. Only in a small number of cases was this not possible as respondents were not comfortable in the presence of the tape recorder, or there was too much interference from outside noises. In these cases extensive notes were taken during the interview and written up immediately afterwards. The interviews were then analysed separately by the two researchers and interpretations compared. In the analysis we were guided in part by the preconceived topics we had set out to investigate. However, several issues that we had not considered previously were brought up by the respondents, so that we then also used a more grounded approach, identifying central themes as arising from the data. Each case study was analysed separately first and systematic comparisons carried out afterwards.

The water and electricity industries in the UK

Both the water and sewerage and the electricity industries in the UK were privatised in 1989. Two separate industry regulators were created to safe-guard the interests of consumers and the public in what remained, essentially, monopoly industries. Prior to privatisation, the public water authorities had not only the function to supply drinking water and treat waste water, but also to regulate the aquatic environment. This function was taken away from the newly privatised water and sewerage companies in 1989 and given to a new environmental regulator, the National Rivers Authority (NRA). This was later merged with other environmental regulatory bodies to form the Environment Agency (EA), now the main environmental regulator in the United Kingdom. Each of the principal activities within the the electricity industry (generation, transmission, and distribution and supply) were allocated to separate companies with the hope of developing a competitive market for electricity within England and Wales.

In this study we have deliberately chosen two industries, water and electricity, that are not normally considered to be highly polluting. Highly polluting industries, such a chemicals, or pulp and paper, have been exposed to concerted regulatory and public pressure for a number of years, which makes environmental policy and performance central to their business and has made them the focus of many empirical studies of corporate greening. However, the aggregate environmental impact of other industries may be more important, or at least as important, in the long run. How and why firms develop environmental policies and practices in the absence of extreme outside pressure is likely to be more instructive about the ways in which the majority of firms and industries can be (or are) brought to greater environ-mental responsibility than studies of highly pressured industries.

While not top polluters, the two industries have significant environ-mental impacts. These are more direct in the case of the water industry, which has been heavily criticised for a variety of negative environmental impacts, such as pollution of rivers and coastal waters by sewage effluent, the dumping of raw sewage at sea, and, more recently, over-abstraction of fresh water from rivers and aquifers. Electricity distribution companies have fewer, although not insignificant direct environmental impacts, mostly through oil and chemical pollution from underground cables networks and transformers. However, their most significant environmental impact may well lie in the product they sell, i.e. electricity, and the associated problems of pollution at generation, depletion of natural resources, and CO_2 emissions.

In this chapter we present case studies of the corporate greening process in six UK water and electricity utilities. Water 1 is a water and sewerage company that has also developed or acquired a number of other businesses, including a waste management division, an environmental consulting business, and a water supply company. Water 2 is also a water and sewerage company which has acquired a large waste management company. Electricity

1 and Electricity 2 are both electricity supply and distribution companies (Regional Electricity Companies, RECs), which have developed a moderate amount of generation capacity as well. Multi-utility is a utility, formed through the merger of a water and sewerage and a regional electricity company. Water 3 is the water business of another multi-utility company, formed in the same way. Water 1, Electricity 1 and Electricity 2 have recently been taken over by foreign companies, whereas the other three companies – Multi-utility , the multi-utility owning Water 3, and Water 2 – remain independent companies.

Change and the individual

The individual as change agent features prominently in both the general literature on strategic and organisational change and much of the environmental management literature. Environmental management is thought to be more successful the stronger top management commitment to it is, the better qualified and well regarded the environmental manager is, and the more, and more influential, environmental 'champions' the company possesses. This emphasis on individual change agents reflects a strong, though controversial tradition in management thinking, which stresses the importance of strong leadership in determining a company's fortunes. The 'change masters' are a popular feature of mainstream strategic management writing, fitting into a 'classical' view of strategic change as the deliberate and planned pursuit of the company's top managers.

This is, however, not an uncontroversial view. 'Evolutionary' and 'processual' models of strategic change have questioned the efficacy, and even sheer possibility of deliberate strategy making. They have also reduced the importance of individual leaders as strategy and change makers, seeing instead any impetus for change either in external market forces or in the complex political and cultural make-up of the organisation.

Let us now see how the role of individuals as change agents in the corporate greening process was perceived by our respondents in the six companies. Individuals seen as particularly important in this respect included (a) top managers, (b) environmental managers and other people with 'environment in the job title' and (c) environmental 'champions' in any position.

The role of top management

The extent to which top managers were regarded as playing an important role in the company's greening efforts varied. At Water 1, Electricity 1 and Water 3, top management was said to have played a permissive rather than a facilitating role. Chairman, chief executive and other top managers in these companies were seen to support environmental management and allow systems to be developed at a lower level but took little active role in moving greening forward.

At Electricity 1, top management was not seen actively to push environmental issues although they were said to take a 'benign interest', even though the chairman was also on the board of the Environment Agency. None the less he was not seen to personally move environmental management in the company. This is partly explained by the role of a chairman, particularly a part-time one, which does not generally include direct involvement in the company's management. However, many respondents in Electricity 1 felt that people were aware that their chairman was on the board of the Environment Agency and that this fact in itself motivated them to act in accordance with environmental policy and guidelines. In the words of one respondent: 'It would be very foolish for any member of staff to embarrass the chairman on the environmental front'.

In the other companies, the role of the chief executive was seen as more crucial – in the sense that a CEO could play an active role in moving environmental issues forward, or hold environmental management back through lack of interest or even hostility. At the water company which is now part of Multi-utility, the previous CEO was considered to have hindered any efforts to establish formal environmental management. While some managers wanted the establishment of an environmental policy and subsequent initiatives, these only became possible when a new CEO was appointed who saw environmental issues as more important. At Electricity 2 the situation was similar. A previous top management team was reported to have appointed an environmental manager and approved an environment policy but had blocked the publication of an environmental report for fear of publicity if certain negative environmental impacts, such as oil leakage from underground electricity cables, were disclosed. It took a new CEO, supported by a new chairman, to change the situation. The new CEO told us that he regarded environmental issues, together with health and safety, as important business issues. He supported and facilitated a number of new initiatives on this front, such as the publication of the first environmental report (including disclosure of oil leakages) and a company-wide awareness raising scheme. Environmentally conscious managers further down in the company hierarchy felt that the CEO's interest gave them significant support in their efforts to green their parts of the organisation.

At Water 2 the situation was slightly different, in so far as none of our respondents reported top management resistance to environmental management. Even so, the support and interest of the CEO were seen as highly important in the company's greening efforts. Respondents felt that, while a previous CEO had been very supportive of environmental issues, the new one was even more pro-environmental. He had officially listed environmental leadership as one of the three key performance indicators for the company (next to customer service and quality) and given talks for all staff on their importance. Staff took this as a sign that environmental issues were considered important and that they were expected to put some effort into environmental management.

The role of other managers

Below the level of the CEO, other senior managers could play an important role. It was generally felt that, where divisional and department managers and directors did not consider environmental issues as important, relatively little environmental progress would be made. Conversely, a committed senior or middle manager could often make a significant difference.

In Multi-utility much of the environmental initiative was seen to emanate from the group technical director. He was reported to have tried for years to establish formal environmental management but was not able to get any-where due to the lack of interest from the CEO. After a change of CEO the technical director renewed his efforts and managed to establish an environ-mental policy, a central health, safety and environment team, and a pro-gramme of environmental policy implementation throughout the company. He was seen as the key environmental champion in the top management team, feeling strongly that bad environmental credentials, from which the company suffered, were a significant problem for a water company.

At middle management level committed individuals could also achieve significant progress. At Electricity 2 the Customer Services Manager had a personal interest in environmental issues (he was a keen bird watcher) and was instrumental in setting up the first environmental policy for the company and in establishing the post of group environmental manager. While no longer as involved in group environmental policy, this manager had then spent significant time and energy on reducing the environmental impact of the customer services department, a department that was regarded by others within the company as exemplary. Similar stories were told in other companies of committed managers making a difference in their own part of the organisation, e.g. a customer services manager in Electricity 1 and a very committed area sewage works manager in Water 2.

The role of environmental champions

Environmental champions could emerge at all levels in the organisation including non-managerial positions. They would first tackle perceived environmental problems in the part of the organisation where they had some direct control, but if their contribution and expertise were recognised their influence could become wider. The environmental issues they tackled were often specific problems, such as waste minimisation or wildlife management on a particular site. If they were successful in tackling a specific issue on their site they were often asked to share their expertise with others in the company, or even manage that issue company wide.

An employee at one of the depots of Electricity 2 became interested in the issue of waste handling, waste segregation and waste minimisation. With the encouragement of the site manager he set up a waste management scheme for his depot and later volunteered to organise a waste management system for the entire company. Another employee in the water supply side of Water 1, who was very keen on wildlife, started some improvement schemes at the sites where he worked. He became known for his interest and commitment and was nominated 'environmental champion' for his area of the company, helping other people on different sites to instigate wildlife improvement schemes. After the company structure was changed to a functional one he no longer officially fulfilled the role of champion for the geographical area but continued to be asked for, and give, advice on an informal basis – mostly in his free time.

Environmental managers as change agents

So far, we have omitted from this discussion those individuals who, by virtue of their position in the company, are expected to foster organisational greening, i.e. environmental managers and other members of the environmental function. Much of the environmental management literature agrees that a 'good' environmental manager is vital in greening the organisation. All the companies in our study employed a full-time environmental manager (the precise title varied) and usually a number of further people with an official environmental brief – either full-time or part-time. The central environmental teams in all six companies were very small, sometimes comprising a single individual, never more than three. Most of the companies also had designated environmental co-ordinators (again, the actual titles varied between the companies) at divisional or departmental level. These individuals occasionally had a full-time environmental brief, but more commonly this was only one of their roles. Additionally, all the water companies had at least one full-time wildlife conservation officer to deal with their statutory obligations regarding conservation, recreation and access to their extensive (and often ecologically valuable) land holdings. A full discussion of the environmental function would be beyond the scope of this chapter. We will therefore limit ourselves to a relatively brief look at some of the ways in which environmental managers and co-ordinators can, and are expected to, effect change.

In all six companies the central environmental manager was charged with developing environmental policy and often with setting up systems for the implementation of such policy. Yet, it became clear from our interviews that the change potential of environmental managers lay less in these formal tasks and more in their ability to persuade and convince other people in the organisation. One respondent described the environmental manager as 'the environmental conscience of the company'. Depending on background and temperament, environmental managers used different persuasion tactics. Thus the environmental manager at Electricity 1 used a business-focused approach, emphasising business risks accruing from a 'less than professional approach' to environmental issues. The environmental manager at Water 1 relied more on a deep-ecology discourse, less concerned with reducing business risks than with promoting genuine ecological concern. While respondents in Electricity 1 found it generally quite easy to identify with the environmental manager's business-focused approach, some respondents in Water 1 had more difficulty in accepting the deep ecology perspective. None the less, both companies seemed to have achieved significant improvements in environmental performance (although this is notoriously difficult to measure). One difference is that the environmental manager at Electricity 1 seemed to feel largely satisfied with the environmental progress the company was making, whereas his counterpart at Water 1 said he often felt frustrated at what he perceived to be slow progress and a lack of true ecological concern by other members of the organisation.

The organisation as the locus for change

Individuals are constrained in their actions by virtue of belonging to organis-ations. Membership of an organisation imposes roles and behaviours on individuals which may be quite different from those shown by the individual in his/her private role. There are two main ways in which organisations take on a meaning of their own, beyond the summed meanings of individuals within them: (1) organisations are given coherence and the capacity to act through a series of tangible aspects, such as their structures, policies, goals, objectives and plans, and their management systems; (2) on a more intang-ible level organisations derive cohesion and a sense of purpose from their organisational culture.

Both of these aspects have found recognition in the environmental manage-ment and organisational greening literature. The tangible aspects are stressed in environmental management standards such as ISO 14000, BS 7750 or EMAS (Eco Management and Auditing Scheme), which have been widely written about. The need for an organisational culture with strong environ-mental values, where environmental effects are considered as a matter of course in everyday decisions and actions, has been stressed by most authors writing about business and the environment. Adherents of deep ecology have usually concentrated on this aspect of organisational change. All the companies in our study experienced at least some change related to environmental issues. At the most basic level all companies had introduced written environmental policies and put in place some sort of environmental management structure, albeit of varying degrees of sophistication. By the end of our research period the companies had also all produced at least one, and at most three, annual environmental performance reports.

Environmental policies

Developing an environmental policy was usually the first step a company took once it was decided to put environmental management on a more formal basis. All the companies in our study had had one, often for several years, although Multi-utility had just developed its policy and was about to launch it formally. Most companies had fairly broad environmental policies, setting out general guidelines and principles but few specific aims. Managers at Multi-utility told us that this needed to be so in order to have a policy that would fit the diverse environmental impacts of a water and an electricity company plus a number of international operations. On the other hand, Electricity 1 had developed a much more detailed environmental policy, which ran to three pages and gave detailed aims and objectives for specific impacts.

Environmental management systems

The six companies varied in their approach to the introduction of an environmental management system. At one end of the spectrum, Water 1 had been one of the pilot companies for the BS 7750 standard as adapted to water and sewerage operations. It had obtained accreditation to BS 7750 for its sewage works in one operating area in 1995 and was looking to obtaining accreditation (to ISO 14000) for all the other areas in due course. At the other end of the spectrum, the environmental manager at Electricity 2 told us she did not believe in environmental management systems *per se*, as they were too bureaucratic and produced little but superfluous paperwork. There were therefore no plans to introduce a formal environmental management system, let alone seek accreditation to BS 7750, ISO 14000 or EMAS. The other companies fell somewhere between these two. Electricity 1 had an environmental management system, modelled on BS 7750, for its electricity distribution business but initially no accreditation was sought. Then, following the building up of some power generation capacity, it was decided to extend the environmental management system to the entire company. Finally, after two years, feeling at top management level was that accreditation to ISO 14000 was both desirable in the increasingly competitive electricity market and achievable within a further two years. The other companies had introduced parts of standard environmental management systems but saw no real benefit in accreditation.

The most important question regarding environmental policies and management systems, and one that was frequently raised by our respondents, is whether they produced any 'real' change in company behaviour and environmental performance. It is impossible to answer this question conclusively, but we have some indication from the opinions of the managers involved. Managers in all companies thought that an environmental policy was an important first statement to their stakeholders. In terms of their effectiveness to promote change within the organisation, environmental policies and management systems received a somewhat mixed response. Virtually everyone we spoke to felt that policies in themselves did not change performance and that implementation was the tricky part. The extent to which policies were seen as generally useful, varied. Managers at Multi-utility , which had only just adopted a new, group-wide policy, agreed that this was an important first step towards more effective environmental management, that it would be embarrassing for the company not to deliver on it, and that stakeholders, including the company's own employees, could use the policy as a lever to demand more environmental action. These sentiments were echoed by many across the companies but there were some dissenting voices. One environmental manager felt that the leverage one could exert through the policy was quite limited. If he tried to use the policy to push forward schemes and changes which went beyond what top management saw as necessary or desirable they could, and would, tell him that they 'never intended the policy to cover this particular issue and he should go and change it'. A manager in Water 2 felt that there was a danger that policies and protocols could become a substitute for action, rather than sparking it: 'Too many protocols, not enough action'.

While an environmental policy is obviously part of an environmental management system, the ability of environmental management systems to prompt change was evaluated separately from that of the policy in isolation. Environmental management systems were seen most positively by managers in those companies that had adopted one, and most sceptically in those that had not and had no intention of doing so. Managers at Water 1 were the most positive about the environmental management system's capacity to induce change. They felt that ISO 14000 had been turned into an 'iron procedure' for the operation of sewage works and that by adopting it they had greatly reduced the likelihood of environmental incidents and thus prosecution by the Environment Agency.[2] They pointed to the fact that Water 1 was now one of the companies with the best prosecution record in the industry as proof that the environmental management system had worked for them. As a word of caution, however, the environmental manager also said that the adoption of the environmental management system had only led to 'real' improvement in areas covered by environmental legislation and that the 'Effects Register' (part of an environmental management system) developed by the company did not cover many wider, non-regulated, impacts.

Environmental performance report

All six companies had produced at least one, and at most three, annual environmental performance reports. In all cases the publication of the first report was preceded by some soul-searching on what to include and how to present the information. The most difficult question in some companies had been whether to report on negative environmental impacts, particularly where these impacts were little known outside the industry. In the electricity industry one such impact was leakage from oil-filled underground electricity cables, probably the most significant direct environmental impact of an electricity distribution company. At Electricity 2 there had been much discussion about whether it was in the interest of the company to disclose this significant pollution. The publication of the first report was delayed by several months as top management was unhappy about this aspect of the report. It was a new top management team that finally gave the go-ahead.

A common problem in producing environmental reports concerned, not the willingness, but the ability, to disclose environmental effects. Managers told us that they often found it impossible to include quantitative information on certain environmental impacts simply because this type of information had never been collected. The process of reporting thus brought about an important change as it forced companies to collect more systematic data about their environmental performance. Managers, particularly in companies that had produced several reports and built up an environmental information system to aid the process, said that they now had a much better understanding of the company's environmental effects and were beginning to collate trend data. Virtually all of our respondents felt that one could only tackle environmental impacts that one could measure and increased quantitative information would be an important step in environmental improvement.

As important as the tangible aspects of organisational greening described above are the intangible aspects of change. These have to do with the culture of an organisation, shared beliefs and attitudes that give an organisation cohesion and a joint sense of purpose. In the analysis of our research data we found three aspects of culture that were important in illuminating change at the organisational level: (1) the overall culture of the organisation, (2) staff morale and enthusiasm, and (3) attitudes towards environmental issues, or what might be termed the 'environmental culture'.

In terms of overall culture, it is important to stress the fact that the organisations used to be public services. In this respect they may be different from typical large companies in the private sector. Many of the managers we spoke to, particularly at top and senior management level, spoke of a significant change in culture since privatisation in 1989, describing how what they called a 'civil service attitude' was slowly giving way to a more customer and market oriented attitude.

Changing the culture

The chief executive of Electricity 2 told us that the company used to have a culture in which the most important task was seen as 'keeping the lights on' and if society wanted electricity it had to accept some of the environmental and safety risks attached to this process. The CEO felt that this was slowly changing towards a culture where it was realised that the company had to take responsibility for such risks and had to try and minimise them. A similar theme was taken up by a senior manager at Electricity 2. He felt that in the past the company had had a civil service attitude. The government was thought to have assumed ultimate responsibility for the risks – including environmental ones – of running an electricity distribution operation. And as an electricity distributor they had seen themselves as a mere extension of the generators who were ultimately responsible for any pollution. This culture, he felt, had slowly given way to one where the company had a perception of itself as a separate corporate entity, which was taking responsibility for the business and societal risks it incurred.

Privatisation had also brought with it, according to many of our respondents, an orientation towards shareholder value and profitability which was absent in the old public water and electricity boards. Particularly, people who had been with the respective organisation for many years tended to find this, and the simultaneously developing customer orientation, problematic. Part of the old civil service mentality was that the *raison d'être* of the organisation was to perform a service to society. Many managers we spoke to still held and valued this attitude. Some of these managers expressed some concern at the new focus on shareholder value and profitability.

Privatisation had not only an orientation towards customers and shareholders, but also a significant restructuring of the organisation. Many companies had lost large numbers of staff. Staff levels at Electricity 2 had decreased by over a third. This brought with it a sharper pace of work and more responsibility for the remaining staff. The industries also saw some significant merger and takeover activity. These had brought, or were expected to bring, further reductions in staffing levels and more restructuring, along with increased insecurity and low morale.

Changing attitudes to environmental issues

Attitudes towards environmental issues – or what could be termed the environmental culture – were also changing. In part this was a consequence of the other changes in culture mentioned above. In our interviews we could detect two opposite streams of thinking, although these were not necessarily neatly separated between companies or even individual respondents. One stream of thought was that the organisation was now more aware of environmental issues, and that environmental management and concern was slowly becoming embedded in the general corporate culture. Respondents felt that this was in part due to the signals sent by a number of tangible measures described in the previous sections, such as a written environmental policy, a formal environmental management system and regular environmental reporting. To a varying extent, the companies had instigated deliberate measures to increase staff awareness of environmental matters. Thus Electricity 2 had run a series of health, safety and environment conferences for the entire company. Managers there felt that this large scale effort had sent the right message, i.e. that these issues were important, and reported a greater motivation for environmental management afterwards. Water 2 had perhaps the most comprehensive environmental staff involvement programme, consisting of regular annual awards for green projects and voluntary green groups throughout the company. The CEO had also given a series of talks to which the entire workforce was invited and where he stressed the importance of environment as one of the three main pillars of the business.

The other stream of thinking was that, while there was more talk about environmental issues, and companies had introduced all sorts of formal measures, the underlying business culture was still largely dominated by operational matters, especially the newly important cost and revenue concerns. Thus, a number of managers at Water 1 and at Water 2 said that, while the company was formally very committed to environmental issues and had introduced a number of environmental management measures, this was not necessarily driven by deep environmental concern. Rather, it was wish to avoid prosecutions (Water 1, through the introduction of ISO 14000) or to build a favourable public image. Some managers at Water 2 regarded the effort of top management to gain environmental awards as motivated by public relations rather than the desire for substantial environmental benefit.

Environmental management as a morale booster

A number of our respondents stressed that environmental management could in itself be good for staff morale and commitment. There was a general view, particularly in the water industry, that many people had originally joined the then publicly-owned Water Boards because they were interested in environmental issues and this work was an opportunity to work for environmental clean-up. These employees, estimated to be between 20 and 30 per cent of the workforce, were naturally attracted and motivated by greater company commitment to environmental management. Although an electricity company would not normally attract such a high proportion of environmental enthusiasts, managers at Electricity 1 also reported that staff were motivated by environmental issues and that the company's greater engagement in these issues over the last few years had, in their opinion, led to an improvement of staff morale.

Change at the wider social and economic level

Organisations do not operate in isolation but are embedded in a wider social and economic context. The interaction between this wider context and the organisation has been conceptualised in various ways. 'Classical' thinking on strategy often emphasises the need for a strategic fit of the organisation with forces in its external environment, and focuses mostly on deliberate change within the organisation to bring about this fit. 'Evolutionary' theories of strategy see the company much more at the mercy of largely uncontrollable external market forces, whereas scholars in the 'systemic' school of strategy stress the fact that the wider environment comprises more than economic aspects, and that managers are strongly influenced by the social, cultural and political context in which they operate. The literature on environmental management and organisational greening has also recognised factors outside the company's boundaries as impacting on its greening efforts. Naturally changes in the natural environment take a prime place in most of these publications, but changing legislative, public and even competitive pressures for greater environmental engagement are also usually mentioned.

There is a large potential number of factors in the wider social and economic environment that one could consider. In our research three aspects became particularly salient: (1) government influence through legislation and regulation, (2) public opinion and (3) changes occurring at a competitive and industry level.

Managers in all six companies told us that environmental legislation that applied to them had increased significantly in recent years and that compliance with the law was one of the major drivers for the environmental management efforts. This was an issue particularly for the water industry, which is specifically subject to extensive environmental legislation such as the European bathing water and urban waste water directives. Water companies as a whole had had a poor compliance record and some companies had been subject to numerous prosecutions on that account. Reducing the number of prosecutions and the resulting bad publicity was therefore a major concern for the water companies in our study. The electricity distribution companies were subject to much less specific environmental legislation. Compliance with the law, while not immaterial, was consequently a much less powerful driver for environmental management in these companies. For instance, several managers at Electricity 1 told us that meeting legislative requirements was the minimum environmental standard that they must achieve, but that their aim was to achieve significantly higher standards.

Privatisation of the two industries in 1989 had brought with it a new regulatory regime, where much of what the companies did was influenced or even decided by the industry regulators. The decisions of the regulators had a significant impact on environmental management as well, particularly in the water industry.

Industry regulators and pricing levels

By setting price levels the regulators in effect determine expenditure to a large extent. The price levels set take account of expenditures that the companies have to make in order to fulfil their legal obligations among others. In the water industry, the years after privatisation saw a rapid increase of sewerage charges to the customer, which were agreed with the regulator in order to ensure that the operations of the companies could be brought up to the standards of national and European environmental legislation, which had not been the case in the past. This resulted in a very large expenditure programme by the companies, whereby sewage works and other installations were upgraded. The electricity distribution industry did not face a comparable backlog in meeting environmental legislation and the regulator had been more concerned with maintaining or even reducing consumer prices, almost from privatisation onwards. After several years of increasing consumer prices in order to meet these expenditure requirements, the water industry regulator was also seen to become more concerned with keeping prices level for consumers.

A number of managers, particularly in the water industry, felt that this cap on their expenditure levels could be in conflict with environmental goals and the expectations of both the public and the environmental regulator, the Environment Agency, who would like them to go beyond the requirements of the law in speeding up environmental clean-up. However, one or two dissenting voices suggested that the amounts of money agreed for environmental expenditure were already very large and that it could be difficult to spend all the money in a sensible way in any given year.

Environmental regulation had also changed in recent years. The re-structuring of environmental regulation in a single regulatory body, the Environment Agency, has already been mentioned. Many of our respondents felt that this restructuring, together with the larger body of environmental legislation that it had to enforce, had led to a much higher workload for the Agency. Managers thought that the Agency did not have the resources to police industry thoroughly and was consequently somewhat dependent on companies' goodwill in supplying necessary information. Perhaps partly because of this the Agency was reported to take a largely non-adversarial stance with the companies in our study and managers did not feel they were under particularly heavy pressure from those quarters.

Public opinion was another strong driver of environmental management in our case study companies. Privatisation of the water and electricity industries had been highly controversial, and in the early 1990s the water industry in particular was subject to a lot of critical media coverage concerning issues such as high executive salaries ('fat cats') and rising consumer prices, water shortages with hose pipe bans and the threat of stand pipes during the drought summers of 1994 and 1995, high leakage rates from water mains, and a number of environmental incidents. Therefore public opinion of the water companies was at times felt to be quite hostile. This did not apply to the same extent to the electricity industry, which had attracted considerably less bad press coverage, but managers there were also highly concerned about their public image. Managers also felt that privatisation, and all the concomitant scrutiny of the newly founded water and electricity companies, had coincided with a generally much higher environmental awareness by the public and interest in companies' environmental performance. Good environmental management and performance were therefore seen as one way in which companies could counter criticisms and gain positive publicity.

Environmental management as public opinion winner

All environmental improvement was considered to be good for public opinion. A few specific examples illustrate this. At Water 2 the annual awards to employees who had suggested particularly good environmental projects was used to generate positive publicity. The awards were given in a public ceremony with as much press coverage as attainable. The award money was to be used by the winning staff member or team to sponsor an environment-related project in the local community. This was said to generate much goodwill locally. Water 3 had carried out two surveys of all its customers in order to discover their priorities for action. Following this exercise, the company decided to channel most of its efforts towards the improvement of local bathing waters. The aim was to obtain blue flags (the European Union recognition for excellent bathing waters) for all its beaches. The management of wildlife conservation on the water companies' large land holdings was also seen to bring public opinion benefits that were much larger than the relatively modest expenditure entailed. Managers in Multi-utility and Water 1 told us that they, and the industry as a whole, were doing significantly more for conservation management than stipulated by the water privatisation act, because they found that it brought them such large benefits in terms of public goodwill.

Significant changes also took place on an industry level. Mergers and acquisitions took place in both industries. By the end of our research period Electricity 2 and Electricity 1 had been taken over by American electricity companies. Water 1 had also been taken over by a foreign company. Multiutility and Water 2 had built up significant overseas business interests. The parents of Electricity 2 and Electricity 1 also had large international interests. There was thus a certain orientation away from the heavily regulated UK utility business. This could have some impact on environmental management. Often, a takeover brought with it significant restructuring of the company, including its environmental function. At Water 1, managers reported that after the takeover environmental issues took less prominence. Among other things this meant that the publication of the second environmental performance report was delayed by a year. At the end of our research period it was still too early to judge conclusively what impact the heavy merger and acquisition activity and the increasing involvement in international business will eventually have on the way companies deal with environmental issues, but there was a feeling that environmental management would not be unaffected.

There was also evidence for a certain degree of institutionalisation of environmental management at industry level. Both industries had, within their industry associations, founded environmental groups which served the purpose of inter-company discussions of environmental issues and their potential solutions. Both industries had industry-wide research and development programmes, many of whose projects were said to have a potential environmental benefit attached. The water industry was in the process of developing a set of uniform environmental indicators that were to be used (voluntarily) by all companies involved in their environmental performance reporting. Through their industry associations the companies also engaged in lobbying processes and negotiations with the regulator.

Discussion and conclusion

In our study of 'corporate greening' we have found evidence for change at all three levels under consideration: the individual, the organisation, and the wider social and economic context. These change processes are interconnected and not always easy to separate. Thus, the convictions and actions of individuals can lead to far-ranging change at the organisational level, for instance when an influential individual persuades others to introduce an environmental management system. Conversely, organisational changes will necessitate changes in individual behaviour, for instance where an environmental management system requires all members of the organisation to assess the adverse environmental impacts of their work and to put into place measures to reduce such impacts and report on them regularly.

Changes at the wider social and economic level interacted with changes at the individual and organisational level. Environmental changes at the organisational level, such as the introduction of environmental management systems and expenditure on environmental clean-up, were strongly influenced or even forced by legislation, regulation and public pressure. Higher environmental awareness in the population at large did, of course, also apply to significant numbers of the people working in the companies, particularly in the water industry where a high proportion of employees were thought already to have an environmental interest.

The findings from our case studies raise a number of questions. One concerns the role of top management in the leadership of corporate greening. Much of the environmental management literature is quite clear that without strong top management commitment no significant greening can happen. Our findings give some support to this assumption in so far as we found several cases where greening efforts were blocked by a hostile top management. It seems that top management must at least allow any greening efforts to happen, if there is to be any change. On the other hand, active involvement by the chief executive in the environmental efforts of the company seemed to be considered a bonus by our respondents but not absolutely necessary. We also have some evidence that the commitment of an environmental 'champion' can make a considerable difference in that part of the organisation that the champion can influence directly. The importance of environmental managers in promoting change seemed to lie less in their formal role and more in their ability to persuade and influence. Thus their effectiveness may well have to do with their personality and the standing they have in the company. This would suggest that merely hiring an environmental manager may not contribute significantly to corporate greening if the manager does not find a receptive audience in other members of the organisation.

Another question concerns the contribution that formal environmental policies, management systems and reports can make to organisational greening. The evidence from our case study suggests that these formal measures can make a contribution if used as a means to an end. Policies as such do not seem to achieve too much, but environmental management systems seem to be able to contribute to specific environmental performance targets by setting up formal procedures which may reduce incidents. Environmental reports seem to contribute something to organisational change in the sense that they can foster the systematic collection of more environmental data and thus alert the company to environmental issues that they may not have considered before.

One of the most noticeable results of our research is perhaps the realisation that environmental management in the companies studied was to a very large extent influenced, even determined, by trends in the wider social and economic environment. This was most noticeable in the water industry, where extensive environmental legislation, together with heightened public awareness and a poor compliance record, had sensitised managers to the external relations aspect of environmental management. Although environmental legislation and thus the question of compliance were less crucial for the electricity companies, heightened public awareness of environmental issues and the public relations backlash to be expected if the company fell foul of environmental expectations still meant that managers were quite aware of external pressures, and tended to cite public pressure together with legislation and regulation as the main drivers for their environmental management efforts.

This strong influence of external factors raises a number of questions. If many of the companies' efforts in environmental management are prompted by legislation and public opinion, this questions the voluntary, proactive and managerialist model of corporate greening presented in much of the environmental management literature. This is despite the fact that some of the companies in our study could probably be considered to exhibit quite advanced levels of environmental management. In some respects we do not consider this to be problematic. It may not matter whether companies try to improve their environmental performance as a result of raised environmental expectations from society or whether their greening efforts are driven by internal vision, so long as environmental performance is improved. And it is a positive sign if public demands are actually being heard by managers who consider themselves to be delivering a public service and who want to be seen to be doing the right thing.

On the other hand, the importance of legislation and regulation in driving corporate greening may give rise to some concerns which have to do with governments' ability and willingness to take a lead in setting the legislative framework for environmental improvement. In an increasingly global economy countries compete for international business. Regulation is seen to be a disincentive for companies to locate in a country. So national governments may find it more and more difficult to regulate industry. This may not apply directly to the companies in our study. Utility services such as water and sewerage and electricity distribution cannot very easily be undertaken on other than a regional or perhaps a national basis, and the companies have a legal obligation to continue delivering these services. Yet, this would not be true for other industries, where relocation to countries with the lightest regulatory pressure may be an option. Even in the industries we studied, privatisation has led to an increasing internationalisation and many of the companies are now part of an international group whose main business interests may not lie in the UK. Less emphasis may therefore be placed on UK operations, which may in turn lead to less attention being paid to business development here, including further environmental improvement.

Notes

1 This chapter is based on research funded by the Economic and Social Research Council's Global Environmental Change Programme, Grant No. L 321 25 3209.
2 After privatisation many water companies had a string of prosecutions by the Environment Agency or its predecessor, the National Rivers Authority, for pollution incidents. These prosecutions were well publicised by a press often perceived to be hostile to privatisation of the water industry and led to significant bad publicity for the industry as a whole.

References

Fineman, S. (1996) Emotional subtexts in corporate greening. *Organisation Studies*, 17 (3), 479–500.
Garrod, B. and Chadwick, P. (1996) Environmental management and business strategy. *Futures*, 28, 1: .37–50.
Gladwin, T.N. (1993) The meaning of greening: A plea for organisational theory. In K. Fischer and J. Schot, (eds) *Environmental Strategies for Industry*, pp. 37–61. Washington, DC: Island Press.
Gladwin, T.N., Kennelly, J.J. and Krause, T.S. (1995) Shifting paradigms for sustainable development: Implications for management theory and research. *Academy of Management Review*, 20 (4), 874–907.
Post, J.E. and Altman, B.W. (1994) Managing the environmental change process: barriers and opportunities. *Journal of Organisational Change Management*, 7 (4), 64–81.
Rennings, K., Brockmann K.L. and Bergmann, H. (1997) Voluntary agreements in environmental protection: Experiences in Germany and future perspectives. *Business Strategy and the Environment*, 6, 245–263.
Roome, N. (1992) Developing environmental management strategies. *Business Strategy and the Environment*, 3 (4), 9–16.
Shrivastava, P. (1994) CASTRATED environment: GREENING organisational studies. *Organisation Studies*, 15 (5), 705–726.
Shrivastava, P. and Hart, S. (1995) Creating sustainable corporations. *Business Strategy and the Environment*, 4, 154–165.
Starik, M. and Rands, G.P. (1995) Weaving an integrated web: Multilevel and multisystem perspectives of ecologically sustainable organisations. *Academy of Management Review*, 20 (4), 908–935.
Stead, W.E. and Stead, J.E. (1994) Can humankind change the economic myth? Paradigm shifts necessary for ecologically sustainable business. *Journal of*

Organisational Change Management, 7 (4), 15–31.

Steger, U. (1993) The greening of the board room: How German companies are dealing with environmental issues. In K. Fischer and J. Schot, (eds) *Environmental Strategies for Industry*, pp. 147–166. Washington, DC: Island Press.

Welford, R. (1992) Linking quality and the environment: A strategy for the implementation of environmental management systems. *Business Strategy and the Environment*, 1 (1), 25–34.

Wilson, D.C. (1992) *A Strategy of Change: Concepts and Controversies in the Management of Change*. London: Routledge.

Zeffane, R., Polonsky, M.J. and Medley, P. (1995) Corporate environmental commitment: Developing the operational concept. *Business Strategy and the Environment*, 3 (4), 17–28.

Part 4

The green organisation?

11 Green myths, green realities

Stephen Fineman

In this final chapter we return to where we began at the start of the book: what can we expect of business in the face of growing environmental concern? Is it a matter of ever more coercion to 'be greener'? Should we look imaginatively at ways we can transform business cultures into environmentally sensitive entities? And if so where, and from whom, should initiatives take place? More pessimistically, are we clutching at green straws, trying to turn the engine of our economic system – industry – into something that it is not, and cannot be? Perhaps we need greater courage, personally and politically, to dismantle and re-form our economy in ways that embed the care of 'nature'. But such fine-sounding sentiments are often just that, remote from the everyday realities and feasibilities of those who 'go to work' and enjoy, or hope to enjoy, the material and other pleasures of twenty-first century industrialism. And it is still easy to suppress, not see, environmental degradation should one choose: human propensities for selective perception and delusion are powerful forces for non-change.

The chapters in this book have illuminated, often in graphic terms, the fragility of eco-modernism – shifting business towards some state that might be called greener. The fragility lies in the ways different actors within business organisations take and value environmental rhetorics and actions, and in the complexity of competing interests and parties that define the wider world of influences on business. What is particularly striking is that there is often an uneasy, or impossible, tension between environmental logics and those of accepted business practice, a strain that is glossed over in the more upbeat presentations of 'green management' and their checklist approach to organisation change. The tussle between 'business' and 'the environment' is not a struggle of equals. In many ways, the environment loses from the outset. But must this be the case?

The social researcher's privilege is to appreciate business close in and also at a distance. In exploring the claims of greening, both perspectives are required, from which theory and philosophical approaches can develop. With this in mind, I invited the authors of this book to disengage from the fine detail of their studies and reflect critically and succinctly on 'the green organisation'. I received six responses, all very thoughtful, some provocative. I reproduce them below.

The green organisation?

Jane Hunt

Business organisations operate within a terrain where modernism, instrumentalism and capitalism are the constituents of business identity. As such, business organisation is deeply antithetical to at least the deeper shades of greening – and even the lighter shades are at best compromised. The embedding of such conventional values and identities makes the possibility of alternatives unthinkable. Attempts at synthesis between the ideologically disparate tenets of greening and modernism *et al.*, such as ecological modernisation and sustainable development, are in essence no more than a reframing and co-optation of 'environment' to make it fit with existing commitments to capitalist organisational forms.

However, that does not mean that greening can have no real meaning for the existing business organisation. On the contrary, what greening does is offer the possibility of change – a more fundamental change, perhaps, than many commentators identify, but still a possibility. Business organisations, far from being soulless, are made up of people engaged in social relationships. Greening provides a vehicle, a vocabulary, a context and a set of categories for these people to express their aspirations for doing things in different ways. It provides the possibility of an alternative – and this alternative is made visible by global attention. Greening sketches out a picture of very different possibilities for business organisation, possibilities that include such conventionally antithetical considerations as compassion, equality and social need rather than profit as the motivation for action.

We can see in the creeping normalisation of a number of green concerns (such as pollution and resource consumption) that business identity is already shifting, that ideas of what it means to be a good and responsible organisation are changing to encompass the (perhaps most mechanistic and instrumental aspects of) green agenda. The 'environment' has shifted from being the preserve of the 'muesli-jumpers' to the legitimate concern of business; concern for issues traditionally well outside the perimeters of organisational attention has crept through the margins and is approaching centre stage. The cusp, though, of the distinction between an organisation which is greening and one that is merely co-opting 'the environment' is found through examining what changes: the organisation, or the idea of greening?

Greening allows for a different future, highlighting that the way we do things now is a choice, not an inevitability. It is the green light which helps us to move from what is to what we can imagine. And it is the now legitimised idea of 'greening' – however woolly and ill-defined – that means that aspirations for a better world, a better way of living, can find expression, not just for the individual, but for the business. That greening does not fit comfortably with existing organisational practices does not mean that greening is impossible; rather, it opens up the potentialities and provides the impetus for organisations to change. So contemporary organisations are antithetical to greening, but greening provides not only the ends but the means by which they can change.

Martin Purvis and Frances Drake

Many current theoretical constructions of the greening of business offer only generalised notions of the processes of change. Organisations, motivated by a combination of external pressures and internal leadership, are assumed to learn about both the necessity and potential competitive rewards of environmental responsibility. Viewed in this way, distinctions between environmental attitudes and practice are blurred. By implication, change in practice, the greening that is measured through environmental indicators, is taken to reflect attitudinal change, a more positive stance towards the environment *per se.*

It is questionable, however, whether attitudinal change is necessarily sufficient to prompt innovations in practice. Individual managers may accept the broad societal importance of environmental issues without translating this into any specific feelings of responsibility or empowerment to make changes in their professional life. Even individual businesses may not have the decisive control over their operations that models of business greening invariably imply. Moreover, such models are often remarkably incurious about the nature of the environmental challenge facing many businesses. The implication that environmental impacts and their solutions can be uncovered by a standard process of auditing is misleadingly optimistic.

Environmental challenges such as ozone depletion and climate change are not the products of the obvious failings of industrial systems, but a hitherto unsuspected result of their normal operation. Nor are environmental concerns always open to unambiguously effective solutions. This caveat does not just apply to the global scale of environmental change. Businesses articulate more immediate dilemmas, for example, over the environmental credentials of recycling schemes for paper, or changing opinion concerning the relative environmental merits of petrol- and diesel-powered vehicles.

Change in practice can also be an inadequate indicator of the greening of business attitudes. In practice, the motives of companies in deciding on environmentally relevant changes may have little to do with explicitly *environmental* learning. Behaviour may tell us as much about the general state of a company and the buoyancy of the markets in which it operates, as it does specifically about environmental attitudes. Businesses whose overall operations are characterised by a high degree of managerial stability, even stagnation, are unlikely to make unforced innovations in any area. By comparison, companies already looking to invest and innovate may, even unconsciously, take action, such as the purchase of new energy efficient equipment, that yields environmental dividends.

More considered reflection upon the motivation underpinning the adoption of innovations that are environmentally relevant takes the argument beyond some of the simple and singular markers of progress used in models of greening. Often it is implied that behaviour that goes beyond current regulatory requirements represents an innovatory stage towards business greening. This may be true, in the sense that the impact of a business on the environment may be reduced. However, such behaviour need not represent any fundamental change of management attitudes and culture, nor any explicitly environmental motivation. Innovations in waste minimisation and resource and energy efficiency are common examples of 'compliance plus' behaviour that often reflects established commercial motives centred on cost and profitability.

Attention to this utilitarian dimension of the greening of business also points to its limits and the need to ground analysis of 'environmental' behaviour more securely in study of business functions as a whole. If companies consider environmental (or environmentally relevant) initiatives to meet particular commercial ends, then we have to recognise that in many instances there are other means to these ends. The existence of these other means can work against environmental innovation; even in a context of basic goodwill towards the environment we might expect companies to opt for the easiest means to achieve their primary commercial objectives. If a company's ultimate aim is cost reduction, then energy efficiency may be an irrelevance if reductions in the wage bill are identified as the best route to savings.

Companies keen to demonstrate their commitment to quality and improvements in production and managerial practice may opt for participation in schemes such as Investors in People, rather than initiatives with an explicitly environmental element. For companies that are concerned to enhance their image, this can be achieved in many different ways that have nothing to do with the environment, for example, through sponsorship of educational, cultural and sporting activities. Environmental initiatives may be seen as temporarily fashionable by business image-makers, but there are many other possibilities for the vast majority of companies not facing particular scrutiny of their environmental performance. Moreover, if attention to the environment reflects perceptions of fashion, or the workings of the issue attention cycle, then greening may stagnate, or even give way to 'degreening', as other avenues present greater opportunities or rewards for business.

Simon Guy

What can we possibly mean by a 'green business'? Is this an organisation that puts aside concern with commercial profit to promote an alternative vision of the future? And if so, of what does this vision comprise? Is it simply to reduce waste and maximise efficient practices of production and consumption? Or does the vision go deeper? Are there forms of business practice that should simply be avoided altogether? And more positively, should we be radically reconsidering the manner in which we conduct business with each other?

These are familiar and longstanding questions in the environmental debate. And yet there seem few easy answers. Beyond the certainties of committed deep green campaigners, who see the roots of the environmental crisis in the very act of economic exchange, attempts to identify the parameters of sustainable business practice appear elusive. What is the problem here?

Perhaps we have to ask what is meant by an organisation? It seems, at times, as if the 'organisation' that populates much environmental literature has a unified mind capable of either wilful immorality or inspired action. Like the sinner blinded by the light on the road to Damascus, the mythological commercial organisation is considered capable of overnight conversion to environmental salvation. Of course, no one suggests that organisations are simply empty vessels swayed only by the prevailing market mood. Instead, these organisations are presumed to be driven by the decisions and strategies of key decision-makers who simply need to be informed and persuaded of the practical economic sense and ethical higher ground of environmentalism to be converted to sustainable business practice. What then prevents this ecological enlightenment? Convinced of both the ethical imperative and rationality of a sustainable approach, the only conclusion is a lack of information, moral outlook or economic interest.

But what if organisations are not capable of autonomous action? What if key decision-makers do not drive organisational change alone? And what if businessmen and women are fully informed, moral citizens able to rationally negotiate economic conditions to achieve complex ends? Considering this possibility suggests that we may have asked the wrong question at the outset. It may be that we should loosen our moral certainties and broaden our research focus to explore the competing dimensions of the environmental problem in relation to business practice. Rather than constructing new checklists of best practice, ecological audits and environmental charters, all measured against a pre-defined notion of sustainability, we may need to recognise multiple interpretations of environmental action. Instead of generating an image of the green organisation in advance, we might have to acknowledge a more heterogeneous set of business practices deriving from multiple sources of environmental motivation.

Seen this way, the green organisation cannot exist in any abstract sense. Framed by rapidly changing social, regulatory and economic contexts, and shaped by an unavoidable negotiative relationship with other businesses, green organisations may follow different pathways of environmental innovation. In this sense, the 'mythical' green organisation may conceal more than it reveals.

Ken Green

A 'green organisation' is a dubious concept. Given the integrated complexity of modern production and consumption, it is only sensible to imagine (and pursue policies to bring about) *green production-and-consumption-systems*. Such systems can be visualised in the form of three interconnecting 'chains':

- the 'materials chain', which describes the physical flows of products and materials;
- the 'supply chain', a term which denotes the pattern of commercial and organisational entities, and
- the 'innovation chain', which governs the patterns of innovation in both processes and products and management systems.

The materials chain – mapping the flows of raw materials and components through manufacturing and use to disposal, re-use, and recycling – is the physical underpinning of the manufacture of products and the delivery of services. The broad structure of any particular chain – the 'technological regime' – may remain relatively stable for decades, due to combinations of knowledge restrictions and institutional rigidities ('lock-in'). Such constraints, however, can be overcome to allow the re-design of, at the least, parts of the material flow, if the firms involved in it collaborate on joint projects.

The way in which the material chain maps to the supply chain will differ for different material flows; for example, compare consumer durables (produced by large companies for many end-users with product design concerned with mechanical and electrical engineering) with construction (many small firms for fewer end-users – property developers – with product design concerned with systems and civil engineering). The size and power of the organisations in that flow is obviously crucial.

Studies of the patterns of innovation have revealed the way in which different types of product and process innovation (e.g. radical vs incremental; science-intensive vs re-design) arise in different industrial sectors at different times in the developmental history of a technology. The 'science-based' industries (electronics, chemicals) are the source of the most fundamental innovations; some other industries however do little more than effect minor product or process innovation. So, some firms in a particular supply chain will be much less able to respond to demands from customers (or regulators) on their own, because the relevant technologies are not directly within that firm's control. For example, a packaged-food manufacturing firm cannot easily respond to demand from retailers for package reduction but must pass such requests to the manufacturer of the packaging materials, who might in turn be limited by the raw materials currently available from chemical companies.

So, rather than seeing the link between customer demand and innovation as a simple one between a firm and its market, we should see it as a *series* of links, with purchaser demands requiring a cascade of similar links up the supply chain. The ability of any particular firm to respond to those demands is dependent on its position in that chain (which is connected to the power it has) but also on its position in the chain of innovative technological knowledge.

The three chains exist in complex relation to each other. Firms dealing with the largest volumes of material may not be the most powerful in a chain or the most critical to green technological innovation. The most commercially powerful firms may not be in a position to effect any green changes that they might favour. The fine structure of the chains – especially how firms relate to each other in terms of their strategic importance in product and process innovation – is crucial to the greening of production and consumption systems. Sustainable systems, yes; sustainable organisations, no.

Barbara Morton

If the 'green organisation' was ever anything more than a myth, it must surely be an increasingly difficult concept to defend. The very use of the word 'green' brings with it problems of definition, while for many organisations, the thorny task of the moment lies in defining what 'sustainability' might mean for them.

But an equally intriguing aspect of the myth is the implied freedom of action of the 'organisation'. In fact, leading organisations recognise the importance of their relationships with the environment – in its widest sense. Far from operating in isolation, therefore, organisations can be seen to represent elements in an increasingly complex web of interactions. Indeed, organisations may be defined by their very 'connectedness' with their stakeholders. One example of the trend is to be found in the electronics products sector, where firms have begun to re-define themselves as 'systems integrators'. For such organisations and for many others, the majority of total environmental impact is associated with goods and services 'bought-in' to the organisation. Dealing with the environmental effects of a product throughout its entire life cycle is notoriously difficult, however, as many organisations have discovered through raising the issue with their suppliers.

Customer organisations have tackled this from a variety of perspectives. These include developing green specifications, adopting life cycle assessment methodologies, asking process-related questions of their suppliers, and imposing deadlines on their suppliers for the adoption of environmental management systems. So many of these approaches have left organisations with more questions than they are able to answer that, in many cases, the whole issue of supplier environmental assessment has had to be put into the 'too difficult' box.

Market structure complicates the picture further. When organisations have found suitable techniques to identify areas of environmental concern, they are able to operate most effectively in circumstances in which they are market makers. Where their market influence is limited they must rely largely on other drivers, such as regulatory pressures, to deliver environmental improvement in that supply chain.

Those involved in public sector procurement walk another tightrope. Can they deliver on commitments by their organisations to be 'green' while at the same time being able to demonstrate fairness, equality of treatment for suppliers and 'best value' for the public purse? Yet public sector expenditure is quoted as a potential cornerstone of policy, such as integrated product policy, which seeks to modify and improve the environmental performance of product systems.

Two trends in supply chain management reinforce the argument for 'green organisations' to be seen in a wider context. One is the outsourcing of goods and services. The second and perhaps the more significant here, is the trend away from the procurement of products as such, towards what might be described as the 'product-plus' scenario. This centres on a concern to specify the 'outcome' required by the purchasing organisation, leaving scope for the supplier to satisfy that requirement through a mix of product, expertise and 'service'.

Under these conditions, leading organisations have seen opportunities for improved performance – including environmental performance, while the notion of the isolated, autonomous 'green organisation' recedes into the distance.

Judith Petts

Since the 1970s, the business literature has been trying to shock, frighten, push and persuade companies out of the 'light green' spectrum into the 'deep'. Being green is not only an environmental, but a social, economic and political imperative. The 'deep green' business is a saviour and a business success. The light or weak green business is a potential failure – the regulator will prosecute you; your customers will desert you; your local community will rise against you; your shareholders will question long-term liabilities. However, lest you should choose to turn a blind eye, the environment is also presented as the ultimate win–win scenario which you can respond to through self regulation to meet your own objectives.

So why are companies who employ over 90 per cent of the UK workforce – i.e. the small and medium-sized enterprises – largely choosing business as usual: institutional conformity with a little green-wash around the edges? We know that, as people, both managers and employees are concerned about the big picture. What happens when they walk into the factory or office? Answer – they have difficulty defining what it means to be green with any degree of business pragmatism, sense of relevance, clear understanding of the environmental benefits that can result, and have difficulty allocating sufficient resources to respond. What impact can one company making widgets and employing 20 people have? If you are subject to no direct regulation what does being compliant mean? What is a good environmental performance? Is this the same as being compliant? Is it the same as being 'green'? What, indeed, is the environment? We await tangible and relevant definitions for most of these.

There is a need to help companies to define the environment clearly in terms of their relationship with it. A good starting point is to make a link between the working and external environment. The environment has to be sold as a business opportunity first and foremost, but it is essential to define and identify specific practical things that can be done. An accredited environmental management system may actually bring few benefits to a particular company, or to the environment. A full-scale energy reduction programme, and nothing else, might – and be a more cost-effective option. There is an urgent need for all environmental regulations to be assessed not just for their cost implications but for their environmental benefits, and for these in turn to be explained in all guidance, codes of practice etc. There is an urgent need to understand the full life-cycle of products manufactured – it is just possible that recycling packaging may be less environmentally friendly than sending it to an energy-from-waste incinerator. Many initiatives appear to be based as much on gut 'green' reactions as robust analysis.

As researchers we need to focus on what companies actually do and how they perform and change over time. Then as teachers of the next generation of business managers we need to build environmental management fully and completely into business and human resource management – not treat it as an optional module. At the same time we need to build business management into the training of environmental scientists and engineers.

The above accounts do much to de-mythologise the green organisation by taking issue with both 'green' and 'organisation'. This is more than academic nit picking. If anything, there is a refreshingly anti-positivist line that allows us (a) to see greening as something that is contested in its meanings and indicators, matters we have to learn live with and 'ride'; and (b) to take enclosed conceptions of the organisation as misleading. Action within an organisation is complexly linked to other chains of influence which both enable and disable business conduct – green or otherwise.

A strong note of pragmatism further punctures the green myth. When greening is presented to business as a route to commercial success rather than a moral imperative, it has to stack up against other possible routes to profit and cost-reduction – some of which are more plausible and more rewarding to the business actor. And when we choose to praise an organisation for its green ventures – such as waste management and recycling – those implementing such policies may have little concern about the environment they are supposedly protecting. Greening, therefore, can come and can go. And for many smaller businesses it has yet to arrive.

But there is a fine line between sensible pragmatism and overstated instrumentality in our analysis. Once the green genie is out of the bottle it is difficult to return it to its original home. Greening has brought with it a discourse that has infused both common and specialist vocabularies. Pollution of the air and water is now known to children at infants' school as well as to their parents. The environment – from threats to wildlife to shrinking icecaps – features in documentary programmes for family viewing. The media dramatises environmental disasters while soap operas regularly highlight the plight of the environment. A whole industry of organisational consultants and public relations experts have turned their skills to selling environmental care, supported by high profile figures in royalty, ecologists and others experts in the burgeoning field of environmental studies. The green discourse is one of conservation and hope, as well as of calamity.

All this may be dismissed as growing fashion which is bound to fade. That is unlikely. Environmental issues have now become institutionalised internationally through legislation and are often represented by government departments. There are political investments at stake as well as professional and academic careers. There are also many new companies that make their profits out of environmental technologies. All this is not going to vanish like last year's fashion in shoes or skirts. The tide may occasionally recede, but the green wave will continue to lap at industry's door.

Index